Butterflies for life

ST. JUDE CHILDREN'S RESEARCH HOSPITAL

"No child should die in the dawn of life."
Danny Thomas

Presented by The Pink Team of Assumption

100% of the profits, after related expenses,
will benefit St. Jude Children's Research Hospital.
The printing costs do not exceed $10.00.

butterfliesforlife.org

Cover art: Butsy Suarez

ISBN: 978-0-9796154-1-2

WIMMER
COOKBOOKS

A CONSOLIDATED GRAPHICS COMPANY

800.548.2537   wimmerco.com

Dedication

"Butterflies For Life" is dedicated to the children, both past and present, of St. Jude Children's Research Hospital, in whose honor this book is written. We find in them the good of the past, the reality of the present and a vision for health and happiness in the future.

Westfield Sugarhouse
Paincourtville, Louisiana

Artist - Christopher Dugas

Home of The Pink Team of Assumption

Assumption Parish, Louisiana

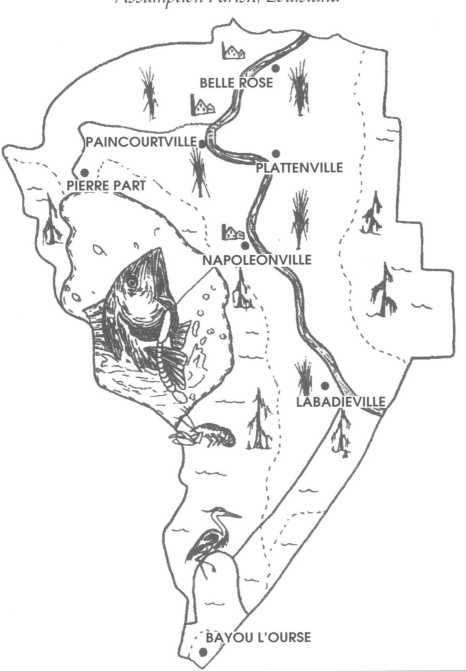

BELLE ROSE

PAINCOURTVILLE

PLATTENVILLE

PIERRE PART

NAPOLEONVILLE

LABADIEVILLE

BAYOU L'OURSE

Along the Bayou ...

Assumption Parish is located in the southern part of Louisiana less than fifty miles from the Gulf of Mexico. The population is scattered along Bayou Lafourche and a myriad of bayous, lakes, swamps and rivers. Our hardworking, industrious people enjoy the easy-going life-style that is synonymous of this area. Many cultures have settled here creating culinary marvels for which Louisiana is famous. Steeped in tradition, these mouthwatering dishes are passed from one generation to the next as part of our heritage.

"Butterflies For Life" was an idea born of the desire to raise money for the much-needed research to fight childhood cancer. At the same time, it also allows families, friends and neighbors who are such good cooks to share their recipes and love of cooking. We hope that all who read and try these recipes will enjoy them as much as we have enjoyed collecting, testing and tasting them.

Bon Appétit
The Pink Team of Assumption

Contributing Artists

Barbara Barras	*Map of Assumption Parish*
Joyce Daigle	*Louisiana Cypress*
Carolyn Dugas	*Madewood*
Christopher Dugas	*Sugarhouse*
Nolia LeBlanc	*Crawfish Boil*
Marie Mabile	*Brown Pelican*
Craig Naquin	*Vegetable Garden*
Sylvia Rochester	*Cattails*
Brenda Romero	*Mallards at Dusk*
Butsy Suarez	*Rural Life and Westfield Sugarhouse*

*We do not know for sure just how the word butterfly came about.
It is thought that it is derived from the Anglo-Saxon word "butterfloege"
which means flying butter. Just how and when the word was first applied to all
butterflies no one knows. In French, the word "Papillion" means butterfly.*

In Memory of

COURTNEY JOY BANTA
MAY 29, 1986 - JUNE 5, 2001

"OUR STORY"

Let me tell you a story, the story of "our team," The Pink Team of Assumption. In the spring of 2001 I received a call from ALSAC of St. Jude Children's Research Hospital in Memphis that would change my life and that of many of my family, friends and the people of our area forever. The call was from a volunteer from St. Jude asking if I would chair a Bike-A-Thon in our small village of Paincourtville, Louisiana, which has a population of fewer than 1,000. I said that I would think it over and would she please call back in a week or so. She said that she would and exactly one week later, she did call back. I hesitantly agreed.

At that time, Courtney Banta, a young girl from Paincourtville, had been in treatment at St. Jude for Neuroblastoma. I went to see her parents and asked to do an "honor ride" for Courtney. They said that she would be thrilled as she loved St. Jude so much.

Next, who would help? That part was easy. I called several friends who are always involved in community activities and they agreed to help. We were on our way to what we thought would be a one-time event.

A few weeks later, Courtney was out of remission and in early June of 2001 she passed away. We were devastated and immediately thought of canceling the Bike-A-Thon. Her parents insisted that she would want the ride to go on as planned. It now became a memorial ride, "The Courtney Banta Memorial Bike-A-Thon."

Our first ride was in September 2001 on a rainy, miserable morning. We watched as some determined riders unloaded their bikes and not only took off, but completed the ride. Our first check to St. Jude Children's Research Hospital was for $7,500 and the rest is history. In 2005, just two weeks after Hurricane Katrina, after receiving such devastating losses and in the most trying of circumstances, our fund-raising efforts generated over $46,000. Our event continues to grow bigger and better each year.

It has been said that a butterfly flapping its wings in Tahiti can in theory produce a tornado in Kansas. It all has to do with mathematics. The Pink Team of Assumption, a grass roots fund raising organization for St. Jude Childrens' Research Hospital, has adopted this theory. We are all about mathematics; raising money for St. Jude. Our team is flapping its butterfly wings in Assumption Parish and expecting to produce a windfall in Memphis, Tennessee. We have adopted a team song, "Angels Among Us," have team colors, pink and purple (Courtney's favorites), a team flag, team shirts and our "mascot" is the butterfly. We are about a united effort to raise money for the hospital. Our dream is to someday raise a million dollars in order to pay the cost of running the hospital for one day. Sure, it's just a dream, but we all have dreams.

Our team started in Paincourtville with twelve members and each year more and more people have joined our fund-raising efforts. We now have more than one hundred members, plus 4-H clubs throughout the parish which have given us so much help and support in so many events. Our entire parish has a population of fewer than 25,000 scattered over 16,000 square miles. Our members are found in the many small communities throughout that area and up and down Bayou Lafourche, a body of water that runs from the Mississippi River to its mouth in the Gulf of Mexico.

This cookbook represents the cooking and lifestyle of the people of Assumption Parish and south Louisiana. It is a collection of "secret" recipes and stories from family and friends shared with love and affection in the hope that all who read it and try the recipes will come to know the people and culture of our area as well as the effort that has been put into helping these children. We hope that you enjoy this book and the recipes as much as we have enjoyed putting it together.

There are so many people to thank for our great success that it cannot possibly be done here without the risk of leaving someone out. Not one person said "no" when asked to give or help. Our people are kind and generous and it is only through "team effort" that ordinary people are able to achieve extraordinary things.

From the "The Pink Team of Assumption," thank you from the bottom of our hearts for a "Wonderful Ride."

Glenda R. Daigle
Coordinator

Table of Contents

Cajun vs Créole Cuisine

Cajun cuisine is sometimes confused with Créole cuisine. Many outside of Louisiana don't know how or why there is a difference.

Cajun cuisine is rooted in French cooking. French immigrants combined their cooking methods with the local ingredients, producing the foods that we consider Cajun today. The Cajun people made use of ingredients that were readily available, namely seafood, rice and wild game. An authentic Cajun meal is usually a three-pot affair, with one pot dedicated to the main dish, one to steamed rice, skillet cornbread or some other grain dish, and the third containing whatever vegetable is plentiful or available.

In Cajun dishes a roux is used as the thickening agent. Added to the roux is what is known as the holy trinity of Cajun cooking: onion, bell pepper and celery. This trio with the roux forms the base for many Cajun dishes.

Créole cooking is more city-urban and inspired by the Spanish, Italian and African influences of New Orleans.

Determining what is Créole and what is Cajun is complicated by the sharing of dishes between the two cuisines, such as gumbo and jambalaya.

Gumbo, the most popular Créole dish, was created in New Orleans and has an African influence with the vegetable okra. Jambalaya is the second in line of fame of Louisiana Créole dishes and there are two recipes for jambalaya. One is Créole and the other is Cajun.

Further complicating this matter is that several famous local restaurants have combined Cajun flavors with Créole ingredients and preparations. Dishes rooted primarily in the New Orleans metropolitan areas such as po-boys or red beans and rice are in reality Créole, not Cajun.

In the last few years both the Cajun and Créole methods of cooking have gained popularity. The tasty, aromatic dishes prepared in these traditions are enjoyed by people around the world.

"Butterflies For Life" embodies both Cajun and Créole cuisines.

Appetizers

M. Mabile

Marie Mabile

Brown Pelican

Louisiana is known as the Pelican State. The pelican has been a symbol of Louisiana since the arrival of the earliest European settlers. They were impressed with the pelican's generous and nurturing attitude toward their young.

Disaster struck in the early 1950's when the use of pesticides caused the Brown Pelican to stop nesting along the Gulf coast. By 1966 the bird had completely disappeared from Louisiana. In spite of that, the Brown Pelican was adopted as the official state bird of Louisiana. The government declared the Brown Pelican an endangered species. Due to repopulation efforts the story has a happy ending. The Brown Pelican has been "recovered" in Louisiana but still remains on the endangered species list.

The symbol is used today on the Louisiana State Flag, the Louisiana State Seal and is featured prominently on the seal of Louisiana State University.

COFFEE MILK

"Café Au Lait"

1½ tablespoons sugar	1 cup hot coffee
1 cup milk	

Caramelize sugar in a heavy skillet. Remove from heat. Slowly heat milk in a saucepan. Add coffee to hot milk. Sweeten with caramelized sugar.

Serves 2

LEMONADE

1 quart simple syrup (recipe page 12)	8 lemons
1 quart water	8 sprigs of mint

Pour simple syrup and water into a 2-quart pitcher. Roll lemons. Cut into halves and juice. Add to water and stir. Add about 8 slices of lemon with rind. Garnish with sprigs of mint.

Makes 8 generous servings

BRIDE'S PUNCH

1½ (46-ounce) cans pineapple juice	1 (10-ounce) can frozen limeade
2 (12-ounce) cans frozen orange juice	1 liter ginger ale

Pour all ingredients into a large punch bowl and stir.

If you have leftover juices or punch add food coloring, cherries, lemon, lime or orange peel and freeze in ice cube trays. Use these ice cubes in your punch bowl at your next party.

CHAMPAGNE PUNCH

1   bottle champagne
1   (46-ounce) can
      pineapple juice
1   (6-ounce) can frozen
      orange juice, thawed

Lemon slices for garnish
Cherries for garnish

Mix first three ingredients together. Freeze. Take out 4 hours before serving and garnish with lemons and cherries.

CRANBERRY PUNCH

1   quart cranberry juice
2   cups pineapple juice

1   cup sugar
1   liter ginger ale

Mix cranberry juice, pineapple juice and sugar together. Place in freezer until ready to serve. Add ginger ale. Stir well.

Makes about 20 (4-ounce) servings

SIMPLE SYRUP

1   cup sugar

4   cups boiling water

Dissolve sugar in water. Pour into a jar and store in the refrigerator until ready to use. Great in lemonade or punches.

LIME SHERBET PUNCH

½ gallon lime sherbet
1   (2 liter) bottle ginger ale

1   (2 liter) bottle lemon lime drink

Place sherbet in punch bowl. Pour ginger ale and lemon lime drink over top. Serve cold.

FRUIT PUNCH

6   quarts ginger ale
5   cups sugar
1½ quarts water
6   cups fresh orange juice
1½ cups fresh lemon juice

1½ quarts pineapple juice
1   (14-ounce) can sliced pineapple, cut
1   (16-ounce) jar cherries

Chill ginger ale. Mix sugar and water and cook until sugar is dissolved. Cool. Place all fruit juices in a large bowl. Mix sugar mixture with juices. Add fruit. Add ginger ale to punch just before serving.

Makes 88 (4-ounce) servings

1 lemon yields *2 tablespoons juice*

1 lime yields *1 tablespoon juice*

1 orange yields *¼ to ½ cup juice, depending on the size of the orange*

TEA

1   tea bag per cup   **1   cup boiling water per bag**

Place tea bag in pot. Pour boiling water over the tea bag and cover the pot. Steep for 3 to 4 minutes. Do not overbrew as the tea will be bitter.

Hint: *Teas do not store well. Make the same day as it is to be used. Good water is important. Do not use chlorinated or ground water. Bottled water is best. Do not use copper or aluminum pans to boil tea bags.*

Tips about Tea

Black tea is fully oxidized and fermented and usually served with milk or lemon and sugar. Lemon peel is preferred over lemon juice for tea. Hold the peel over the tea and twist to release the oil. Drop the peel into the tea. When using sugar, cane sugar is preferred.

Green tea skips the oxidizing process and has a more delicate taste and lighter color. Because of the delicate flavor nothing needs to be added.

Oolong tea is partly oxidized and is a cross between black and green tea in color and taste.

Apache Dip

1   (8-ounce) container sour
    cream
1   (8-ounce) package
    cream cheese, softened
1   (10-ounce) can diced
    green chilies
1   (4-ounce) can chopped
    black olives

8   ounces sharp Cheddar
    cheese, grated
1   tablespoon
    Worcestershire sauce
8   ounces ham, diced
1   round bread

Mix sour cream, cream cheese, green chilies, olives, Cheddar cheese, Worcestershire sauce and ham. Refrigerate. When ready to serve place in round, hollowed out bread and heat at 350 degrees for approximately 15 to 20 minutes or until thoroughly heated.

Serves 30

Artichoke Dip

2   (14-ounce) cans
    artichoke hearts
1½ ounces grated Parmesan
    cheese
½   cup olive oil

2   cups Italian bread crumbs
½   teaspoon Worcestershire
    sauce
    Red pepper to taste

Drain artichokes and reserve liquid. Cut each artichoke into 4 pieces. Place artichokes in casserole dish. Mix reserved liquid, Parmesan cheese, olive oil, bread crumbs, Worcestershire sauce and red pepper. Add to artichoke. Heat and serve.

Hint: *Can also be served cold.*

SHRIMP AND ARTICHOKE DIP

5 (8-ounce) cans artichokes
   Juice of 1 lemon
½ cup capers, drained
¾ cup chopped onion
2½ cups mayonnaise
¼ cup dried basil

   Seasoned salt to taste
   Hot sauce to taste
   Black pepper to taste
5 pounds shrimp, boiled
   and peeled

Drain, rinse and quarter artichokes. Set aside. Mix lemon juice, capers, onion, mayonnaise, basil, salt, hot sauce and black pepper. Stir in shrimp. Gently fold in artichokes. Adjust seasonings if necessary. Refrigerate at least 4 hours before serving.

SPINACH AND ARTICHOKE DIP

2 (10-ounce) packages
   frozen spinach
1 (15-ounce) can artichoke
   hearts
1 tablespoon butter
1 teaspoon minced garlic
4 ounces cream cheese
4 ounces shredded Swiss
   cheese
4 ounces shredded
   Monterey Jack cheese

1 cup chopped green
   onions
1 tablespoon
   Worcestershire sauce
1 tablespoon Créole
   seasoning
1 teaspoon hot sauce
¼ teaspoon thyme

Grease a 9x13-inch casserole. Set aside. Drain and chop spinach. Set aside. Drain and chop artichoke hearts. Set aside. Melt butter and sauté garlic. Add cheeses, green onions, Worcestershire sauce, Créole seasoning, hot sauce, thyme, spinach and artichoke hearts. Pour into prepared casserole. Refrigerate at least 4 hours. Bake at 350 degrees 35 to 40 minutes.

LAYERED BEAN DIP

- 1 (9-ounce) can bean dip
- 1 (1-ounce) package avocado dip
- ½ cup sour cream
- ½ cup mayonnaise
- 5 tablespoons picante sauce
- 1 (1-ounce) package taco seasoning
- 1 large tomato, chopped
- ¼ cup chopped green onions
- 8 ounces grated sharp Cheddar cheese
- 1 (4-ounce) can chopped black olives

Spray a 9x9-inch dish with cooking spray. Layer the bean dip on the bottom of the dish. Place the avocado dip on top. Combine sour cream, mayonnaise, picante sauce and taco seasoning. Spread on top of avocado dip. Layer tomato on top of sour cream mixture. Sprinkle with green onions and cheese. Garnish with black olives. Refrigerate.

BROCCOLI DIP

- 1 (10-ounce) box broccoli florets
- 1 (10-ounce) can cream of mushroom soup
- ⅓ stick butter
- 1 (6-ounce) roll garlic cheese
- ⅛ teaspoon pepper

Cook broccoli according to directions on box. Set aside. Combine soup, butter and cheese. Microwave on high 6 minutes in a covered dish. Chop broccoli in food processor. Add broccoli to soup mixture. Microwave on high 6 minutes. Add pepper.

HOT CHICKEN DIP

1　cup mayonnaise
1　(8-ounce) package
　　cream cheese
1　(10-ounce) can tomatoes
　　with chili peppers
1　(10-ounce) can cream of
　　chicken soup
1　(12-ounce) can chicken,
　　drained
1　teaspoon Créole
　　seasoning
¾　cup chopped green
　　onions

Preheat oven to 350 degrees. Grease a 9x9-inch casserole. Set aside. Mix mayonnaise, cream cheese, tomatoes, soup and chicken in a heavy saucepan. Heat over low heat until cream cheese is melted. Stir until well blended. Add Créole seasoning and green onions. Pour into prepared casserole. Bake 20 to 30 minutes.

CRAB DIP

1　stick butter
1　large onion, chopped fine
1　(8-ounce) package
　　cream cheese
1　(10-ounce) can cream of
　　mushroom soup
1　pound crabmeat
　　Salt to taste

Melt butter in a saucepan. Add onion and sauté until wilted. Stir in cream cheese and cook until melted. Add soup, crabmeat and salt. Simmer about 5 minutes. Serve warm.

CRAB ÉLÉGANT

½ cup chopped, green onions

½ cup chopped parsley

1½ sticks butter

1 pound crabmeat

1 tablespoon white wine (optional)

1 level tablespoon flour

1 pint half-and-half

Salt and pepper to taste

Sauté green onions and parsley in butter. Add crabmeat and wine. Cook 5 minutes. Mix flour and half-and-half. Gradually add to the crab mixture and simmer until thick. Add salt and pepper to taste.

Hint: *Can be served in tart shells or with crackers.*

CRAWFISH DIP

1 stick butter

1 large onion, chopped

1 bell pepper, chopped

1 clove garlic, minced

¼ cup chopped parsley

1 pound Louisiana crawfish tails, peeled

Salt and pepper to taste

Hot sauce to taste

1 (8-ounce) package cream cheese

Melt butter. Sauté onion and bell pepper in butter until onion is clear. Add garlic, parsley, crawfish, salt, pepper and hot sauce. Cook 10 minutes over medium heat. Add cream cheese. Stir until smooth.

Makes 3 cups

Hint: *Serve in mini tart shells, with Melba toast or with crackers.*

Shrimp Dip

2	(8-ounce) packages cream cheese	2	teaspoons Worcestershire sauce
1	pound boiled shrimp, peeled	2	teaspoons horseradish
½	cup mayonnaise	½	teaspoon celery salt
⅓	cup chili sauce		Greens onions, garnish (optional)
3	tablespoons ketchup		

In a large bowl soften cheese. Chop shrimp and add to cheese, mix thoroughly. Add mayonnaise, chili sauce, ketchup, Worcestershire sauce, horseradish and celery salt. Blend well. Serve with crackers.

Hot Tamale Dip

1	(28-ounce) can hot tamales	8	ounces jalapeño cheese, cubed
1	(15-ounce) can chili		

Unwrap and slice tamales into small pieces. Place tamales in a heavy saucepan. Add chili and cheese. Stir until well mixed. Cook over medium heat until cheese is melted. Pour into bowl and serve with your favorite chips.

Having a Party?

Allow 12 hors d'oeuvres per person and if you have:

10 people	*Serve 3 varieties of hors d'oeuvres*
20 people	*Serve 4 to 5 varieties of hors d'oeuvres*
50 or more people	*Serve 8 or more varieties of hors d'oeuvres*

Suggestions: Finger sandwiches, dips, canapés, mini desserts, etc.

ARTICHOKE BREAD

1   stick butter
1   cup sour cream
1   cup grated Monterey Jack cheese
1   (14-ounce) can artichoke hearts, drained and chopped

Green onions and parsley to taste, chopped
1   large loaf French bread
Grated Cheddar cheese to taste

Preheat oven to 400 degrees. Melt butter. Add sour cream, Monterey Jack cheese, artichoke, green onions, and parsley. Blend thoroughly. Split bread in half lengthwise. Push soft part of bread down and fill both halves with the artichoke mixture. Sprinkle with Cheddar cheese. Bake 25 to 30 minutes or until hot and bubbly.

CHEESE BREAD

1	stick butter, softened	1	tablespoon minced garlic
¾	cup mayonnaise	2-3	cups grated mozzarella cheese
½	cup chopped green onions	1	loaf French bread

Preheat oven to 400 degrees. Mix together butter and mayonnaise. Stir until well blended. Add green onions, garlic and cheese. Blend thoroughly. Cut bread in half lengthwise. Spread butter mixture evenly over both halves of bread. Bake 20 to 25 minutes until cheese is lightly brown.

SPINACH BREAD

1	(10-ounce) package frozen chopped spinach	½	cup shredded Cheddar cheese
1	medium onion, finely chopped	½	cup shredded mozzarella cheese
1	stick butter	1	loaf French bread

Preheat oven to 350 degrees. Cook spinach according to package directions. Drain. Set aside. Sauté onion in butter. Stir in spinach. Remove from heat. Add cheeses. Mix thoroughly. Slice bread in half lengthwise. Spread mixture evenly on both halves of bread. Wrap each loosely in foil. Bake 30 minutes.

CRAWFISH BREAD

1 (10-ounce) package frozen chopped spinach
¾ cup chopped onion
1 loaf French bread
1 cup mayonnaise
2 tablespoons butter
1 pound Louisiana crawfish tails, peeled and chopped
¾ cup chopped green onions
1 teaspoon pureed garlic

1 teaspoon chopped parsley
1 teaspoon Créole seasoning
1 (8-ounce) package cream cheese, softened
3 tablespoons mayonnaise
½ cup grated Parmesan cheese
¾ cup shredded jalapeño cheese
Paprika and parsley to taste

Preheat oven to 375 degrees. Boil spinach and onion until tender. Drain well. Set aside. Cut bread in half lengthwise. Place on cookie sheet and spread with mayonnaise. Set aside. In butter, sauté crawfish, green onions, garlic and parsley 5 to 10 minutes. Stir in Créole seasoning. In a large bowl, blend crawfish mixture, spinach mixture, cream cheese and mayonnaise. Spread evenly on both sides of bread. Top with Parmesan cheese, jalapeño cheese, paprika, and parsley. Bake 15 minutes and then broil 2 minutes.

May the wings of the butterfly kiss the sun and find your shoulder to light on, to bring you luck, happiness and riches today, tomorrow and beyond.

Irish Blessing

SAUSAGE BITES

1	(16-ounce) package breakfast sausage	2	teaspoons chopped parsley
½	cup chopped onion	1	egg, beaten
2	cups baking mix	1	teaspoon hot sauce
1	cup grated Swiss cheese	⅔	cup milk
½	cup Parmesan cheese	¼	cup mayonnaise

Preheat oven to 400 degrees. Grease a 9x13-inch pan and set aside. Brown sausage and onion. Drain. Set aside. Combine baking mix, Swiss cheese, Parmesan cheese and parsley. Mix well. Add sausage mixture, egg, hot sauce, milk and mayonnaise. Stir thoroughly. Spread in prepared pan. Bake 25 to 30 minutes. Cut into small squares.

HOLIDAY BRIE

1	large sheet frozen puff pastry	½	cup dried cranberries, softened
1	pound Brie cheese round	¼	cup sliced almonds
2	tablespoons light brown sugar	1	egg, slightly beaten
½	cup peach preserves	1	teaspoon water

Preheat oven to 400 degrees. Roll pastry on floured surface into a 14-inch square. Place on baking sheet. Place Brie in center and sprinkle with brown sugar. Spoon preserves over sugar. Sprinkle cranberries and almonds over preserves. Mix egg and water. Brush edges of pastry with egg mixture. Bring edges over top of Brie. Pinch edges together to make a pretty bundle. Make sure edges are sealed. Brush entire pastry with egg mixture. Bake 20 minutes or until golden brown. Let stand 1 hour before serving.

HOT AND SPICY BRIE

1	(12-ounce) can crescent rolls	1	(8-ounce) jar jalapeño raspberry preserve
1	(8-ounce) Brie cheese round	1	egg white, slightly beaten
½	cup chopped walnuts		

Preheat oven to 350 degrees. Lightly grease baking sheet. Set aside. Roll out crescent rolls, pinching seams together to make one pastry shell. Place on prepared baking sheet. Place Brie in center, sprinkle with walnuts and pour preserves on top. Bring dough over the cheese and wrap in a nice shape. Pinch edges to seal. Brush with egg white. Bake 30 minutes or until golden brown.

RASPBERRY BRIE

1	sheet puff pastry	¼	cup chopped pecans, toasted
1	(8-ounce) Brie cheese round	½	cup raspberry jam
1	tablespoon light brown sugar	1	egg, beaten

Preheat oven to 375 degrees. Lightly grease baking sheet. Set aside. Roll pastry out 2 inches on each side. Place on prepared baking sheet. Place Brie in middle of pastry. Sprinkle Brie with brown sugar and pecans. Spread jam on top of sugar mixture. Bring edges of pastry together. Pinch edges to seal. Brush with egg. Bake 25 minutes or until golden brown.

Chocolate Chip Cheese Ball

1 (8-ounce) package cream cheese	½ cup semisweet mini chocolate chips
1 teaspoon vanilla	2 tablespoons brown sugar
¾ cup confectioners' sugar	1 stick butter

Mix all ingredients thoroughly. Chill 2 hours. Shape into a ball. Chill 1 hour.

Hint: *Serve with chocolate graham cracker sticks.*

Nutty Cheese Ball

1 cup mayonnaise	1 cup chopped green onions
2 cups finely shredded Cheddar cheese	1 (8-ounce) jar hot pepper jelly, red or green
2 cups chopped pecans	

Mix mayonnaise and cheese. Add pecans and green onions. Mix well. Shape into a ball. Chill. Before serving, spoon pepper jelly over ball. Serve with crackers of choice.

Party Cheese Nibbles

1 stick butter	1½ teaspoons Créole seasoning
1 cup grated sharp Cheddar cheese	1 cup flour

Preheat oven to 400 degrees. Cream together butter, cheese and Créole seasoning. Add flour to butter mixture. Mix until dough consistency. Roll into 1-inch balls and place on a cookie sheet. Press with a fork to slightly flatten. Bake 15 minutes or until golden brown.

Makes 4 dozen

CHICKEN GLACÉ

8	cups water	1	cup chopped bell peppers
1	(3½-pound) whole chicken		Salt and pepper to taste
1	cup chopped onion	2	(1-ounce) boxes unflavored gelatin
1	cup chopped celery		

Cut up chicken. Pour water in large stock pot with chicken. Boil until chicken can easily be deboned. Remove chicken reserving water. Dice chicken meat and set aside. To the water add onion, celery and bell pepper. Add salt and pepper to taste. Cook until vegetables are very tender and liquid is reduced to about 4 cups. Add chicken. Gradually add gelatin. Stir until gelatin is completely dissolved. Bring to a boil. Remove from heat. Pour into a 9x13-inch pan. Refrigerate to gel.

Hint: *This makes a great appetizer to serve with crackers. For extra flavor, green onions may also be added.*

CAJUN "FIRE" CRACKERS

1	(1-pound) box saltine crackers	1	(1-ounce) package dry ranch dressing mix
1½	cups vegetable oil		
1	tablespoon crushed red pepper		

Place crackers in a two-gallon container with lid. Mix together oil, red pepper and dressing mix. Stir until dissolved. Pour over crackers. Cover. Rotate crackers gently so that oil mixture will cover bottom of crackers. Turn container upside down and rotate again. Turn container every 5 to 10 minutes for 1 hour. Best after 12 hours.

Hint: *For very spicy crackers, use 2 tablespoons crushed red pepper.*

PARTY MEATBALLS

1 stick butter
1½ cups brown sugar
1 (14-ounce) can crushed pineapple
1 (8-ounce) can pineapple juice

2 (16-ounce) bottles barbecue sauce
2 (3-pound) bags cooked Italian style meatballs

Melt butter. Add sugar. Cook until sugar is dissolved. Add crushed pineapple and pineapple juice. Stir in barbecue sauce. When mixture is hot, slowly add meatballs, coating all meatballs with sauce. Heat thoroughly.

STUFFED MUSHROOMS

12 large mushrooms
1 stick butter
1 onion, finely chopped
2 ribs celery, finely chopped
Worcestershire sauce, to taste
½ pound shrimp, chopped
1 pound crabmeat
½ lemon, juice only

2 teaspoons parsley
1½ cups Italian bread crumbs
Salt and red pepper to taste
Garlic powder to taste
Hot sauce to taste
½ cup white wine
½ cup melted butter
Parmesan cheese (optional)

Preheat oven to 350 degrees. Clean and remove stems from mushroom. Set aside. Chop mushroom stems. Set aside. Melt butter. Add onion, celery and mushroom stems. Cook until limp. Add Worcestershire sauce, shrimp, crabmeat, lemon juice, parsley, bread crumbs, salt, pepper, garlic powder and hot sauce. Cook slowly for about 15 minutes. Stuff mushrooms with mixture. Place in a baking dish. Top with wine and ½ cup melted butter. Bake 10 to 15 minutes.

QUICK MINI PIZZAS

1	pound ground beef	1½	pounds Velveeta
1	pound hot breakfast sausage	2	(24-count) packages party rye bread

Preheat oven to 350 degrees. Cook beef and sausage until brown. Drain, retaining some oil. Add Velveeta. Mix thoroughly. Place a teaspoonful of mixture on each slice of bread and flatten mixture. Place on a cookie sheet. Bake 8 to 10 minutes.

Makes 4 dozen

Hint: *Place on a cookie sheet to freeze. Then store in freezer bags until ready to serve.*

LEMON WINGS

24	chicken wings		Minced garlic
	Lemon pepper		Honey
	Créole seasoning	½	stick butter
2-3	lemons		

Preheat oven to 350 degrees. Remove tips of each wing to the joint. Use only the flat portions and drumettes. Season to taste with lemon pepper and Créole seasoning. Place in a large shallow baking pan. Grate fresh lemon zest over the wings. Sprinkle with minced garlic. Squirt honey lightly over the wings. Dab butter randomly over wings. Cover with foil. Bake 25 minutes. Remove foil. Cook additional 25 minutes turning to brown both sides. Do not overcook, wings must be moist.

RED-HOT WINGS

Vegetable oil for frying
40 chicken wings, tips removed
1 (12-ounce) bottle hot sauce
1 (1-ounce) package Italian salad dressing mix
2 sticks butter, melted
1 (16-ounce) bottle Bleu cheese dressing

Preheat oven to 350 degrees. Line a cookie sheet with foil. Set aside. Heat oil. Fry wings about 10 minutes until almost crisp. Drain. In medium bowl, combine hot sauce, salad dressing mix and butter. Dip wings in butter mixture. Place a single layer of wings on the prepared cookie sheet. Bake 10 minutes. Remove and coat with butter mixture. Return to oven and bake until crispy. Serve with Bleu cheese dressing.

NUTS AND BOLTS

1 stick butter
1 teaspoon celery salt
1 teaspoon onion salt
1 teaspoon garlic salt
1½ tablespoons Worcestershire sauce
1 tablespoon hot sauce
2½ cups Wheat Chex
2½ cups thin, stick pretzels
2½ cups Rice Chex
1 cup peanuts

Preheat oven to 250 degrees. Melt butter in large shallow baking pan. Stir in celery salt, onion salt, garlic salt, Worcestershire and hot sauce. Add Wheat Chex, pretzels, Rice Chex and peanuts. Mix until well coated. Bake 1 hour. Stir every 15 minutes. Spread on paper to cool. Store in tightly covered containers.

PINK TEAM MIX

2 cups Cheerios cereal
1 (8-ounce) bag Chex Sweet 'n Salty Trail Mix
1 (14-ounce) bag kissable candy
1 (12-ounce) bag white chocolate chips
3 tablespoons oil

Line 2 baking sheets with wax paper. Set aside. Mix cereal, trail mix and candy in a large bowl. Microwave chocolate chips and oil on high. Stir every 20 seconds until chocolate melts and mixture is smooth. Immediately pour over cereal mixture. Toss with large spatula until well coated. Drop by spoonfuls onto prepared baking sheets. Freeze 15 minutes. Remove and store in covered container.

SUGARHOUSE TRASH

1 (12-ounce) box Crispix cereal
1 (16-ounce) bag tiny twist pretzels
1 (16-ounce) bag pecans
1 stick butter
½ cup dark corn syrup
1 cup dark brown sugar

Preheat oven to 250 degrees. Lightly grease roasting pan. In the roasting pan mix together cereal, pretzels and pecans. Combine butter, corn syrup and sugar in a saucepan. Cook until sugar is dissolved. Pour sugar mixture over cereal mixture. Bake 1 hour, stirring every 15 minutes. Pour into a brown paper bag. Shake the bag 10 minutes.

Hint: *Peanuts or walnuts may be substituted for pecans.*

MAYONNAISE

4 eggs, boiled	Lemon juice or vinegar
1 egg yolk, raw	to thin
1 pint vegetable oil	

Mash boiled yolks. Add raw egg yolk. Mix until well blended. Add oil a few drops at a time mixing well after each addition. Repeat until all the oil is used. After all the oil is added, lemon juice or vinegar may be used to thin the mayonnaise if desired.

Hint: *Adding a large amount of oil at one time will cause the mixture to separate.*

MOM'S FAVORITE BARBECUE SAUCE

¾ cup chopped onion	2 tablespoons mustard
1 stick butter	3 tablespoons
¾ cup ketchup	Worcestershire sauce
¾ cup water	2 teaspoons salt
⅓ cup lemon juice	½ teaspoon pepper
3 tablespoons sugar	Liquid smoke (optional)

Sauté onion in butter until soft. Add ketchup, water, lemon juice, sugar, mustard, Worcestershire sauce, salt and pepper. Simmer 15 minutes. Refrigerate leftover sauce.

CRANBERRY SAUCE

3 cups fresh cranberries
1 cup cold water

1¼ cups sugar

Wash and clean berries. Place in a saucepan, add cold water and sugar. Stir over medium heat until berries pop. Cook until thick. Cool and store in refrigerator in a covered container.

JAZZY SAUCE

1 (18-ounce) jar pineapple preserves
1 (18-ounce) jar apple jelly
1 (5-ounce) jar prepared horseradish

1 (1-ounce) jar dry mustard
1 tablespoon coarse black pepper

Place all ingredients in a medium-size bowl and beat with wire whisk until well blended. Store in refrigerator.

Makes 2 pints

Hint: *Serve over cream cheese.*

"There is nothing in a caterpillar that tells you it's going to be a butterfly."

Richard Buckminster Fuller

SWEDISH MEATBALL SAUCE

1 (16-ounce) jar grape jelly   1 (16-ounce) jar barbecue
                                                                    sauce

Mix jelly and barbecue sauce and heat to boiling. Serve hot.

Hint: *Meatballs and/or sausages may be added.*

EASY PARTY MEATBALL SAUCE

1 (26-ounce) jar spaghetti   ½ cup sugar
    meat flavored sauce   1 (18-ounce) bottle brown
1 (26-ounce) jar spaghetti   sugar barbecue sauce
    roasted garlic and
    onion sauce

Combine meat sauce, garlic and onion sauce, sugar and barbecue sauce in slow cooker. Add your favorite meatballs and/or sausage. Bring to a boil. Simmer 20 minutes.

"Beautiful and graceful, varied and enchanting, small but approachable, butterflies lead you to the sunny side of life. And everyone deserves a little sunshine."

Jeffreey Glassberg

Biscuits, Bread
& Breakfast

Carolyn
Dugas

Carolyn Dugas

Madewood

Louisiana was a promised land at the end of the 18th century. Profitable river trade along the Mississippi, the influx of foreign merchants through the bustling Port of New Orleans, and the fertile Mississippi Delta fields lured entrepreneurial men to the banks of the river.

Thomas Pugh of North Carolina moved to the Bayou Lafourche region of Louisiana. He hired New Orleans architect Henry Howard to design a house that would be the gem of the bayou.

For four years Thomas cut, fashioned and cured his timbers, mostly cypress. The title "Madewood" came naturally, as the house was built essentially of the plantation's own wood. Madewood was set apart from all its neighbors by its Greek-Revival style of architecture in the middle of the cane fields.

Fortunately, the Civil War spared Madewood. Today it is a gracious home-away-from-home that travelers from around the world can enjoy. As one sits on the shaded porches looking out at the majestic oaks dripping with Spanish moss, one can smell the sweet magnolias and be transported back into a simpler time and life along Bayou Lafourche.

Carolyn Dugas

ANGEL BISCUITS

4	cups biscuit mix	2	sticks butter, melted
1	teaspoon baking powder	1½	cups milk
1	heaping tablespoon sugar		Extra biscuit mix if needed
1	teaspoon salt		

Preheat oven to 400 degrees. Sift biscuit mix, baking powder, sugar and salt in a large bowl. Make a well in center. Put butter in center and pour milk over butter. Mix well. More biscuit mix may be needed to reach the desired consistency to form mixture into balls about 1½ to 2 inches in diameter. Place on cookie sheet and bake 10 to 12 minutes or until golden brown.

Hint: *These can be frozen until ready to use.*

Use shortening or oil when greasing pans. These absorb nicely into the dough and make a nicer crust.

BASIC BISCUITS

2½	cups flour	2	tablespoons sugar
1½	tablespoons baking powder	¾	cup solid shortening
½	teaspoon salt	⅔	cup milk

Preheat oven to 450 degrees. In a large bowl, mix flour, baking powder, salt and sugar. Cut in shortening with pastry blender until coarse. Add milk and stir until dough holds together. Place on floured surface and knead lightly. Roll out to 1-inch thickness and cut with biscuit cutter dipped in flour. Place on baking sheet and bake 15 to 20 minutes or until golden brown.

Hint: *If you wish to freeze biscuits, bake 10 to 15 minutes, allow to cool. Put in bags and freeze until ready to finish baking. Freezes well.*

BUTTERFLY BISCUITS

1 stick butter	1 cup biscuit mix, separate bowl
4 cups biscuit mix	
1 cup lemon lime soda	
1 (8-ounce) container sour cream	

Preheat oven to 350 degrees. Melt butter and pour into a 9x13-inch baking dish and set aside. Mix biscuit mix, lemon lime soda and sour cream. Drop by spoonfuls into the separate bowl of biscuit mix. Form into a patty and lay in the baking dish coating both sides with the melted butter. Bake 10 to 15 minutes or until golden brown.

Makes 20 to 25 biscuits

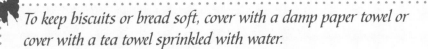 *To keep biscuits or bread soft, cover with a damp paper towel or cover with a tea towel sprinkled with water.*

LOUISIANA SWEET POTATO BISCUITS

1 cup cooked and mashed sweet potato	½ cup light brown sugar
2 cups biscuit mix	2 tablespoons butter
½ teaspoon baking powder	3 tablespoons solid shortening
½ teaspoon baking soda	½ cup milk

Preheat oven to 400 degrees. Place biscuit mix, baking powder, baking soda and brown sugar in mixing bowl and stir. Add sweet potato and blend. Add butter, shortening and blend with pastry blender until mixture is coarse. Add milk and mix well. Place on floured surface and roll out to about 1-inch thickness. Cut with biscuit cutter dipped in flour. Place on baking sheet and bake 15 to 20 minutes or until golden brown.

Makes 10 to 12 biscuits

SAUSAGE AND CHEESE BISCUITS

3 cups biscuit mix	8 ounces shredded mild Cheddar cheese
1 pound hot bulk sausage	¼ cup milk
8 ounces shredded sharp Cheddar cheese	

Preheat oven to 350 degrees. Sift biscuit mix, crumble and add uncooked sausage. Add cheeses. Add milk and mix well. Shape into 1-inch balls and bake 20 to 25 minutes or until brown.

Hint: *Freezes well.*

Store leftover biscuit dough in an airtight container. Dough will not rise until the container is opened.

BREAKFAST CUPCAKES

10 slices bacon	10 tablespoons salsa
1 can (10) buttermilk biscuits	½ cup shredded Cheddar cheese
10 eggs	

Preheat oven to 350 degrees. Fry bacon and set aside. Using a cupcake pan, press one biscuit into each cup and up the side to form a cup. Break an egg into each biscuit. Spoon 1 tablespoon of salsa over each egg. Crumble 1 slice of bacon in each cup and sprinkle with cheese. Bake 15 minutes.

Putting a small dish of water in the oven when baking bread or rolls will help the crusts from getting too hard or too brown.

HOMEMADE BREAD

2	cups warm water	6½	cups bread flour
2	teaspoons salt	2	tablespoons shortening
2	tablespoons sugar	1	stick butter
1	package yeast		

Preheat oven to 350 degrees. In a large bowl, mix water, salt, sugar and yeast thoroughly. Add 2 cups of flour at a time and mix well. Continue with flour until consistency of dough forms. Grease another large bowl with shortening and place the dough in bowl. Cover with a large dishtowel to keep drafts from touching dough. Let rise 1 hour. Grease hands with shortening and knead to remove all bubbles. Form the dough into loaves or dinner rolls and let rise another 15 to 20 minutes. Bake 25 to 30 minutes or until bread is golden brown. Remove from oven and spread butter on bread.

Makes 2 loaves or 12 dinner rolls

To glaze rolls and bread: Before baking, brush with a beaten egg yolk for a dark shiny finish. Brush with melted butter or margarine for a light shiny finish.

BEIGNETS

1 package dry yeast	1 large egg, well beaten
1 cup warm water	4-5 cups flour
¾ cup evaporated milk	3 cups vegetable oil
¼ cup sugar	¼ cup confectioners' sugar
1 teaspoon salt	

Combine yeast and warm water in large glass measuring cup. Let stand 5 minutes. Combine yeast mixture, evaporated milk, sugar, salt and egg in a large bowl. Gradually add enough flour to make soft dough. Cover and refrigerate about 8 hours. Place dough on a well floured surface and knead several times. Roll into a rectangle ¼-inch thick. Cut into 2½-inch squares. Fry in hot oil (375 degrees) 1 minute on each side. Drain on paper towels. Sprinkle with confectioners' sugar.

Makes about 2½ dozen beignets

Milk makes the texture of bread finer. Water makes the texture coarser.

FRIED BREAD DOUGH

1 package frozen bread dough	3 cups vegetable oil
	¼ cup confectioners' sugar

Place frozen dough in refrigerator overnight to defrost. Remove from refrigerator and let rise until double in size. Break off pieces about the size of a golf ball. Each piece should be stretched by hand to at least twice its size. Put slits in the middle of each piece of dough after it is stretched. Fry in hot oil (375 degrees) 3 to 4 minutes browning on both sides. Place on paper towels and sprinkle with confectioners' sugar or serve with syrup.

Hint: *You may also use 1 package of bread dough from the bakery.*

CAJUN DOUGHNUTS

6 cups flour	3 eggs, beaten
1 tablespoon baking powder	3 tablespoons shortening
1 teaspoon baking soda	1 cup milk
1 cup sugar	1 tablespoon vanilla
	½ cup confectioners' sugar

Mix flour, baking powder and baking soda and set aside. Cream sugar, eggs and shortening together until light and fluffy. Add flour mixture while alternately adding milk, mixing thoroughly between additions. Add vanilla. Place on a floured surface and knead gently several times. Roll dough out to ½-inch thickness and cut into rectangular pieces. Cut 2 slits in each piece to allow the dough to brown when frying. Fry in hot oil (375 degrees) until golden brown. Drain on paper towels. Sprinkle with confectioners' sugar. Serve while hot.

Makes about 36 doughnuts

Hint: *Cinnamon sugar may also be used in place of confectioners' sugar.*

BANANA BREAD

1 stick butter	2 cups flour
⅔ cup sugar	1½ teaspoons vanilla
2 eggs	1 cup chopped pecans (optional)
3 ripe bananas, mashed	
1 teaspoon baking soda	

Preheat oven to 350 degrees. Grease and flour a loaf pan, set aside. Cream butter and sugar. Add eggs and blend well. Add bananas, baking soda, flour, vanilla and pecans. Mix well. Pour into prepared pan. Bake in a loaf pan 45 minutes.

MONKEY BREAD

Bread

Nonstick cooking spray	½ teaspoon cinnamon
20 small biscuits	½ cup sugar

Topping

1½ sticks butter	1 cup brown sugar
1 teaspoon cinnamon	½ cup chopped pecans

Preheat oven to 350 degrees. Spray Bundt pan. Set aside. Quarter biscuits. Mix cinnamon and sugar in a bowl. Roll biscuits in sugar mixture. Place biscuits in prepared pan. To make the topping, melt butter in a small saucepan. Add cinnamon and brown sugar. Bring to a boil. Cook 2 minutes. Pour cinnamon sugar mixture over biscuits. Top with pecans. Bake 25 minutes. Cool 10 minutes before inverting on a platter.

PUMPKIN BREAD

3 cups sugar	1 (15-ounce) can pumpkin
2 teaspoons cinnamon	1¾ cups raisins
1 teaspoon nutmeg	3½ cups flour
1 teaspoon ginger	2 teaspoons baking powder
1 teaspoon vanilla	2 teaspoons baking soda
1 cup vegetable oil	1 teaspoon salt
4 eggs	¾ cup water

Preheat oven to 375 degrees. Spray 3 loaf pans or one 9x13-inch pan with nonstick cooking spray. Put sugar, cinnamon, nutmeg and ginger in a large mixing bowl and mix well. Add vanilla and oil and mix. Add eggs, one at a time, mixing thoroughly after each egg. Mix in pumpkin and raisins. Sift together flour, baking powder, baking soda and salt. Add this mixture to the pumpkin mixture alternating with the water. Mix well after each addition. Pour into prepared pans. Bake 1 hour.

RAISIN ZUCCHINI BREAD

2	cups sugar	1	teaspoon salt
1	cup oil	1	teaspoon baking powder
3	eggs, beaten	1	teaspoon baking soda
3	cups finely shredded zucchini	1	tablespoon cinnamon
1	tablespoon vanilla	1	cup raisins
3	cups flour	1	cup chopped pecans

Preheat oven to 350 degrees. Grease and flour 2 loaf pans or one 9x13-inch pan and set aside. Blend sugar and oil. Add eggs, zucchini and vanilla, mix well. In separate bowl combine flour, salt, baking powder, baking soda and cinnamon. Combine flour mixture and zucchini mixture and stir well. Add raisins and pecans, mix well. Pour into prepared pans. Bake 1 hour. Let cool 10 minutes before removing from pan.

STRAWBERRY BREAD

2	(10-ounce) packages strawberries	1	tablespoon cinnamon
2	cups flour	4	eggs
1	teaspoon baking soda	1¼	cups vegetable oil
1	teaspoon salt	2	cups sugar
		1¼	cups chopped pecans

Defrost strawberries. Preheat oven to 350 degrees. Grease and flour 2 loaf pans and set aside. Sift flour, baking soda, salt and cinnamon. In a large bowl, beat eggs and add oil and sugar. Gradually stir in flour mixture. Add strawberries (do not drain) and pecans. Pour into prepared pans. Bake 60 minutes or until toothpick inserted in center comes out clean.

Makes 2 loaves

COUNTRY CORNBREAD

- 3 cups yellow cornmeal
- 1 cup flour
- 6 tablespoons sugar
- 1 teaspoon salt
- 2 tablespoons baking powder
- 1 cup milk
- 1 cup nonfat plain yogurt
- ¼ cup unsalted butter, melted
- ¼ cup vegetable oil
- 4 large eggs, lightly beaten
- 1 (15-ounce) can cream corn

Preheat oven to 400 degrees. Grease two 8-inch square baking pans. Combine cornmeal, flour, sugar, salt and baking powder in a bowl. In another bowl, combine the milk, yogurt, butter, oil and eggs. Add this to the cornmeal mixture. Stir until just moistened. Add the cream corn. Pour the batter into the prepared pans and bake until the top is golden brown and a toothpick inserted in the center comes out clean, about 45 minutes. Cool and cut into squares.

Makes 12 to 18 squares

Before the Acadians left Canada they adopted Our Lady of the Assumption as the patroness of their people. The Acadians settling in this area of Louisiana named their parish Assumption after Our Lady.

CRACKLING CORNBREAD

Cracklings
2   cups 1-inch pieces salt pork

Cornbread

2   cups yellow cornmeal
1½ teaspoons baking powder
½   teaspoon baking soda
1¼ cups crackling crumbs

1   cup buttermilk
¼   cup crackling drippings
2   eggs, well beaten

Preheat oven to 400 degrees. Make cracklings by frying pieces of salt pork until they are brown and crumbling. Set aside crumbs and reserve the drippings. Grease a 9x13-inch baking pan and set aside. To make the cornbread, combine cornmeal, baking powder and soda. Blend thoroughly and add crackling crumbs. Add buttermilk and drippings to the eggs. Mix well. Stir into cornmeal mixture. Pour into prepared baking pan. Bake 25 to 30 minutes.

Makes 8 servings

Hint: *Bacon may be substituted if cracklings are unavailable.*

The wings of some butterflies are marked with patterns that look very much like letters of the alphabet, as well as numerals.

CRAWFISH CORNBREAD

1 onion, chopped	½ teaspoon Créole seasoning
1 bell pepper, chopped	
3 jalapeños (optional)	½ teaspoon baking soda
½ stick butter	⅓ cup vegetable oil
1 pound Louisiana crawfish tails, peeled	2 eggs, beaten
	1 (15-ounce) can cream style corn
1 cup yellow cornmeal	
1 teaspoon salt	8 ounces Cheddar cheese, grated

Preheat oven to 350 degrees. Grease 9x13-inch pan and set aside. Sauté onion, bell pepper and jalapeño in butter until wilted. Add crawfish and cook 5 minutes. Set aside. In a large bowl, combine cornmeal, salt, Créole seasoning and baking soda. Add oil, eggs, corn, cheese and crawfish mixture. Mix well. Pour into prepared pan. Bake 40 to 45 minutes or until golden brown.

EASY SPOON BREAD

3 cups milk	1 stick butter
1½ cups cornbread mix	6 eggs, separated

Preheat oven to 375 degrees. Grease a 2-quart casserole. Place milk in a large saucepan and bring to a boil. Stir in cornbread mix gradually and cook until very thick. Stir until mixture leaves the side of the pan. Remove from heat. Add butter and stir until completely melted. Allow to cool. Beat egg yolks and stir into cooled cornmeal mixture. Beat egg whites until stiff, but not dry. Blend into cornmeal mixture. Pour into prepared casserole and bake 45 to 50 minutes or until golden brown. Serve warm with butter, syrup or powdered sugar.

Hint: *This dish is usually eaten with a spoon.*

OATMEAL BREAKFAST CAKE

1	cup flour	1	teaspoon baking soda
1	cup old-fashioned oats	½	teaspoon cinnamon
1	cup graham cracker crumbs	½	teaspoon salt
		½	cup vegetable oil
¾	cup brown sugar, packed	1	cup buttermilk
½	cup sugar	3	eggs
1	teaspoon baking powder		

Preheat oven to 350 degrees. Coat a 12-cup Bundt pan with cooking spray. Combine flour, oats, crumbs, sugars, baking powder, baking soda, cinnamon and salt. In a separate bowl, whisk together oil, buttermilk and eggs. Add buttermilk mixture to dry ingredients and whisk until combined. Spoon batter into prepared Bundt pan. Bake 40 minutes or until a toothpick inserted in the center comes out clean. Cool on wire rack 5 minutes. Remove from pan and cool completely on wire rack.

Serves 16

BREAKFAST IN A HURRY CASSEROLE

1	(16-ounce) package bulk sausage	1	teaspoon chopped parsley
6	eggs	2	tablespoons chopped green onions
2	cups milk		
2	cups grated Cheddar cheese	1	teaspoon Créole seasoning
1	cup biscuit mix		

Preheat oven to 350 degrees. Cook and drain sausage. Put into an 8x11-inch casserole. In a large mixing bowl mix eggs, milk, cheese, biscuit mix, parsley, green onions and seasoning until well blended. Pour egg mixture over sausage. Bake uncovered 40 to 45 minutes.

MERE'S CRÊPES

2	eggs	1	cup milk
¼	teaspoon salt	1	cup flour
¼	teaspoon sugar		Oil for skillet or crepe pan
1	cup water		

Beat eggs thoroughly. Stir in salt and sugar. Mix water and milk. Add ½ of the milk mixture to the egg mixture. Add flour and mix well. Add the remaining milk mixture and mix thoroughly. Batter should be smooth and the consistency of light cream. Let stand 15 to 20 minutes. Oil and heat skillet or crepe pan. Pour ¼ cup of batter into the skillet. Move pan around so that the entire surface is coated. When golden brown on bottom turn and brown other side. Butter, roll and set aside to be filled. Fill with jam, preserves, cream cheese, syrup or filling of your choice.

Makes 15 to 20 crêpes

EGG AND SAUSAGE PIE

1	(8-inch) pie shell	6	eggs
1	egg white	½	cup evaporated milk
1	pound bulk breakfast sausage	1	cup grated Cheddar cheese

Preheat oven to 350 degrees. Brush pie shell with egg white. Bake 10 minutes. Remove from oven. Brown and drain sausage. Beat eggs. Add milk, cheese and sausage to eggs. Pour into pie shell. Bake 30 to 40 minutes or until eggs are firm. Allow to set 10 minutes before cutting.

Serves 4

Hint: *Any cheese may be used.*

EGG AND SAUSAGE CASSEROLE

8	slices bread, buttered	½	teaspoon salt
1½	pounds bulk pork sausage	½	teaspoon black pepper
3	cups grated Cheddar cheese	½	teaspoon dry mustard
6	eggs, slightly beaten	½	teaspoon Worcestershire sauce
2½	cups milk	½	teaspoon Créole seasoning
1	small onion, minced	½	cup chopped parsley
1	clove garlic, minced		

Assemble the casserole the day before serving. Grease a 3-quart casserole. Trim bread and cut into cubes. Place in prepared casserole. Cook and drain sausage. Combine sausage, cheese, eggs, milk, onion, garlic, salt, pepper, mustard, Worcestershire sauce, seasoning and parsley, stirring with a wire whisk. Pour mixture over bread. Chill at least 24 hours. Bake uncovered at 325 degrees for 1 hour.

Serves 8 to 10

Hint: *Unbaked casserole can be frozen; thaw before baking.*

Add a little milk or water to eggs when scrambling to make them light and fluffy.

If in doubt about the freshness of an egg, immerse it in cold water, if it floats, do not use.

EGGS BEL-MAR

White Sauce

½ stick butter
¼ cup flour
2 cups milk

1 teaspoon salt
½ teaspoon pepper

Bel-Mar

1 (6-ounce) package Canadian bacon
½ pound bulk pork sausage
6 tablespoons butter, melted
¼ cup chopped green pepper

¼ cup chopped red pepper
¼ cup chopped green onions
½ pound mushrooms, sliced
18 eggs, slightly beaten
1 cup soft bread crumbs

Preheat oven to 350 degrees. Grease a 9x13-inch casserole. To prepare white sauce, melt butter in a heavy saucepan. Add flour, stirring until smooth. Cook 1 minute, stirring constantly. Gradually add milk and cook over medium heat, stirring constantly, until sauce thickens and bubbles. Add salt and pepper and set aside. To prepare the Bel-Mar, cook bacon and pork sausage, drain and set aside. Put 3 tablespoons butter in a saucepan and sauté peppers, green onions and mushrooms until tender. Drain and add to bacon and sausage mixture. Coat a large skillet with 1 tablespoon butter and add eggs. Cook over low heat until eggs begin to set. Stir frequently with a wide spatula until eggs are thickened, but not dry. Remove from heat and set aside. Gently stir bacon and sausage mixture into white sauce. Add this to the eggs and stir thoroughly. Spoon this mixture into prepared casserole. Combine bread crumbs with remaining 2 tablespoons of butter and mix well. Sprinkle over the egg mixture. Bake uncovered 20 to 25 minutes or until thoroughly heated.

Makes 12 servings

SUNDAY SCRAMBLED EGGS

½ stick butter
1½ cups sliced mushrooms
½ cup diced red bell pepper
½ cup diced green bell pepper
1 medium tomato, chopped
¼ cup chopped green onions
1 teaspoon salt
½ teaspoon black pepper
12 large eggs
½ cup heavy whipping cream

In a large nonstick skillet, melt butter over medium heat. Add mushrooms, peppers, tomato, green onions, salt and pepper. Cook 5 to 6 minutes, stirring frequently or until vegetables are tender. In a medium bowl, whisk together eggs and cream. Pour egg mixture into pan with vegetables. Cook 4 to 5 minutes, stirring occasionally, until eggs set. Serve immediately.

Makes 6 to 8 servings

OVERNIGHT FRENCH TOAST

1 loaf French bread, day old
1 stick butter, melted
1½ cups light brown sugar
1 teaspoon cinnamon
8 eggs
2 cups milk
⅛ teaspoon salt

Grease a 9x13-inch baking dish and set aside. Cut bread into 1-inch thick slices. In a small bowl, mix together butter, brown sugar and cinnamon. Press this mixture in the bottom of the prepared baking dish. Place bread slices over this mixture. Press pieces tightly together to hold them in place. In a separate bowl, beat eggs, milk and salt. Carefully pour over bread. Make sure the bread stays on the bottom of the pan and does not float. Cover tightly and refrigerate overnight. Bake at 350 degrees for 45 minutes. Cool 5 minutes before serving.

Serves 6 to 8

GRILLADES

1	(2 pound) round steak	½	cup vegetable oil
½	teaspoon salt	1	medium onion, chopped
½	teaspoon pepper	2	cloves garlic, minced
2	tablespoons vinegar	¾	cup water
1	tablespoon Worcestershire sauce	1	heaping teaspoon cornstarch
½	cup flour		

Cut round steak into thin strips. Place steak in a bowl and add salt, pepper, vinegar and Worcestershire sauce. Marinate for at least 1 hour. Remove meat, drain and dredge in flour. Heat oil and fry meat until brown. Add onion and garlic to meat and cook until onion is caramel color. Add ½ cup water, cover and let simmer on low heat for about 1½ hours or until meat is tender. Dissolve cornstarch in remaining water and add to pot. Let liquid come to a boil to thicken gray. Stir so the gravy will not have lumps. Meat should be tender enough to cut with a fork.

Hint: *Serve over piping hot grits.*

"I've watched you for now a full half-hour, self-poised upon that yellow flower and, little butterfly, indeed I know not if you sleep or feed."

Author unknown

BAKED CHEESE GRITS

¾ cup quick grits, uncooked
1 egg
¼ teaspoon salt
1 cup shredded Cheddar cheese

2 tablespoons butter
⅛ teaspoon garlic powder
⅛ teaspoon red pepper

Preheat oven to 350 degrees. Grease 1½-quart baking dish. Prepare grits according to directions on box. Beat egg and add a small amount of grits to beaten egg until all of the grits and egg are mixed. Return grits and egg mixture to stove. Add salt, cheese, butter, garlic powder and red pepper. Cook over low heat 1 minute or until cheese is melted. Pour into prepared casserole. Bake 30 to 40 minutes or until top is set and slightly puffed. Allow to stand 5 minutes before serving.

Makes 4 to 6 servings

HAVARTI CHEESE GRITS

2 (14-ounce) cans chicken broth
14 ounces water
1 (12-ounce) can evaporated milk

1 stick butter
2 cups grits
1 (8-ounce) block Havarti cheese
Salt to taste

In a large saucepan mix chicken broth, water, milk and butter and bring to a boil. Add grits and cook 5 to 7 minutes. Add cheese and cook until cheese is melted. Salt to taste.

SHRIMP AND GRITS

	Grits, uncooked	1½	tablespoons lemon juice
	Salt and pepper to taste	2	tablespoons chopped parsley
1	stick butter		
2	cups shredded Cheddar cheese	1	cup thinly sliced green onions
8	slices bacon	1	large clove garlic, minced
1	pound shrimp		

Cook grits according to package, (enough for 4 people). Add salt, pepper, butter and cheese to cooked grits. Set aside and keep warm. Fry the bacon in a large skilled until crisp. Drain bacon on paper towel. Add the shrimp to the bacon drippings and cook over medium heat until pink, about 6 minutes. Do not overcook. Add the lemon juice, parsley, green onions and garlic to the shrimp. Remove from heat. Pour grits into individual serving bowls. Pour ¼ of shrimp mixture over each serving of grits. Garnish with crumbled bacon. Serve hot.

Makes 4 main course or 8 appetizers

Hint: *Use both the white and green parts of the green onions.*

Save bacon dripping for use in sautéing or cooking. Drippings are great for flavoring beans.

JUST GRITS

5	cups water	1	teaspoon salt
4	tablespoons butter	1	cup grits

In a heavy saucepan (nonstick is best) heat water to boiling. Add butter and salt. Pour grits slowly into boiling water, stirring constantly to prevent lumping. When grits is completely mixed cover and reduce heat to low and cook 20 to 30 minutes. Stir frequently.

HASH BROWNS BREAKFAST CASSEROLE

1½ pound bag hash browns	2	cups grated sharp Cheddar cheese
2	pounds bulk breakfast sausage	8 eggs
1	cup vegetable seasoning blend	1 cup cream
		Salt and pepper to taste

Defrost hash browns. Preheat oven to 350 degrees. Grease a 9x13-inch baking dish. Place defrosted hash browns into prepared baking dish in an even layer. Brown and drain sausage. Add seasoning blend and cook until vegetables are soft. Spread sausage mixture evenly over the hash browns. Sprinkle cheese on top of the sausage mixture. In a separate bowl, beat eggs, cream, salt and pepper. Pour egg mixture over the cheese. Make sure that all the cheese is covered. Bake 50 to 60 minutes.

Makes 10 to 12 servings

LOST BREAD

"Pain perdu"

1	French bread, day old	½	teaspoon vanilla
2	eggs	½	cup sugar
½	cup evaporated milk	¼	cup vegetable oil
½	cup milk		

Slice bread into ¾-inch slices. Set aside. Beat eggs. Add milks, vanilla and sugar. Place each slice of bread in mixture and soak both sides. Heat oil in a large skillet. Fry bread on both sides until deep golden brown. Sprinkle with powdered sugar or serve with syrup. Best when served hot.

Note: *Because of the resourcefulness of the Cajuns they found a use for stale bread. Bread that had become stale was no longer used. It was thrown away or as the Cajuns thought "lost". This dish was created to use that "lost" bread.*

"If anyone desires a wish to come true they must capture a butterfly and whisper that wish to it. Since they make no sound, they can't tell the wish to anyone but the Great Spirit. So by making the wish and releasing the butterfly it will be taken to the heavens and be granted"

Author unknown

BLUEBERRY STREUSEL MUFFINS

Muffins

1¾ cups flour	¾ cup milk
2¾ teaspoons baking powder	⅓ cup vegetable oil
¾ teaspoon salt	1 cup blueberries
½ cup sugar	1 tablespoon flour
2 teaspoons lemon zest	1 tablespoon sugar
1 large egg, lightly beaten	

Streusel

¼ cup sugar	½ teaspoon cinnamon
2½ tablespoons flour	1½ tablespoons butter

Preheat oven to 400 degrees. Grease muffin pan. Set aside. Combine 1¾ cups of flour, baking powder, salt, sugar and lemon zest in a large bowl. Make a well in the center of the mixture. Combine egg, milk and oil. Stir well. Add to dry ingredients mixing just until moistened. Combine blueberries, 1 tablespoon each of flour and sugar. Toss gently to coat. Fold blueberry mixture into batter. Spoon batter into prepared muffin pan. Fill each cup ⅔ full. To make the streusel, combine sugar, flour and cinnamon. Cut in butter with pastry blender until mixture is crumbly. Sprinkle over batter in cups. Bake 18 minutes or until golden brown. Remove from pan immediately.

Makes 1 dozen

Hint: *If using frozen blueberries thaw and drain and pat dry with paper towel. This will prevent discoloration of batter.*

CARROT MUFFINS

2	eggs	2	cups grated carrots
1	cup sugar	2	cups flour
1	cup vegetable oil	1	teaspoon cinnamon
½	teaspoon vanilla	1	teaspoon salt
1	cup orange juice	2	teaspoons baking powder

Preheat oven to 350 degrees. Grease muffin pan. Set aside. In a bowl, beat eggs, continue to beat while adding sugar, oil, vanilla and orange juice. Stir in carrots. Sift flour, cinnamon, salt and baking powder into a large bowl. Add egg mixture to dry ingredients and mix until just moist. Spoon into the prepared muffin pan. Fill cups about ⅔ full. Bake 30 minutes or until golden brown.

Makes 15 to 20 muffins

POPPY SEED MUFFINS

1¾	cups flour	1	(8-ounce) container sour cream
¼	teaspoon baking soda		
½	teaspoon salt	1	large egg, beaten
½	cup sugar	½	stick butter, melted
3	tablespoons poppy seeds	2	teaspoons vanilla

Preheat oven to 400 degrees. Grease muffin pan. Set aside. Combine flour, baking soda, salt, sugar and poppy seeds in a mixing bowl. Make a well in the center of the mixture. Combine sour cream, egg, butter and vanilla. Add to dry ingredients and stir until just moistened. Spoon into the prepared muffin pan filling cups ⅔ full. Bake 18 to 20 minutes or until light brown. Remove from cups immediately.

Makes 12 muffins

CRABMEAT OMELET

1	tablespoon butter	1	teaspoon chopped parsley
¼	cup chopped green onions	2	tablespoons sherry
¾	cup cooked crabmeat	¼	cup heavy cream
1	teaspoon flour		Salt and pepper to taste
1	teaspoon tarragon	3	eggs

Melt butter in a large skillet. Add green onions and sauté until soft. Stir in crabmeat, flour, tarragon, parsley and sherry. Cook on low heat for 4 to 5 minutes or until crabmeat is heated thoroughly. Stir in cream and season with salt and pepper to taste. Beat eggs and spoon crabmeat mixture in when the eggs are ready to pour into the skillet to make the omelet.

Hint: *Crawfish or shrimp may be substituted.*

BAKED PUFF PANCAKE

½	stick butter, melted	½	cup flour
2	eggs	⅛	teaspoon cinnamon
½	cup milk	⅛	teaspoon nutmeg

Heat oven to 400 degrees. Place butter in a large ovenproof skillet. In a mixing bowl beat eggs until fluffy. Blend in milk, flour, cinnamon and nutmeg until smooth. Pour into prepared skillet. Bake uncovered 15 to 20 minutes and golden brown. Serve immediately with syrup.

Makes 2 servings

CRÉOLE PANCAKES

4 eggs, beaten	½ cup flour
1 cup sour cream	1 tablespoon sugar
1 cup cottage cheese, small curd	¼ teaspoon baking soda
	⅛ teaspoon salt

Mix eggs, sour cream, cottage cheese, flour, sugar, baking soda and salt. Stir until thoroughly mixed. Fry on greased griddle as you would any other pancake.

CINNAMON STREUSEL BREAKFAST PUDDING

1 loaf French bread	3 cups milk
1 stick butter, melted	2 tablespoons vanilla
4 large eggs	¾ cup light brown sugar
1 cup sugar	¼ cup chopped pecans
¼ teaspoon salt	2 tablespoons cinnamon

Grease a 9x13-inch pan with 2 tablespoons butter. Slice bread into 1 to 1½-inch thick slices. In a large mixing bowl beat eggs until frothy. Slowly add in sugar, salt, milk and vanilla. In a smaller bowl combine brown sugar, pecans and cinnamon. Arrange ½ of the bread on the bottom of the prepared baking pan. Fit tightly together. Brush with ½ of the remaining melted butter. Slowly pour half of the egg mixture evenly over the bread. Sprinkle half of the sugar cinnamon mixture over the top. Layer the other ½ of the bread and brush with remaining butter. Pour remaining egg mixture over bread. Sprinkle remaining sugar cinnamon mixture over the top. Cover and refrigerate for at least 2 hours or overnight. Remove from refrigerator and allow pudding to reach room temperature. Bake uncovered in a 375 degree oven 45 to 50 minutes.

BREAKFAST PIZZA

1 (12-ounce) package bacon	1½ cups shredded cheese
1 package crescent rolls	¼ cup chopped green onions
5 eggs, beaten	¼ cup sliced olives
¼ cup milk	¼ cup chopped bell pepper
¼ teaspoon oregano	Sliced avocado (optional)
⅛ teaspoon pepper	Chopped tomatoes (optional)
Salt to taste	

Preheat oven to 375 degrees. Lightly grease 12-inch pizza pan. Fry, drain and crumble bacon and set aside. To make crust, unroll crescent rolls. Separate into triangles. Place triangles on prepared pizza pan with points toward center. Press triangles together to cover the bottom and ½ inch up the sides of the pan. Bake 10 to 12 minutes or until lightly browned (do not remove crust from oven), While pizza crust is baking, combine eggs, milk, oregano, pepper and salt. Pull out oven rack and carefully pour egg mixture onto the crust. Bake 8 to 10 minutes or until egg mixture is set. Sprinkle with bacon, cheese, green onions, olives, bell pepper and other choices of topping. Bake 3 to 5 minutes or until cheese melts. Cut into wedges.

Serves 6

Hint: *Cheddar, Swiss or mozzarella cheese may be used.*

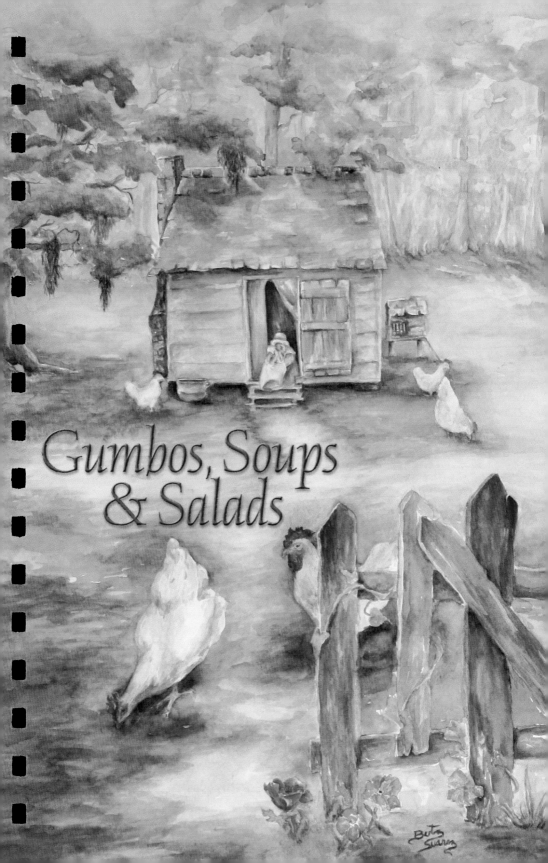

Gumbos, Soups
& Salads

Butz Suarez

Rural Life

Nestled along Bayou Lafourche and the swamps and bodies of water of Assumption Parish in south Louisiana, there are many villages and small settlements. The quiet, laid-back lifestyle is depicted in the family life and traditions of this rural area.

Many people still raise chickens, pigs and livestock, and their children learn to care for them at a very early age. It is not uncommon to see gardens tucked into many back yards. These tiny plots of prized vegetables are tenderly watched over and cared for until the time of harvest. Tomatoes, corn, squash, eggplant, okra, cucumbers, bell pepper, snap beans...the list is almost endless. So, it is not unusual that many of the basic ingredients found in the recipes in this book have been raised by the people who cook them.

Traditions are strong and so are the families who have handed them down from generation to generation. Stories are told and retold as a living document of the life and times of their ancestors. Families are close-knit and any occasion can be a reason for a family dinner or get-together. Neighbors are often included as extended family and always arrive with a covered dish to enjoy the festivities. And.....so is the life in south Louisiana.

To remove excess oil from the top of soup, gumbo or gravy, place a piece of paper towel over the surface and remove when saturated. Repeat if necessary.

SHRIMP AND CORN CHOWDER

½ stick butter

2 large onions, chopped

2 ribs celery, chopped

1 bell pepper, chopped

1 clove of garlic, minced

2 pounds shrimp

4 (10-ounce) cans cream of mushroom soup

4 (10-ounce) cans cream of potato soup

3 (14-ounce) cans cream style corn

3 (14-ounce) cans whole kernel corn

1 pint half-and-half

Salt, pepper and Créole seasoning to taste

½ cup chopped green onions

Melt butter in a stock pot and sauté onion, celery, bell pepper and garlic until wilted. Add shrimp to vegetable mixture and cook 20 minutes. Add mushroom soup, potato soup, cream corn, whole kernel corn and half-and-half. Add salt, pepper and Créole seasoning to taste. Cook over low to medium heat, stirring, about 40 minutes. Add green onions and simmer additional 15 minutes.

Hint: *Milk can be added for desired consistency of chowder. Louisiana crawfish or crab can be substituted for the shrimp.*

The Louisiana Native Americans, the Choctaw Indians, gave us filé. Filé is a powder made from dried sassafras leaves. Filé is used to thicken gumbos. It is easily home grown.

CHICKEN AND SAUSAGE GUMBO

1 chicken, cut up
2 links smoked sausage
½ cup vegetable oil
¾ cup flour
1 cup chopped onion
1 cup chopped bell pepper
1 cup chopped celery
¼ cup chopped parsley
2 cloves garlic, minced
6 quarts water
   Salt and pepper to taste
1 cup chopped green
   onions
   Filé to taste (optional)
   Hot sauce (optional)

Preheat oven to 350 degrees. Place chicken in 9x13-inch pan. Bake covered 35 minutes. Set aside. Cut sausage into bite size pieces and set aside. Heat oil in a stock pot on medium heat. Add flour and stir until dark brown (roux). Add onion, bell pepper, celery, parsley and garlic. Cook vegetables, stirring, until wilted. To this mixture add water, salt and pepper. Bring to a boil. Lower heat and simmer 30 minutes. Add chicken and sausage simmer 30 additional minutes. Stir in green onions and cook 5 minutes. Adjust salt, pepper and hot sauce to taste. Serve over hot cooked rice.

LENTEN GREEN GUMBO

"Gumbo Verte"

1 small cabbage	½ cup vegetable oil
1 bunch Swiss chard	½ cup flour
1 (10-ounce) package frozen spinach	1 large onion, chopped
1 (10-ounce) package frozen mustard	2 ribs celery, chopped
1 (10-ounce) package frozen turnip tops	4 cloves garlic, minced
	1 pound shrimp
	Salt and pepper to taste

Chop cabbage and chard. Boil spinach, mustard and turnip top until tender, following package directions. Drain and reserve all liquids. Heat oil in stock pot and add flour stirring until golden brown (roux). Add onion, celery and garlic. Sauté until wilted. Add shrimp to the roux. Sauté 10 to 15 minutes. Add cabbage, chard, spinach, mustard and turnip tops and sauté 10 to 15 minutes. Pour in reserved liquids. Add salt and pepper. Cook on medium heat for about 30 minutes until mixture is creamy. Serve over rice.

Hint: *A 15-ounce can of any green vegetable can be substituted. A small chicken or 1 pound of sausage can replace the shrimp.*

CRAB AND CORN BISQUE

4 cups corn	4 cups milk
¼ cup chopped onion	1 cup heavy cream
½ stick butter	Salt and pepper to taste
2 tablespoons flour	1 pound crabmeat

Chop corn in food processor and set aside. Sauté onion in butter and add flour. Stir and cook 2 minutes. Add corn and cook additional 5 minutes. Blend in milk, cream, salt and pepper. Bring to a boil. Stir in crabmeat lower heat and cook 10 minutes.

OKRA SEAFOOD GUMBO

1	cup vegetable oil	2	teaspoons lemon juice
1	cup flour		Hot sauce to taste
2	large onions, chopped		Worcestershire sauce to taste
¼	cup chopped green onions		Créole seasoning to taste
3	cloves garlic, minced	3	bay leaves
3	pounds shrimp		Salt and pepper to taste
1	(28-ounce) can diced tomatoes	½	cup chopped parsley
4	quarts stock or water	1	pint oysters
1	quart cooked okra		Filé to taste (optional)
2	pounds crabmeat	12	gumbo crabs (optional)
½	teaspoon liquid crab boil (optional)		

In a stock pot on medium, heat oil and add flour, stirring until flour is dark brown (roux). Add onion, green onions and garlic cooking until vegetables are wilted. Add shrimp, cook 2 minutes. Remove shrimp from pot and set aside. Add the tomatoes. Cook 5 minutes. Add water, okra, crabmeat, crab boil, lemon juice, hot sauce, Worcestershire, Créole seasoning, bay leaves, salt, pepper and parsley. Cover and simmer over medium heat 1 hour, stirring occasionally. Add shrimp, oysters and crabs. Cook additional 30 minutes. Add filé if desired.

Serves 15 to 20

Hint: *Stock can be made by boiling discarded shells and heads of shrimp in 4 quarts of water until liquid is reduced by half. Strain.*

Gumbo comes from the African word, kingombo, which means okra. Africans first brought okra, a crucial ingredient in gumbo recipes, to Louisiana.

AFTER-THANKSGIVING TURKEY GUMBO

Leftover turkey with bones
2 pounds andouille, cut into pieces
1½ cups vegetable oil
1½ cups flour
2 onions, chopped
2 cups chopped celery
2 bell peppers, chopped
4 cloves garlic, minced

6 quarts broth, from turkey and andouille
2 cups cooked okra (optional)
½ cup finely chopped green onion tops
Parsley to taste
Salt and pepper to taste
Filé (optional)

Remove large pieces of turkey from body and cut into cubes. Set aside. Place turkey body and bones in a large stock pot. Cover with water. Boil 1 to 1½ hours or until meat can easily be pulled from bones. Remove turkey. Strain broth. Reserve 3 quarts of broth. Set aside. De-bone turkey. Set aside. Boil andouille about 20 minutes. Strain and reserve at least 3 quarts of broth. Set aside. Heat oil and add flour. Cook stirring until flour is the color of peanut butter (roux). Add onion, celery, bell pepper and garlic. Cook until vegetables are wilted. Add turkey and andouille. Mix well and add broths. Cook about 1½ hours. Add okra, green onions and parsley. Simmer about 10 minutes. Salt and pepper to taste. If more liquid is needed add hot water. Remove from heat and add filé. Serve with rice.

Hint: *Smoked sausage may be used if andouille is not available.*

Andouille (ahn-do'-ee) is a spicy country sausage used in gumbos and other Cajun dishes.

ARTICHOKE AND OYSTER SOUP

1 (10-ounce) can artichoke
   hearts
3 dozen oysters
½ stick butter
¼ cup chopped green
   onions
3 bay leaves
¼ teaspoon thyme

Red pepper to taste
2 tablespoons flour
1 (14-ounce) can chicken
   broth
2 tablespoons chopped
   parsley
½ cup half-and-half
⅛ teaspoon nutmeg

Drain and chop artichoke, reserve liquid. Set aside. Drain and chop oysters. Reserve liquid. Set aside. Melt butter in a saucepan. Sauté green onions, bay leaves, thyme and red pepper until wilted. Add flour and stir. Add broth and reserved liquid from artichokes and oysters. Simmer 15 minutes. Add artichoke hearts, oysters and parsley. Simmer 10 minutes. Remove from heat. Remove bay leaves. Stir in half-and-half and nutmeg.

BROCCOLI AND CRAB SOUP

1 (14-ounce) box broccoli
   florets
1 large onion, chopped fine
¾ stick butter
1 (10-ounce) can cream of
   mushroom soup

4½ cups milk
1 cup half-and-half
1 pound Mexican Velveeta
½ pound crabmeat
1 teaspoon basil

Steam broccoli until softened. Sauté onion in butter. Add broccoli, soup, milk, half-and-half, cheese, crabmeat and basil. Simmer on low heat 10 minutes continually stirring.

CAJUN SWEET POTATO SOUP

8	medium sweet potatoes	1	(64-ounce) can chicken broth
1	cup chopped onion		
1	cup chopped bell pepper	4	chili peppers, chopped
3	cloves garlic, minced	1	(14-ounce) can diced tomatoes
1	teaspoon yellow curry powder		
		1	can light coconut milk
	Salt and pepper to taste	1	cup chunky peanut butter
3	tablespoons peanut oil	1	pound medium shrimp
		1	pound crabmeat

Peel and dice sweet potatoes and set aside. In a large stock pot, sauté onion, bell pepper, garlic, curry powder, salt and pepper in oil until wilted. Add sweet potato and cover with broth about ½ inch over sweet potato. Add chili pepper and tomato and boil 15 to 20 minutes. Add milk, peanut butter, and shrimp. Cook 5 minutes. Add crabmeat and simmer 5 minutes.

CALICO CHEESE SOUP

½	cup finely chopped carrots	½	stick butter
		3	tablespoons flour
½	cup finely chopped celery	2	pints half-and-half
1	cup boiling water	2	cups chicken broth
	Salt to taste	2	cups shredded Cheddar cheese
2	tablespoons minced onion		

Place carrots and celery in boiling salted water; cover and cook until tender. Drain. Puree and set aside. Sauté onion in butter until wilted. Stir in flour, half-and-half and broth. Continue cooking, stirring constantly, until slightly thickened. Add cheese and stir until melted. Add vegetable mixture. Cook 10 minutes.

CORN, CRAB AND CRAWFISH SOUP

2	pounds Louisiana crawfish tails, peeled	3	(14-ounce) cans cream corn	
¼	cup vegetable oil	1	(14-ounce) can whole tomatoes, diced	
3	medium onions, chopped			
1	medium bell pepper, chopped	1	(8-ounce) can tomato sauce	
4	cloves garlic, minced	1	(10-ounce) can tomatoes with green chilies	
3	ribs celery, chopped			
1	bunch green onions, chopped		Water or seafood stock	
			Salt and pepper to taste	
3	(15-ounce) cans corn	1	pound crabmeat	

Sauté crawfish in oil. Add onion, bell pepper, garlic, celery, green onions and cook until vegetables are wilted. Add corn, cream corn, tomatoes, tomato sauce and tomatoes with green chilies. Add enough water for desired thickness of soup. Bring to a slow boil and simmer 45 minutes. Lower heat. Add salt, pepper and crabmeat. Cook 10 minutes more.

"What the caterpillar calls the end of the world, the master calls a butterfly."

Richard Bach

CRAWFISH BISQUE SOUP

½ cup chopped onion
½ cup chopped green onions
1 stick butter
1 pound Louisiana crawfish tails, peeled
2 (10-ounce) cans cream of potato soup
1 (10-ounce) can cream of mushroom soup
1 (15-ounce) can yellow corn, drained
1 (15-ounce) can white corn, drained
1 (8-ounce) package cream cheese
1 pint half-and-half
Créole seasoning to taste
Salt and pepper to taste

Sauté onion and green onions in butter until wilted. Add crawfish and cook 5 minutes. Add potato soup, mushroom soup, yellow corn, white corn and cream cheese. Cook stirring until cream cheese melts. Add half-and-half. Mix well. Add Créole seasoning, salt and pepper. Cook 15 minutes on low to medium heat. Serve with French bread.

FRENCH ONION SOUP

1 loaf French bread
4 onions, minced
1 tablespoon olive oil
2 tablespoons butter
1 teaspoon sugar
Salt and red pepper to taste
1 quart chicken broth
4 tablespoons grated Parmesan cheese

Preheat oven to 350 degrees. Cut French bread in small rounds and toast. Set aside. Sauté onion in oil and butter until wilted. Add sugar, salt and pepper. Pour into a 2-quart casserole dish and add broth. Place prepared French bread on top of soup mixture and sprinkle with cheese. Bake 20 minutes.

Serves 4

LENTIL SOUP

2 tablespoons olive oil
2 medium onions, chopped
3 ribs celery, chopped
1 bell pepper, chopped
1 tablespoon minced garlic
1 (14-ounce) can diced tomatoes
1 (14-ounce) can chicken broth
½ cup dry sherry

2 tablespoons soy sauce
2 tablespoons Worcestershire sauce
2 tablespoons hot sauce
1 teaspoon salt
3 quarts hot water
1 pound dry lentils, rinsed
1 cup chopped spinach
½ cup picante sauce

In a stock pot mix in oil, onion, celery, bell pepper, garlic and tomatoes with liquid. Cook over medium heat 10 minutes. Stir. Add chicken broth, sherry, soy sauce, Worcestershire sauce, hot sauce and salt. Cook 10 minutes. Add hot water, lentils and spinach. Bring to a boil, reduce heat to medium and cook 40 minutes. Stir. Add picante sauce and extra water if needed for desired consistency. Reduce heat. Cook loosely covered 1½ hours or until lentils are tender. Stir.

Serves 10

The lentil has a range of colors from yellow to red-orange to green, brown and black. Lentils have a short cooking time and a distinctive earthy flavor. Lentils are used to prepare inexpensive and healthy soups.

Potato Soup

8	slices bacon	1½	teaspoons dried basil
1	cup diced onion	1½	teaspoons salt
⅔	cup flour	1½	teaspoons hot sauce
6	cups chicken broth	1½	teaspoons black pepper
4	cups cooked, diced white potatoes	1	cup grated Cheddar cheese
2	cups whipping cream	¼	cup chopped green onions
¼	cup chopped parsley		
1½	teaspoons minced garlic		

Fry bacon crisp, crumble and set aside. Sauté onion in bacon drippings over medium heat about 3 minutes. Add flour, stirring until smooth. Cook 5 minutes, stirring, until golden. Gradually whisk in chicken broth until liquid thickens. Add potatoes, cream, bacon, parsley, garlic, basil, salt, hot sauce and black pepper. Simmer 10 minutes. Do not boil. Add Cheddar cheese and green onions. Cook until cheese melts.

Hint: *Garnish with extra cheese and green onions if desired.*

*"His talent was as natural as the pattern
that was made by the dust of a butterfly's wings."*

Ernest Hemingway

RED BEAN SOUP

½ cup oil
½ cup flour
4 large onions, chopped
5 ribs celery, chopped
1 large bell pepper, chopped
3 cloves garlic, minced
½ cup chopped green onions
2 pounds smoked sausage, sliced
2 pounds andouille, diced
6 (15-ounce) cans red beans
5 quarts chicken broth
2 (8-ounce) cans sliced mushrooms
1 cup chopped parsley
Salt and pepper to taste

In a large stock pot, heat oil over medium heat. Add flour, stirring until golden brown (roux). Add onion, celery, bell pepper, garlic and green onions. Cook 10 minutes. Add sausage and andouille. Cook 15 minutes. Add beans and chicken broth. Stir. Bring to a boil. Reduce heat and simmer 1½ hours. Add mushrooms and simmer to desired thickness. Stir in parsley, salt and pepper. Serve over rice.

Beans have long been known for their low cost and high nutritional value. A pound of cooked dried beans will make about 9 servings, compared to 4 servings per pound of meat, poultry or fish.

SHRIMP AND ARTICHOKE SOUP

2 (14-ounce) cans
   artichoke hearts
1½ pounds shrimp
2 tablespoons hot sauce
1 tablespoon Créole
   seasoning
2 tablespoons olive oil
2 medium onions, chopped
1 pound mushrooms, sliced
½ stick butter, melted

½ cup flour
2 (14-ounce) cans chicken
   broth
2 cups hot water
⅔ cup dry sherry
½ teaspoon white pepper
2 teaspoons salt
1 tablespoon
   Worcestershire sauce
3 pints half-and-half

Drain and coarsely chop artichokes and set aside. Toss together shrimp, hot sauce and Créole seasoning in a bowl. Marinate 1 hour in the refrigerator. In a stock pot combine olive oil and onion. Sauté on medium heat 10 minutes. Add mushrooms cook 5 minutes. Reduce heat and slowly stir in butter and flour cooking for a few minutes. Slowly blend in broth. Add water, sherry, pepper, salt, Worcestershire sauce and artichoke hearts. Bring to a boil and cook 15 minutes. Stir. Add shrimp mixture. Bring to a boil and cook 15 minutes. Stir. Reduce heat to simmer and slowly blend in half-and-half. Do not boil. Stir. Remove from heat. Cover and allow to rest 30 minutes.

The artichoke was introduced to the United States in the 19th century, by French immigrants in Louisiana. It is preferable not to cover the pot while artichokes are boiling so that the acids will boil out into the air. Covered artichokes can turn brown.

SHRIMP AND CORN SOUP

½ cup oil
½ cup flour
1 medium onion, chopped
1 (10-ounce) can tomatoes with green chilies
2 (15-ounce) cans corn
1 (15-ounce) can cream corn
1 (10-ounce) can cream of shrimp soup
1 quart water
½ teaspoon liquid crab boil (optional)
Salt and pepper to taste
1 pound small shrimp
1 tablespoon parsley flakes

Heat oil in stock pot. Add flour, stirring until golden brown (roux). Add onion and sauté until wilted. Add tomatoes with green chilies, corn, cream corn, soup, water, crab boil, salt and pepper. Bring to a boil. Lower heat and simmer 45 minutes. Add shrimp and parsley flakes. Simmer 15 minutes.

OYSTER AND HAM SOUP

1 onion, finely chopped
2 ribs of celery, finely chopped
2 tablespoons butter
¼ cup flour
½ pound ham, cubed
1 (14-ounce) can chicken broth
Browning liquid for color
1 pint oysters, drained
2 cups oyster water, strained
Red pepper and salt to taste
½ cup chopped green onions

Sauté onion and celery in butter until wilted. Add flour and cook until golden. Add ham, broth, browning liquid and cook 10 minutes. Add oysters, oyster water, red pepper, salt and green onions. Cook 10 minutes

Hint: *Chicken broth can be substituted for oyster water.*

If you have over-salted a soup or vegetables, add a cut raw potato and discard once it has cooked and absorbed the salt.

TORTILLA SOUP

1	jalapeño pepper	4	(14-ounce) cans chicken broth
½	stick butter		
½	cup oil	1	(14-ounce) can tomatoes
1	large onion, chopped	1	teaspoon cumin
2	large carrots, diced	1	teaspoon chili powder
6	ribs celery, chopped	1	teaspoon salt
3	chicken breasts, cubed	1	teaspoon lemon pepper
½	cup flour	1	teaspoon hot sauce

Seed and chop jalapeño. Set aside. Melt butter and oil in stock pot. Add onion, jalapeño pepper, carrots and celery. Sauté until vegetables are wilted. Add chicken. Cook 3 minutes. Stir in flour cooking 2 to 3 minutes. Slowly stir in broth, tomatoes with juice, cumin, chili powder, salt, lemon pepper and hot sauce. Simmer 1 hour.

Makes 12 cups

Hint: *Serve with tortilla chips, Cheddar cheese, avocado or a spoonful of sour cream.*

"A caterpillar who wanted to know itself well would never become a butterfly."

Andre Gide

TRI-COLOR BELL PEPPER SOUP

2	red bell peppers	2	(14-ounce) cans chicken broth
2	yellow bell peppers		
1	green bell pepper	1	(10-ounce) can cream of chicken soup
¼	cup olive oil		
½	stick margarine	1	(12-ounce) can evaporated milk
2	medium onions, chopped		
5	cloves garlic, minced		Salt, black pepper and white pepper to taste
1	rib celery, chopped		

Bake red, yellow and green bell peppers in 350 degree oven until thin layer of skin can be removed. Peel skin and cut into large pieces. Heat oil and margarine in a saucepan and add all peppers, onion, garlic and celery. Sauté 15 minutes until vegetables are wilted. Pour vegetable mixture into a blender, add broth and soup. Blend until creamy. Return to saucepan and simmer 30 minutes. Slowly stir in milk and simmer 10 minutes. Add salt, black pepper and white pepper to taste. Serve with crackers.

"We are like butterflies who flutter for a day and think it is forever."

Carl Sagan

VEGETABLE SOUP

2	pounds stew meat	1	(10-ounce) can tomatoes with green chilies
	Créole seasoning to taste		
¼	cup olive oil	1	(14-ounce) can diced tomatoes
2	medium onions, chopped		
4	ribs celery, chopped	3	(10-ounce) cans corn
1	small bell pepper, chopped	2	(10-ounce) cans green beans
1	small cabbage, chopped	2	medium potatoes, cubed
¼	cup chopped parsley	3	medium turnips, cubed
½	cup chopped green onions	4	quarts water
			Salt and pepper to taste
½	pound carrots, sliced	½	(16-ounce) package vermicelli

Season meat with Créole seasoning and set aside. In a stockpot heat olive oil, add meat and cook until brown. Add onion, celery and bell pepper, cook until vegetables are wilted. Add cabbage, parsley, green onions, carrots, tomatoes with green chilies, diced tomatoes, corn, green beans, potatoes, turnips, water, salt and pepper. Cook 2 hours on medium heat. Add vermicelli cook 5 to 10 minutes.

Hint: *Stew meat can be pork, beef or venison. Other vegetables of choice may be added.*

"No shade, no shine, no butterflies, no fruits, no flowers, no leaves, no birds . . . November."

Thomas Hood

Salad dressing should be added just before serving.

BLUE CHEESE DRESSING

1 cup mayonnaise	1 tablespoon fresh lemon juice
2 tablespoons minced onion	¼ cup crumbled blue cheese
1 teaspoon minced garlic	Salt, black and red pepper to taste
¼ cup chopped parsley	
½ cup sour cream	

Combine all ingredients and mix thoroughly. Chill 3 to 4 hours before serving.

CHEESE DRESSING

½ cup olive oil	2 cloves garlic, minced
½ cup vegetable oil	1 cup Parmesan cheese
2½ tablespoons lemon juice	¼ cup feta cheese
1½ tablespoons white wine vinegar	¾ teaspoon salt

Mix all ingredients together. Pour over salad and toss.

SWEET AND PEPPERY DRESSING

¼ cup red wine vinegar	½ cup olive oil
¼ cup sugar	2 tablespoons pepper jelly

Mix all ingredients together. Pour over favorite salad.

ITALIAN DRESSING

1⅓ cups vinegar
1 (0.35-ounce) packet
   artificial sweetener
1 teaspoon olive oil

1 teaspoon lemon juice
1 teaspoon garlic powder
1 (0.6-ounce) envelope dry
   Italian mix

Mix all ingredients together. Store in a cruet.

POPPY SEED DRESSING

¾ cup sugar
1 teaspoon mustard
1 teaspoon salt
¼ small onion, pureed

5 tablespoons white vinegar
1 cup salad oil
1½ tablespoons poppy seeds

In a blender mix sugar, mustard, salt, onion and vinegar until
sugar is dissolved. Stream salad oil into mixture until thickened.
Stir in poppy seeds. Refrigerate.

SENSATIONAL DRESSING

½ cup vegetable oil
⅓ cup water
¾ cup white vinegar
2 tablespoons sugar
2 tablespoons minced
   garlic
2 tablespoons chopped
   green onions

½ teaspoon black pepper
3 tablespoons granulated
   garlic
¼ cup grated Parmesan
   cheese
¾ cup shredded Romano
   cheese

Mix all ingredients together. Chill.

STRAWBERRY VINAIGRETTE

1	teaspoon Créole mustard	1	tablespoon finely chopped tarragon
1	tablespoon balsamic vinegar		Salt and pepper to taste
4	tablespoons pomegranate juice		Fresh strawberries
¾	cup olive oil		Toasted pecans
1	tablespoon finely chopped thyme		Fresh Parmesan cheese

Whisk mustard, vinegar and juice in a deep bowl. Slowly whisk in the oil in a steady stream until all is incorporated. Add thyme, tarragon, salt and pepper. Serve over fresh strawberries, toasted pecans and grated Parmesan cheese.

Hint: *Spinach or any combination of greens may be used.*

BROCCOLI SALAD

Dressing

1	cup mayonnaise	2	tablespoons red wine vinegar
½	cup sugar	1	red onion, chopped

Salad

1	large bunch broccoli	6	slices bacon, fried crisp and crumbled
1	(8-ounce) package mozzarella cheese		

To make dressing blend mayonnaise and sugar until smooth. Add vinegar, stir. Mix in onion. Prepare salad by washing and breaking broccoli into small pieces. In a large bowl, toss broccoli, cheese and bacon. Stir dressing into the broccoli mixture. Chill before serving.

ASPARAGUS SALAD

Dressing

1   (0.6-ounce) packet
    Italian dressing mix

Balsamic vinegar
Canola oil

Salad

2   bunches fresh asparagus

1   (14-ounce) can artichoke
    hearts, drained

1   (14-ounce) can hearts of
    palm, drained

1   large bell pepper, diced

1   (2-ounce) can small
    black olives, drained

2   ounces lite feta cheese,
    crumbled

To make dressing, mix Italian dressing, vinegar and oil according to directions on package. Set aside. To make the salad cut asparagus into 2-inch pieces, steam until just soft. Cool rapidly in ice water, drain, place in a bowl. Set aside. Cut artichokes and hearts of palm into bite size pieces. Add bell pepper, artichoke, hearts of palm, olives and cheese to the asparagus. Toss salad with prepared Italian dressing and refrigerate 30 minutes before serving.

Look for asparagus with a fresh green color. The tips should be compact, tightly closed, and dark green or purplish in color. The thicker, more mature stalks are considered more tender and flavorful.

BABY BLUE SALAD

Balsamic Vinaigrette

½   cup balsamic vinegar
3   tablespoons Créole
    mustard
3   tablespoons honey
2   cloves garlic, minced

2   small green onions,
    minced
¼   teaspoon salt
¼   teaspoon pepper
1   cup olive oil

Salad

¾   pound mixed salad
    greens
4   ounces blue cheese,
    crumbled

2   oranges, peeled and
    thinly sliced
1   pint fresh strawberries,
    quartered

To make vinaigrette whisk together vinegar, mustard, honey, garlic, green onions, salt and pepper. Gradually whisk in olive oil. Prepare salad by tossing greens with vinaigrette and cheese. Arrange orange slices and strawberries over greens.

Serves 6

Balsamic vinegar is highly appreciated by chefs and gourmet food lovers. Young vinegars (3-5 years) are used in salad dressing. Mid-age vinegars (6-12 years) are used to enhance sauces and pastas. Old vinegars (12 years plus), which are very rich and thick, are used sparsely to enhance plain meat, fish, fresh fruit or even drunk from a small glass to conclude a meal.

BRIDESMAID CHICKEN SALAD

1½ cups mayonnaise
¾ cup fruit chutney
1 cup halved green grapes
1 teaspoon curry powder
2 teaspoons grated lime zest
¼ cup fresh lime juice
½ teaspoon salt
4 cups diced, cooked, chicken breast

2 (13-ounce) cans pineapple chunks, drained
2 cups chopped celery
1 cup chopped green onions
½ cup toasted almonds

Blend mayonnaise, chutney, grapes, curry, lime zest, lime juice and salt. Fold chicken, pineapple, celery, green onions and almonds into the mayonnaise mixture. Chill 4 to 6 hours. Toss before serving.

Makes 8 to 10 servings

Hint: *Serve on salad greens.*

When sending out invitations to a bridal shower, place an index card in the envelope. Request that the guest write her favorite recipe on the card and bring it to the shower. If it will be a large bridal shower, request that some guest bring desserts, some a main dish, and etc. Write the category on the top of the card. Place a pretty box on the sign in table ready to accept the recipes.

CHICKEN SALAD

4	chicken breasts	6	eggs, boiled
1-2	onions	1	(10-ounce) jar sweet pickle relish
1	bell pepper	1	cup mayonnaise
	Salt and pepper		Salt and pepper to taste
	Water		

Boil chicken, onion, bell pepper, salt and pepper in enough water to cover the chicken and vegetables. Cook until chicken is tender. Drain. Chop chicken meat, eggs, onion and bell pepper in a food processor. Add sweet relish and mayonnaise. Mix well. Salt and pepper to taste.

CHICKEN AND RICE SALAD

2	cups cooked yellow rice	½-1	cup mayonnaise
2	cups cubed cooked chicken	½	cup plain yogurt
1	(14-ounce) can artichoke hearts, drained, chopped	1	tablespoon curry
			Juice of ½ lime
¼	bell pepper, finely chopped	½	cup dry roasted peanuts
½	cup chopped stuffed olives	½	cup chopped green onions

Combine rice, chicken, artichoke hearts, bell pepper, olives, mayonnaise, yogurt and curry. Squeeze lime juice over this mixture. Mix well. Arrange on a platter. Sprinkle with peanuts and green onions.

HOT CHICKEN SALAD

½ cup slivered almonds

4 cups diced cooked chicken

2 cups chopped celery

¼ cup chopped onion

¼ cup chopped pimento, drained

1 (4-ounce) jar sliced mushrooms, drained

1 (8-ounce) can sliced water chestnuts, drained

½ teaspoon salt

½ teaspoon pepper

2 cups shredded Cheddar cheese

1 cup mayonnaise

½ cup sour cream

3 tablespoons lemon juice

1 cup crushed potato chips

1 cup shredded Parmesan cheese

Preheat oven 350 degrees. Lightly grease a 9x13-inch baking dish. Set aside. Bake almonds in a shallow pan 5 to 10 minutes until toasted. Stir together almonds, chicken, celery, onion, pimiento, mushrooms, chestnuts, salt and pepper. In a separate bowl mix 1 cup Cheddar cheese, mayonnaise, sour cream and lemon juice until blended. Stir into chicken mixture. Spoon into a prepared baking dish. Top with remaining Cheddar cheese, potato chip crumbs and Parmesan cheese. Bake 30 minutes or until thoroughly heated.

Makes 12 servings

"And what's a butterfly? At best, but a caterpillar, at rest."

John Grey

CHICKEN NOODLE SALAD

Dressing

2 chicken ramen noodle flavor packets
4 tablespoons sugar
1 cup olive oil

2 teaspoons salt
1 teaspoon pepper
6 tablespoons red wine vinegar

Salad

6-8 chicken breasts, cooked and cubed
1 (4-ounce) bag almonds, toasted

1 (16-ounce) package shredded cabbage
2 (3-ounce) packages chicken ramen noodles, broken

To make dressing, mix together flavor packets, sugar, oil, salt, pepper and vinegar. Refrigerate. Prepare salad by mixing chicken, almonds, cabbage and noodles in a large bowl. Stir in dressing and serve.

COLESLAW

2 pounds cabbage, shredded
2 medium carrots, minced
¼ cup sugar
2 teaspoons Créole seasoning

1¼ cups mayonnaise
3 tablespoons vinegar
½ onion, minced

Place cabbage in a large bowl. Add carrots, toss. Sprinkle with sugar and Créole seasoning, stir well. Combine mayonnaise, vinegar and onion, stir until well blended. Pour over cabbage mixture and toss until completely coated.

Hint: *Best when prepared ahead and allowed to chill.*

Break lettuce. Do not cut with a knife as edges will turn brown.

COLORFUL COLESLAW

Dressing

1 cup vegetable oil
6 tablespoons white vinegar
2 tablespoons sugar
1 teaspoon salt

1 teaspoon pepper
2 packets chicken ramen
   soup seasoning

Salad

1 cup slivered almonds
3 tablespoons sesame
   seeds
2 (3-ounce) packages
   ramen soup noodles,
   broken
1 small red cabbage

4 cups broccoli stems
1 red bell pepper
1 yellow bell pepper
1 red onion
5 green onions, finely
   chopped

Preheat oven to 350 degrees. To make dressing, combine oil, vinegar, sugar, salt, pepper and seasoning packets. Stir until well blended. Prepare salad by baking almonds, sesame seeds and noodles 5 minutes and set aside. Julienne cut cabbage, broccoli stems, red bell pepper, yellow bell pepper and red onion. Place these vegetables in a large bowl with green onions, almonds, sesame seeds and noodles. Add dressing and toss well.

CRUNCHY COLESLAW

1 medium cabbage, chopped fine

¼ cup finely chopped green onions

2 (3-ounce) packages ramen noodles

2½ ounces sliced almonds

½ cup sesame seeds

1½ sticks margarine

⅔ cup vegetable oil

½ cup vinegar

½ cup sugar

2 teaspoons soy sauce

Mix cabbage and green onions. Refrigerate. Brown noodles, almonds and sesame seeds in margarine. Drain on paper towel. Refrigerate. Blend together oil, vinegar, sugar and soy sauce. Refrigerate. Blend all ingredients together when ready to serve.

CORN SALAD

6 slices bacon

4 cups white shoe peg corn, drained

1 large tomato, diced

3-4 green onions, chopped

Créole seasoning to taste

2-3 tablespoons mayonnaise

Fry bacon crisp and crumble. Mix together bacon, corn, tomato, green onions and Créole seasoning, stir in mayonnaise. Refrigerate. Serve cold.

CRÉOLE OLIVE SALAD

3 tablespoons olive oil
2 tablespoons red wine vinegar
2 tablespoons Créole mustard
1 tablespoon minced green onions
1 teaspoon sugar
¼ teaspoon Cayenne pepper

1 (16-ounce) package shredded coleslaw mix
1 (14-ounce) can artichoke hearts, drained, chopped
1 (7-ounce) jar pimiento stuffed olives, drained, halved

In large bowl, combine oil, vinegar, mustard, green onions, sugar and pepper. Mix well. Add coleslaw mix, artichoke hearts and olives. Mix thoroughly. Cover and chill at least 1 hour before serving.

LAYERED SALAD

1 small head lettuce, bite size pieces
2 ribs celery, chopped
3 medium carrots, grated
1 small red onion, chopped
1½ cups frozen green peas, boiled 1 minute, drained

1½ cups mayonnaise
4 eggs, boiled, chopped
2 cups grated Cheddar cheese
1 (3-ounce) bottle bacon bits

In a 9x13-inch dish layer vegetables in the order listed. Cover. Refrigerate.

Serves 10 to 12

WINTER SALAD

Salad

8	slices bacon	½	cup chopped onion
1	head broccoli, florets only	½	cup golden raisins
½	head cauliflower, florets only	½	cup pecans

Dressing

1	cup mayonnaise	3	tablespoons vinegar
½	cup sugar		

To make salad, fry bacon crisp and crumble. Set aside. In a serving bowl, combine broccoli, cauliflower, onion, raisins and pecans. Set aside. For dressing, mix mayonnaise, sugar and vinegar. Stir well. Blend into vegetable mixture. Top with bacon.

Hint: *Mushrooms and water chestnuts may be added*

POTATO SALAD

12	medium red potatoes	1	tablespoon minced parsley
6	eggs, boiled		Salt and pepper to taste
½	cup Italian salad dressing		Paprika and parsley for garnish (optional)
¾	cup mayonnaise		
2	tablespoons pickle relish		

Boil and cube potatoes. Set aside. Separate egg whites from yolks. Chop egg whites and add to potatoes. In a medium size bowl mash egg yolks. Slowly pour in salad dressing, stirring constantly. Stir in mayonnaise, relish, parsley, salt and pepper. Blend mayonnaise mixture with potato mixture. Stir well. Garnish with paprika and parsley.

Serves 12

RASPBERRY SUPREME SALAD

Salad

1 (15-ounce) can crushed pineapple

1 (6-ounce) package raspberry gelatin

1½ cups boiling water

¾ cup pineapple juice

1 (15-ounce) can whole cranberries

Topping

2 (8-ounce) packages cream cheese, softened

½ cup sugar

1 cup sour cream

To make salad, drain pineapple. Reserve ¾ cup of juice. Set aside. Stir boiling water in gelatin until dissolved. Add juice, pineapple and cranberries. Stir. Pour into a large casserole dish. Refrigerate until firm. To make topping, mix cream cheese, sugar and sour cream. Blend until smooth. Spread over firm gelatin salad.

SEAFOOD SALAD

1 (16-ounce) package elbow pasta

1 pound shrimp, boiled

1 pound Louisiana crawfish, boiled

1 pound crabmeat, cooked

½ cup chopped bell pepper

½ cup chopped celery

½ cup chopped green onions

1 cup mayonnaise

Cook pasta to package directions. In a large bowl combine pasta, shrimp, crawfish, crabmeat, bell pepper, celery and green onions. Fold mayonnaise into pasta mixture. Salt and pepper to taste.

HOT TURKEY SALAD

2 cups diced cooked
   turkey
1 cup diced celery
1 cup mayonnaise
1½ tablespoons lemon juice
1 tablespoon grated onion

½ teaspoon salt
½ cup chopped, toasted
   almonds
½ cup shredded American
   cheese
1 cup crushed potato chips

Preheat oven to 425 degrees. Combine turkey, celery,
mayonnaise, lemon juice, onion, salt and almonds. Toss lightly
and place in a casserole dish. Top with cheese and potato
chips. Bake 10 minutes.

Serves 5 to 6

VEGETABLE SALAD

1 (15-ounce) can petit pois,
   drained, rinsed
1 (15-ounce) can green
   beans, drained, rinsed
1 (4-ounce) jar pimento
3-4 ribs celery, chopped
1 bell pepper, slivered

2 medium onions, sliced
½ cup chopped green
   onions
1 cup sliced fresh
   mushrooms
1 bottle red wine French
   dressing

Mix first 8 ingredients together. Marinate in red wine French
dressing. Refrigerate.

Vegetables

18 USC 707

Craig Naquin

Assumption Parish 4-H

I pledge

My Head to clearer thinking, My Heart to greater loyalty, My Hands to larger service,
My Health to better living, for my Club, my Community, my Country and my World.

Those are the words that seven-million 4-H youths across America recite as part of the 4-H tradition. The roots of the 4-H can be traced back to as early as 1908.

Assumption citizens have enjoyed 4-H since 1914 when the Cooperative Extension service was established. Currently in Assumption Parish, the 4-H program reaches approximately 3000 youths from grades pre-K through high school. The 4-H program has an emphasis on community service.

The Assumption Parish 4-H youth decided to partner with the Pink Team of Assumption in 2003 to help them in their goal to raise money for St. Jude Children's Research Hospital. Since then, in addition to the Bike-A-Thon, the 4-H has been an integral part of the Pink Team's fundraising efforts.

HOLLANDAISE SAUCE

1 stick butter, no substitute	¼ cup half-and-half
¼ cup lemon juice	2 teaspoons dry mustard
4 egg yolks, room temperature	½ teaspoon salt
	Hot sauce to taste

Melt butter in top of double boiler. Add lemon juice. Lightly beat egg yolks. Add egg yolks, half-and-half, mustard, salt and hot sauce. Stir until thoroughly blended. Cook in double boiler until desired thickness. Cover and refrigerate. Heat when ready to use. Add cream if it becomes too thick.

CHEESE SAUCE FOR VEGETABLES

2 tablespoons butter	1½ cups milk
2 tablespoons flour	4 ounces American cheese

In a saucepan, over medium heat, melt butter. Add flour to form a thick paste. Gradually add milk, stirring constantly until mixture thickens. Add cheese and stir until melted and well blended.

ARTICHOKE HEARTS AND GREEN BEANS

2 teaspoons olive oil	1 teaspoon onion powder
1 medium onion, chopped	1 teaspoon garlic powder
2 cloves garlic, minced	1 teaspoon sweet basil
2 (15-ounce) cans French-style green beans, drained	½ cup Italian bread crumbs
	½ cup grated Parmesan cheese
1 (15-ounce) can artichoke hearts, drained and quartered	Salt to taste
	Bread crumbs, for topping

Preheat oven to 350 degrees. Grease a casserole dish and set aside. Heat olive oil in a large skillet; add onion and sauté until tender. Add garlic. Cook 1 minute. Add green beans and artichoke hearts. Stir until heated thoroughly. Add onion powder, garlic powder, sweet basil, bread crumbs and cheese. Mix well. Pour mixture into prepared casserole dish. Cover with additional bread crumbs. Bake 20 to 25 minutes.

FRESH SNAP BEANS

3 slices bacon	2 cups water
Bacon drippings	½ teaspoon garlic powder
1 small onion, chopped	Créole seasoning to taste
1 pound fresh snap beans	

Fry bacon, drain and crumble. Set aside. Sauté onion in bacon drippings. Add beans, water, garlic powder and Créole seasoning. Bring to a boil. Add bacon and reduce heat. Cover and simmer 30 to 40 minutes or until tender.

Asparagus Casserole

1	cup crushed saltine crackers	1	(15-ounce) can cream of celery soup
½	stick butter, melted	1	cup grated mild Cheddar cheese
3	eggs, hard boiled		
1	(15-ounce) can asparagus spears	½	teaspoon white pepper

Preheat oven to 350 degrees. Butter a 1-quart casserole dish. Mix crackers with butter. Slice eggs. Drain asparagus spears. Layer ingredients in the casserole dish by placing a layer of ½ of the crackers, asparagus, eggs, soup and cheese. Repeat layering. Save a small amount of crackers to sprinkle on the top layer of cheese. Sprinkle with pepper. Bake 30 minutes.

Baked Beans

6	slices bacon	½	cup brown sugar
3	(32-ounce) cans pork and beans	½	cup cane syrup
		½	cup ketchup
3	onions, chopped	2	tablespoons mustard
3	cloves garlic, minced	½	cup barbecue sauce
2	teaspoons hot sauce	1	(10-ounce) can mushrooms, drained
3	tablespoons Worcestershire sauce		

Preheat oven to 350 degrees. Grease a casserole dish and set aside. Fry bacon, drain, crumble and set aside. Combine pork and beans, onion, garlic, hot sauce, Worcestershire sauce, brown sugar, cane syrup, ketchup, mustard and barbecue sauce. Mix thoroughly. Add mushrooms and bacon. Pour into prepared casserole dish. Bake 45 to 50 minutes or until bubbly.

RED BEANS

2	pounds red beans		Salt and pepper to taste
10	cups water		Créole seasoning to taste
1	large onion, chopped	1	pound smoked sausage,
3	cloves garlic, minced		sliced

Wash beans and soak in water (2-inches above beans) 1 hour. Drain. Add water, onion and garlic. Bring to a boil. Lower heat to simmer. Cook until beans are tender. Stir occasionally to avoid sticking. Water may need to be added to obtain volume. For creamy beans, mash against side of pot while stirring or remove 2 cups of beans, mash with a potato masher and return to pot. Season to taste with salt, pepper and Créole seasoning. Add sausage and cook beans for an additional 30 minutes or until gravy is creamy.

SWEET GREEN BEANS

2	tablespoons olive oil	½	teaspoon minced garlic
2	tablespoons flour	½	teaspoon black pepper
½	medium onion, chopped	1	tablespoon sugar
4	ounces tasso, slivered	1	(16-ounce) can chicken
1	(16-ounce) bag cut green beans		broth

Heat oil in a medium saucepan. Add flour and cook over medium heat until flour is the color of peanut butter (roux). Stir constantly. Add onion and tasso. Stir until onion is soft. Add green beans. Stir. Add garlic, pepper and sugar. Mix thoroughly. Stir in broth. Bring to a boil. Cook over medium heat 10 minutes. Cover and reduce heat. Cook 20 to 25 minutes until beans are tender and gravy is thick.

Makes 4 to 6 servings

Hint: *Tasso is a highly seasoned smoked beef, pork or turkey meat used in vegetable dishes and gravies.*

VIKING BEANS

1 pound ground beef
1 pound bacon, diced
1 cup chopped onion
1 (32-ounce) can pork and beans
2 (15-ounce) cans kidney beans

2 (15-ounce) cans lima beans, drained
½ cup ketchup
¾ cup brown sugar
1 teaspoon vinegar
1 teaspoon mustard

Preheat oven to 325 degrees. Grease a large casserole dish and set aside. Fry beef and bacon together. Drain. Add onion and cook about 5 minutes, until onion is tender. Remove from heat. Add pork and beans, kidney beans and lima beans. Stir well. In a separate dish, mix ketchup, sugar, vinegar and mustard. Pour mixture over beans. Stir and mix thoroughly. Place in prepared casserole dish. Cover and bake 30 minutes. Remove the cover. Bake an additional 30 minutes.

WHITE BEANS

1 pound dried white beans
12 cups water
½ cup minced onion

½ cup cooking oil
½ pound salt pork
¼ cup chopped green onions

Wash beans and soak in 6 cups of water overnight in the refrigerator. Put beans to cook in the same water in which they were soaked. Boil until hulls start to detach from beans. Drain water. Add remaining water. Add onion and oil. Wash salt pork and cut into bite size pieces. Add to beans. When mixture comes to a boil, lower heat to medium. Stir occasionally to make sure beans don't stick. For creamy beans, mash beans against side of pot while stirring. Cook beans until tender, 1 to 2 hours. Add green onions 15 minutes before beans are completely cooked.

CRUNCHY BROCCOLI

Broccoli

1   bunch broccoli, cut into florets

Salt to taste

Sauce

¼   cup olive oil
1   small onion, chopped
2   tablespoons flour
1½ cups milk
½   cup grated Parmesan cheese

1   tablespoon chopped parsley
Salt and pepper to taste

Crunchy Topping

3   tablespoons olive oil
1   clove garlic, minced

6   tablespoons bread crumbs

Preheat oven to 400 degrees. Grease pie pan and set aside. Cook broccoli in boiling salted water 4 minutes. Drain, refresh under cold water and drain again. Pat dry with paper towels and transfer to a bowl. To make the sauce, heat oil in medium saucepan over medium heat. Add onion and cook until tender. Add flour and stir until foamy. Pour in milk and cook. Stir continuously until mixture comes to a boil and thickens. Stir in cheese and parsley. Cook until cheese is melted. Season with salt and pepper. Coat broccoli evenly with sauce. Transfer broccoli to prepared pie pan. To make the topping, heat oil in nonstick skillet. Add garlic. Cook until golden. Add bread crumbs and toss until lightly browned. Sprinkle topping over sauce coated broccoli. Bake 20 minutes or until hot and bubbly.

Makes 4 servings

BROCCOLI WITH CHEESE

½ stick butter
1 onion, chopped
3 packages broccoli, chopped
1 (10-ounce) can cream of mushroom soup

6 ounces garlic cheese
1 small can sliced mushrooms, drained
¾ cup chopped almonds
½ cup bread crumbs

Preheat oven to 325 degrees. Grease a 9x13-inch casserole dish and set aside. Sauté onion in butter. Add broccoli and cook until tender. Add soup, cheese, mushrooms and ½ cup almonds. Pour into prepared casserole dish. Sprinkle with bread crumbs and remaining almonds. Bake until bubbly.

Makes 10 servings

CRÉOLE CABBAGE

1 cabbage
3 tablespoons vegetable oil
1 onion, chopped
1 teaspoon minced garlic
½ teaspoon chopped parsley

1 teaspoon sugar
1 teaspoon Créole seasoning
2 cups water

Cut cabbage into large pieces. Wash and drain. In a large skillet, heat oil and sauté onion. Add cabbage. Stir until mixture begins to cook down. Stir in garlic, parsley, sugar and Créole seasoning. Pour water over mixture and cover. Cook 20 to 25 minutes until cabbage is soft. A small amount of liquid should remain.

Now, This is Cabbage!

1 medium cabbage	1½ cups grated Cheddar cheese
½ stick butter	
1 medium onion, chopped	¾ cup bread crumbs
1 (10-ounce) can cream of mushroom soup	

Preheat oven to 350 degrees. Grease a casserole dish and set aside. Break cabbage and boil in salted water until tender. Drain and set aside. Melt butter in large saucepan. Add onion and sauté until soft. Stir in soup. Remove from heat. Add cabbage and 1 cup of cheese. Mix thoroughly. Pour into prepared casserole dish. Top with remaining cheese. Sprinkle with bread crumbs. Bake covered 45 minutes or until mixture bubbles.

A container of vinegar next to the stove when cooking something with a strong smell (i.e. cabbage) will help to absorb the smell.

Sweet Buttered Baby Carrots

1 pound baby carrots	1 tablespoon sugar
1 small onion, chopped	½ teaspoon salt
½ stick butter	
½ teaspoon chopped parsley	

Preheat oven to 350 degrees. Grease a casserole dish and set aside. Boil carrots 10 minutes or until tender. Drain and set aside. In a small saucepan, sauté onion in butter until tender. Spread carrots in prepared casserole dish. Sprinkle with parsley, sugar and salt. Pour butter and onion mixture over the carrots. Bake 20 to 25 minutes.

CARROTS AU GRATIN

3 tablespoons butter
5 cups thinly sliced carrots
3 tablespoons minced green onions
2 tablespoons flour
2 tablespoons chopped parsley

Salt and pepper to taste
1 cup milk
1 cup shredded Colby-Monterey Jack cheese blend
1½ cups crushed potato chips

Preheat oven to 350 degrees. Lightly grease a 9-inch baking dish. In a large skillet, melt butter over medium heat. Add carrots and green onions. Cook 6 minutes. Stir occasionally. Stir in flour, parsley, salt and pepper. Cook 2 minutes. Stir occasionally. Add milk. Cook 2 to 3 minutes or until thickened. Stir in cheese. Spoon mixture into prepared baking dish and top with potato chips. Bake 30 minutes or until hot and bubbly.

Parsley will keep in a covered jar in the refrigerator if placed in the jar slightly damp.

CARROT SOUFFLÉ

1¾ pounds carrots
1 cup sugar
1½ teaspoons baking powder
1½ teaspoons vanilla

2 tablespoons flour
3 eggs, beaten
1 stick butter, softened
¼ cup confectioners' sugar

Preheat oven to 350 degrees. Grease a 2-quart casserole dish. Peel and boil carrots until very soft. Drain. Place carrots in a large mixing bowl. Add sugar, baking powder, vanilla and flour. Beat until smooth. Add eggs and butter. Mix thoroughly. Pour into prepared casserole dish. Bake 1 hour or until top is light brown. Sprinkle with confectioners' sugar.

Makes 6 to 8 servings

CAULIFLOWER AND CHEESE

1	head cauliflower	½	cup chopped green onions
2	tablespoons butter	¼	cup bread crumbs
2	tablespoons flour	2	tablespoons grated mild Cheddar cheese
1	cup milk		
½	teaspoon salt		
½	teaspoon pepper		

Preheat oven to 375 degrees. Break cauliflower into florets and cook in boiling water 15 to 20 minutes. Drain well. Place in buttered baking dish. Melt butter in saucepan over medium heat. Add flour. Stir in milk and cook until smooth and thick. Add salt, pepper and green onions. Stir. Pour mixture over cauliflower. Sprinkle with bread crumbs and cheese. Bake 20 minutes or until light brown.

Makes 6 servings

CREAMY CAULIFLOWER

1	head cauliflower	1	(10-ounce) can cream of shrimp soup
1	(8-ounce) package cream cheese, softened		

Preheat oven to 325 degrees. Grease a casserole dish and set aside. Break cauliflower into florets. Boil in salted water 15 minutes or until tender. Place in prepared casserole dish. Cube cream cheese and place over cauliflower. Pour soup over entire mixture. Be sure that the cauliflower is completely covered. Bake 20 to 25 minutes.

Quick and Easy Corn Pudding

½	stick butter	2	eggs, slightly beaten
1	medium onion, chopped	⅔	cup bread crumbs
2	(15-ounce) cans whole corn, drained	1	cup sour cream
2	(15-ounce) cans cream style corn	1	teaspoon salt
		1	teaspoon white pepper

Preheat oven to 350 degrees. Butter a 3-quart casserole dish and set aside. Melt butter in saucepan. Sauté onion until tender. Add whole corn, cream style corn, eggs, bread crumbs, sour cream, salt and pepper. Mix thoroughly. Pour into prepared casserole dish. Bake 35 to 40 minutes or until firm.

Makes 8 to 10 servings

Stewed Corn and Tomatoes

"Maque choux"

1	onion, chopped	1	(15-ounce) can diced tomatoes
2	tablespoons chopped bell peppers	1	teaspoon Créole seasoning
1	clove garlic, minced	1	teaspoon sugar
6	tablespoons butter		
4	cups corn		

Sauté onion, bell pepper and garlic in butter. Add corn, tomatoes, Créole seasoning and sugar. Stir and simmer over low heat 30 to 40 minutes.

Note: *This is a Native American Indian dish adapted for their use by the Créoles.*

BAKED CUSHAW

Cushaw

1 medium cushaw
(pumpkin)
½ cup water
1 tablespoon cooking oil
3 cups brown sugar

½ teaspoon salt
1 teaspoon cinnamon
½ teaspoon nutmeg
1 stick butter

Topping

1 tablespoon brown sugar
1 tablespoon cinnamon

2 tablespoons butter

Preheat oven to 375 degrees. Grease a 2-quart casserole dish and set aside. To prepare cushaw, pierce rind and place whole in a 325 degree oven. This makes it easier to peel and cut. Remove rind and seeds. Cut into cubes. Place in a large, heavy saucepan with water and oil. Cover and cook on medium heat until soft. Add sugar, salt, cinnamon, nutmeg and butter. Continue cooking on medium heat approximately 1 hour or until dark brown. Stir occasionally to prevent sticking. Spread in a prepared casserole dish. To prepare topping sprinkle brown sugar and cinnamon over casserole. Dot with butter. Bake until heated thoroughly and a brown crust is formed.

Hint: *Great side dish.*

Cushaw (kuh-SHAW; KOO-shaw) is a very large, hard-shelled squash with a crooked neck. It is popular in Cajun and Créole cooking. The meat of the cushaw is yellow. To prepare cushaw place it in a 325 degree oven for about 15 minutes before peeling and cutting.

FRIED EGGPLANT CASSEROLE

3	eggplants	1	teaspoon minced garlic
2	cups Italian seasoned bread crumbs	2	eggs, slightly beaten
½	cup grated Parmesan cheese		Olive oil for frying
½	cup chopped parsley	1	(15-ounce) can stewed tomatoes

Preheat oven to 350 degrees. Grease a 2-quart casserole dish and set aside. Peel eggplants and slice. Set aside. Mix bread crumbs with ⅓ cup cheese, parsley and garlic. Dip slices of eggplant into eggs and then into bread crumbs. Fry in oil until golden brown. Drain. Place in prepared casserole dish. Top with tomatoes and sprinkle with remaining cheese. Bake 20 to 25 minutes or until completely heated.

SOUTHERN STYLE GREENS

2	pounds collard greens	1½	cups water
2	strips bacon, thick cut	2	tablespoons sugar
½	cup chopped onion	⅓	teaspoon crushed red pepper flakes
2	large garlic cloves, minced	⅓	cup cider vinegar

Wash greens in cold water. Drain. Wash a second time. Drain. Remove heavy stems. Tear leaves into bite size pieces. Set aside. In a 6-quart Dutch oven, cook bacon until lightly brown. Add onion. Cook over medium heat 5 to 7 minutes. Stir occasionally until onion softens and starts to brown. Stir in garlic. Add water. Stir to loosen any particles from bottom of pan. Stir in sugar and pepper. Continue cooking until the mixture boils. Add greens to boiling water. Reduce heat. Cover and simmer 30 minutes. Stir in vinegar. Cook an additional 20 to 25 minutes or until desired tenderness.

SMOTHERED OKRA

½ cup vegetable oil	1 onion, chopped
2 pounds fresh okra, sliced	½ bell pepper, chopped
3 tomatoes, peeled and chopped	1 teaspoon salt
	1 teaspoon red pepper

Preheat oven to 275 degrees. In a heavy roasting pan, heat oil. Add okra, tomatoes, onion, bell pepper, salt and pepper. Place roasting pan in oven. Cover and cook 1½ to 2 hours. Stir occasionally.

Hint: *Great to use to thicken gumbos. Can also be used as a side dish.*

PETIT POIS

1 (16-ounce) can petit pois	¼ cup shredded lettuce
2 tablespoons butter	1 teaspoon chopped parsley
¼ cup chopped onion	
¼ teaspoon salt	1 teaspoon cornstarch
1 tablespoon sugar	1 tablespoon butter

Drain peas, reserving 2 to 3 tablespoons of liquid. Combine peas, butter and reserved liquid in a saucepan. Add onion, salt and sugar. Lay shredded lettuce on top. Add parsley. Cover and cook until lettuce wilts and cooks into the peas. Cream cornstarch and butter. Add to peas. Cook 1 to 2 minutes.

'Southern field peas' refers to hundreds of varieties subdivided into four main groups; field peas, Crowder peas, cream peas and black-eyed peas. They were originally brought to the United States in the colonial days. Field peas became a staple food among many residents in the Deep South as they are drought resistant and easily adapt to various soils.

FIELD PEAS

1	pound salt pork, cubed	3	cloves garlic, minced
¼	cup vegetable oil	2	cups water
1½	quarts field peas		Salt and pepper to taste
3	medium onions, chopped	1	teaspoon sugar

Brown meat in oil. Add peas, onion and garlic. Cook over medium heat 20 to 30 minutes. Stir often. Add water, salt, pepper and sugar. Stir. Cover and simmer 1½ hours. Stir frequently adding water as needed. Remove one cup of peas and mash (this will thicken peas). Return to pot and cook 30 minutes.

"Happiness is a butterfly, which when pursued, is always just beyond your grasp, but which, if you will sit down quietly, may light upon you."

Nathaniel Hawthorne

Snap Peas with Roasted Garlic Dressing

Roasted Garlic Dressing

1   clove garlic
⅔   cup olive oil
¼   cup white wine vinegar
2   tablespoons Dijon
       mustard

¼   teaspoon salt
¼   teaspoon pepper

Snap Peas

4   cups frozen sugar snap
       peas
1   red bell pepper, sliced
1   purple onion, sliced
¼   cup roasted garlic
       dressing

⅓   cup crumbled feta
       cheese
½   teaspoon salt
½   teaspoon pepper

To make dressing, sauté garlic in 1½ tablespoons olive oil. Place remaining olive oil in blender and add sautéed garlic, vinegar, mustard, salt and pepper. Blend until smooth. To prepare peas, cook peas, bell pepper, onion and roasted garlic dressing over low heat 5 minutes or until thoroughly heated. Stir constantly. Remove from heat. Stir in cheese, salt and pepper. Top with dressing. Serve immediately.

Makes 8 to 10 servings

Did you know that peas are the world's oldest crop? "We are old and we are wise. We are one of the matriarchs of the garden. More than food we are healers of the soil, which is so much needed today." ... Message from the pea essence ...

CONFETTI SCALLOPED POTATOES

½	cup chopped onion	1	(16-ounce) package frozen hash brown potatoes
¼	cup chopped bell pepper		
2	tablespoons butter		
1	(10-ounce) can cream of mushroom soup	1	cup grated sharp Cheddar cheese
½	cup milk	½	teaspoon salt
½	cup sour cream	¼	teaspoon pepper
		¼	cup melted butter
		1	cup Ritz cracker crumbs

Preheat oven to 375 degrees. Grease a shallow casserole dish and set aside. Sauté onion and bell pepper in butter. Add soup, milk and sour cream. Stir until well blended. Add potatoes, cheese, salt and pepper. Pour into prepared casserole dish. Mix butter with cracker crumbs. Spread on top of entire casserole. Bake 35 to 40 minutes.

Makes 6 to 8 servings

POTATO STEW

½	cup vegetable oil	6	medium red potatoes, cubed
½	cup flour		
1	onion, chopped		Salt and pepper to taste
½	bell pepper, chopped	3	green onions tops, chopped fine
6	cups water		

Heat oil, add flour and cook over medium heat until flour is the color of peanut butter (roux). Stir constantly. Add onion and bell pepper. Cook over low heat until soft and clear. Add water and bring to a boil. Reduce heat. Cover and cook 1 hour. Season cubed potatoes with salt and pepper. Add potatoes and green onions to gravy. Cook until potatoes are tender.

Makes 6 to 8 servings

STUFFED POTATOES

2	medium potatoes	1	(8-ounce) package Velveeta, chopped
4	large potatoes, baked		
6	slices bacon, fried crisp	1	cup milk
1	medium onion, chopped	8	ounces sour cream
½	cup chopped green onions	1½	teaspoons black pepper
½	stick butter		Cheddar cheese for topping

Preheat oven to 350 degrees. Peel and chop medium potatoes. Boil until tender and drain. Cut baked potatoes in half and scoop out centers. Set skins aside. Fry bacon. Remove, drain and crumble. Set aside. Sauté onion in bacon drippings. Add green onions. Add boiled potatoes and potatoes scooped from baked potatoes. Break up large pieces. Add butter and Velveeta. Stir until melted. Add milk, sour cream and pepper. Mix thoroughly. Spoon mixture into potato skins. Top with Cheddar cheese. Sprinkle bacon on top of potatoes. When ready to serve bake until entire potato is heated and cheese is melted.

CREAMED SPINACH

4	packages frozen spinach, chopped
1	stick butter
¼	cup flour
1	small onion, chopped
1	cup evaporated milk
1	cup liquid from spinach
1	teaspoon Créole seasoning
1½	teaspoons garlic salt
12	ounces Mexican cheese, chopped in small pieces
2	teaspoon Worcestershire sauce
	Salt and pepper to taste
	Bread crumbs to sprinkle

Preheat oven to 350 degrees. Grease a casserole dish and set aside. Cook spinach according to package directions. Drain and reserve liquid. Melt butter in heavy saucepan. Add flour. Stir until lumps disappear. Add onion and cook until soft. Add milk and liquid from spinach. Continue stirring over medium heat until thick and smooth. Add Créole seasoning, garlic salt, cheese, Worcestershire sauce, salt and pepper. Stir until melted. Pour over spinach. Mix thoroughly. Place in prepared casserole dish. Sprinkle with bread crumbs. Bake 30 minutes until lightly brown.

SQUASH CASSEROLE

½	cup chopped onion
1	stick butter
6	medium yellow squash, unpeeled and sliced
1	(10-ounce) can cream of celery soup
32	crushed butter flavored crackers
½	cup Italian bread crumbs

Preheat oven to 350 degrees. Grease a 2-quart casserole dish and set aside. Sauté onion in butter. Add squash and cook until tender. Stir in soup and cracker crumbs. Pour into prepared casserole dish. Top with bread crumbs. Bake 25 minutes.

FRIED SWEET POTATOES

2 **large sweet potatoes**   ½ **cup sugar**
1 **cup oil**

Boil sweet potatoes (with skins on) until fork tender. Cool. Peel and slice lengthwise into ½-inch slices. Heat oil. Fry slices in hot oil. Brown on both sides. Remove and drain on paper towel. Sprinkle hot potatoes with sugar. Serve hot.

The sweet potato is a new world plant and the yam was brought to us from Africa

SWEET POTATO WEDGES

4 **medium sweet potatoes**   ½ **cup brown sugar**
½ **stick butter, melted**   1 **tablespoon cinnamon**

Cut unpeeled sweet potatoes into large wedges. Place in slow cooker. Pour butter over potatoes. Sprinkle with sugar and cinnamon. Cook on low 4 hours or until potatoes are fork tender. Reduce drippings and pour over potatoes. Serve hot.

BAKED TOMATOES FLORENTINE

1 (10-ounce) package frozen spinach, chopped
1 cup seasoned bread crumbs
½ cup chopped green onions
3 eggs, slightly beaten
¾ cup melted butter
¼ cup grated Parmesan cheese
¼ teaspoon Worcestershire sauce
½ teaspoon minced garlic
¼ teaspoon salt
¼ teaspoon pepper
½ teaspoon dried thyme
⅛ teaspoon hot sauce
9 tomato slices, thick
  Parmesan cheese, additional for topping

Preheat oven to 350 degrees. Butter a baking dish and set aside. Cook spinach using the butter method on the package directions. Add bread crumbs, green onions, eggs, butter, cheese, Worcestershire sauce, garlic, salt, pepper, thyme and hot sauce. Mix well. Arrange the tomato slices in a single layer in prepared baking dish. Mound equal amounts of spinach mixture onto each tomato slice. Sprinkle lightly with additional cheese. Bake 15 minutes.

Makes 9 servings

Hint: *This may be made ahead and frozen for later use.*

The tomato is actually a fruit; therefore, it should be treated like one, which means not storing it in the refrigerator. Tomatoes stored at room temperature have the best flavor.

FRIED VEGETABLES

Vegetables

Cauliflower	Okra
Broccoli	Squash
Eggplant	

Batter

2 eggs	¼ teaspoon Créole
½ cup milk	seasoning
1 cup flour	Vegetable oil to deep fry
½ teaspoon salt	

To prepare vegetables boil cauliflower and broccoli in salted water 5 minutes. Let cool and separate broccoli into florets. Slice eggplant and soak in salted water 5 minutes. Cut okra into ½-inch slices, wash and drain. Cut squash into ½-inch slices. To prepare batter beat eggs and milk. Mix flour, salt and Créole seasoning. Dredge prepared vegetables in flour and then in egg mixture and again in flour. Deep fry in hot oil, 375 degrees, until brown. Drain on paper towels.

TRI-COLORED VEGETABLES

4 carrots	1 (8-ounce) bag fresh sugar
1 yellow bell pepper	snap peas
2 tablespoons butter	¼ teaspoon minced garlic
2 tablespoons olive oil	½ teaspoon salt
½ small onion, chopped	¼ teaspoon pepper

Cut carrots into ¼-inch strips. Boil carrots 3 minutes. Drain. Set aside. Slice yellow bell pepper into ¼-inch strips. Set aside. In a medium saucepan, heat butter and oil over medium to high heat until butter is melted. Sauté onion until soft. Add carrots, bell pepper and peas. Sauté 5 minutes or until tender crisp. Add garlic, salt and pepper. Sauté 1 minute.

VEGETABLE MEDLEY

2 (16-ounce) bags frozen mixed vegetables
2 cups finely chopped onion
2 cups finely chopped celery
2 cups grated Cheddar cheese
1 cup mayonnaise
1 roll of Ritz crackers, crushed
1 stick butter, melted

Preheat oven to 350 degrees. Grease a 9x13-inch casserole dish and set aside. Prepare vegetables according to directions on package and drain. Mix vegetables, onion, celery, cheese and mayonnaise. Place in prepared casserole dish. Mix cracker crumbs with butter and spread on top vegetables. Bake 30 minutes.

PRALINE TOPPED YAMS

Yams

3½ cups yams
2 eggs
1 cup sugar
½ teaspoon salt
1 teaspoon vanilla
1 stick butter, melted
½ cup half-and-half

Topping

1 cup light brown sugar
1 cup chopped pecans
⅓ cup flour
1 stick butter, melted

Boil, peel and mash yams. Preheat oven to 350 degrees. Beat eggs. Add yams, sugar, salt, vanilla, butter and half-and-half. Mix well. Pour into a 9x11-inch glass baking dish. Bake 15 to 20 minutes. Remove from oven. To prepare topping mix sugar, pecans, flour and butter. Sprinkle over casserole. Bake 20 minutes. Praline top will form.

Hint: *Canned sweet potatoes may be used.*

Louisiana ranks third in the nation in rice production.

BLACK-EYED PEA JAMBALAYA

1¼ cups rice

1 (15-ounce) can black-eyed peas with jalapeño

1 pound smoked pork sausage, chopped

1 (14-ounce) can beef broth

1 stick butter, melted

1 bell pepper, chopped

1 medium onion, chopped

In a large bowl, mix all ingredients and pour into rice cooker. Set cooker. Let jambalaya remain in covered cooker 10 minutes after cooking has been completed (bell will chime).

BROWN RICE

1 stick butter

½ (1-ounce) envelope dry onion soup mix

2 (10-ounce) cans consommé

1 cup rice

1 (4-ounce) can sliced mushrooms, drained

Preheat oven to 350 degrees. Melt butter in casserole dish. Add soup mix, consommé, rice and mushrooms. Stir well. Bake covered 1 hour.

Makes 6 servings

PLANTATION RICE

8	slices bacon, crumbled	1¼	cups rice
1	medium onion, chopped	1	teaspoon salt
4	teaspoons butter	2¼	cups water
1	cup coarsely chopped pecans	2	tablespoons chopped parsley

Fry bacon in a large skillet until almost crisp. Add the onion and sauté lightly. Remove bacon and onion and set aside. Add butter and pecans to the drippings. Sauté over medium heat just until fragrant. Remove the pecans and set aside. Stir the rice and salt into the pan, coating the rice well. Add water and bring to a boil. Simmer covered, 25 to 30 minutes or until the rice is tender and liquid is absorbed. Stir in bacon, onions, pecans and parsley.

WILD RICE AND MUSHROOM CASSEROLE

1	(6-ounce) package wild rice mix	4	(4-ounce) cans sliced mushrooms, drained
1	cup chopped onion	1	(10-ounce) can cream of mushroom soup
1	cup chopped celery		
½	stick butter	1	cup whipping cream

Preheat oven to 350 degrees. Grease a 9x12-inch baking dish. Cook rice according to package directions. Sauté onion and celery in butter. Add mushrooms and soup to mixture and stir. Remove from heat and stir in rice, mixing well. Stir in whipping cream. Mix completely. Pour into prepared baking dish. Bake 1 hour.

Dressing Mix

1½ pounds ground beef
1½ pounds ground pork
1 large onion, chopped
1 large bell pepper, chopped
2 stalks celery, diced
3 cloves garlic, minced
½ cup chopped green onions

3 tablespoons cornstarch
2 (14-ounce) cans beef broth
Salt, pepper and Créole seasoning to taste
1 quart oysters, drained (optional)
¼ cup chopped parsley

Brown beef and pork, drain well. Add onion, bell pepper, celery, garlic and green onions. Sauté until vegetables are wilted. Dilute cornstarch in broth. Add to meat mixture. Season to taste with salt, pepper and Créole seasoning. Add oysters and parsley. Simmer 35 to 40 minutes.

3 to 4 cups cooked rice may be added to dressing mix for a rice dressing.

4 packages of cornbread mix, prepared, may be added to dressing mix for a cornbread dressing.

Hint: *Wonderful stuffing for your holiday turkey.*

 Rice always triples in volume, so be sure to take this into account when choosing an appropriate cooking pot.

CORNBREAD DRESSING

4 (6-ounce) packages cornbread mix

2 pounds ground beef

2 onions, chopped

1 bell pepper, chopped

3 cloves garlic, minced

1 cup chopped celery
Salt and pepper to taste

2 (14-ounce) cans chicken broth

1 (10-ounce) can cream of mushroom soup

1 (4-ounce) can mushroom steak sauce

1 teaspoon browning liquid

¼ cup chopped parsley

¼ cup chopped green onions

2 teaspoons poultry seasoning

2 teaspoons sage

3 eggs, beaten

Preheat oven to 350 degrees. Bake cornbread mix according to package directions. Cool, crumble and set aside. Brown beef and drain. Add onion, bell pepper, garlic and celery. Salt and pepper to taste. Cook until vegetables are wilted. Add chicken broth. Cook slowly 30 minutes, stirring often. Add soup, steak sauce, browning liquid, parsley and green onions. Remove from heat. Add cornbread, poultry seasoning and sage, slowly stir in beaten eggs. Spoon mixture into a large casserole dish. Bake 30 to 45 minutes.

Cornbread Tips

1. Sprinkle a little cornmeal in the hot pan before adding the batter. It will brown and add a crispier texture.
2. Use muffin or corn stick pans, (preferably iron), to vary the shape of the cornbread.
3. Instead of baking, fry the batter like pancakes.

SEAFOOD CORNBREAD DRESSING

1 package cornbread mix	1¼ cups water
½ cup chopped onion	1 cup chopped uncooked shrimp
3 tablespoons vegetable oil	
½ cup chopped red bell pepper	1 cup crabmeat
	1 cup oysters, drained
½ cup chopped green bell pepper	Créole seasoning to taste
	½ cup chopped green onions
½ cup chopped celery	
1 clove garlic, minced	1 cup chopped jalapeño cheese
1 (10-ounce) can cream of shrimp soup	

Preheat oven to 350 degrees. Grease a 9x13-inch baking dish. Mix and bake cornbread according to package directions. Sauté onion in oil until wilted. Add bell peppers, celery and garlic. Sauté 5 minutes or until vegetables are tender. Stir in soup, water, shrimp, crabmeat, oysters and Créole seasoning. Bring to a boil over medium heat, stirring constantly. Crumble cornbread into seafood mixture. Stir in green onions and cheese. Spoon into prepared baking dish. Bake 30 to 40 minutes or until golden brown.

Cornbread was popular during the American civil War because it was very cheap and could be made in many different forms. It could be fashioned into high-rising, fluffy loaves or simply fried for a fast meal.

BAYOU RICE DRESSING

2	tablespoons vegetable oil	1	(14-ounce) can beef broth
2	tablespoons flour		
1	large onion, chopped	4	cups cooked rice
1	pound ground beef	1	teaspoon salt
1	pound ground pork	1	teaspoon black pepper
2	cloves garlic, minced		
2	tablespoons chopped parsley		

Heat oil and add flour. Cook until the color of peanut butter, (roux). Add onion and sauté until wilted. Brown beef and pork. Drain and add to roux. Stir in garlic and parsley. Cook over medium heat for 5 minutes. Add broth. Cover and cook over low heat 20 to 25 minutes. Add rice, salt and pepper and mix thoroughly. Simmer 5 minutes.

Rice was brought to the American colonies in the early 1600's, and commercial production began in 1685. The first cultivators of rice in America did so by accident. A storm damaged ship docked in Charleston, South Carolina. The captain of the ship gave a small bag of rice to a local farmer as a gift.

OYSTER DRESSING

1 pint oysters	1 (14-ounce) can chicken broth
¼ cup vegetable oil	
1 medium onion, chopped	1½ cups water
½ bell pepper, chopped	1 teaspoon red pepper
1 rib celery, chopped fine	1 teaspoon Créole seasoning
2 cloves garlic, minced	
½ pound chicken livers, chopped (optional)	2 cups rice

Drain oysters (keep liquid and strain). Cut up oysters and set aside. Heat oil and sauté onion, bell pepper, celery and garlic. Add liver and oysters and cook 5 minutes. Add chicken broth, water, oyster liquid, red pepper, Créole seasoning and rice. Bring to a boil, cover and reduce heat to low. Stir once after 15 minutes (do not uncover too often). Cook approximately 15 more minutes or until rice is cooked and all liquid is absorbed.

Hint: *Deboned chicken may be added.*

FETTUCCINE ALFREDO

1 (16-ounce) bag fettuccine	1 cup heavy cream
	Salt and pepper to taste
1½ teaspoons olive oil	⅛ teaspoon nutmeg
1½ tablespoons minced garlic	¼ cup Parmesan cheese

Boil fettuccine and set aside. Heat olive oil in medium pan. Add garlic, sauté on low heat 5 minutes. Add cream and bring to a boil. Simmer on low 4 to 5 minutes until cream thickens. Add salt, pepper and nutmeg. Turn off heat and add cheese, a little at a time, stirring with a whisk. Mix with hot pasta.

Easy Sticky Spaghetti and Cheese

1 (16-ounce) bag spaghetti	2 tablespoons butter
1 pound Velveeta	¼ teaspoon garlic powder
1 (12-ounce) can evaporated milk	¼ teaspoon onion powder
	½ teaspoon Créole seasoning

Boil spaghetti and drain. Cut cheese in small cubes and place in pot. Add milk and butter. Top with hot spaghetti. Add garlic powder, onion powder and Créole seasoning. Cover and cook on low heat until cheese and butter are melted. Pour into a casserole, cover and serve hot.

Baked Spaghetti and Cheese

1 (16-ounce) bag #3 spaghetti	¼ teaspoon onion powder
3 large eggs	½ teaspoon Créole seasoning
1 cup milk	2 (8-ounce) bags shredded cheese
¼ teaspoon garlic powder	

Boil spaghetti, drain and set aside. Preheat oven to 350 degrees. Spray a 9x13-inch baking dish with nonstick spray. Beat eggs and milk until blended. Add garlic powder, onion powder and Créole seasoning. Add spaghetti to this mixture and stir well to coat all spaghetti. Add one bag of cheese and mix well. Pour mixture into baking dish and top with remaining cheese. Bake until cheese begins to brown, approximately 40 to 50 minutes.

STUFFED MIRLITON

4	mirlitons	1½ pounds ground beef
2	tablespoons vegetable oil	Créole seasoning to taste
1	large onion, diced	1½ cups seasoned bread
2	teaspoons minced garlic	crumbs

Grease a casserole dish and set aside. Cut mirlitons in half lengthwise, remove seeds. Place in a large pot and cover with water. Boil until tender. Scoop out centers. Mash slightly and set aside. Reserve outer skins for stuffing. Heat oil. Add onion and garlic and sauté until clear. Add ground beef and brown. Season to taste with Créole seasoning. Add mirlitons to the ground meat mixture. Cook 15 to 20 minutes. Add 1 cup of bread crumbs and stir until thoroughly mixed. Fill mirliton skins. Place in prepared casserole dish. Sprinkle with remaining ½ cup bread crumbs. Bake at 350 degrees for 30 minutes.

In Louisiana the mirliton is sometimes called "alligator pear" because they are shaped like a pear and when held sideways they resemble an alligator's head.

Main
Dishes

S.Rochester

Sylvia Rochester

Cattails

CATTAIL JAMBALAYA

3	tablespoons butter	1	pound Louisiana crawfish
2	cups julienne cut cattail shoots	1	teaspoon Creole seasoning
1	cup chopped green onions	¼	cup chicken stock
2	cloves garlic, minced	3	cups cooked rice

Heat butter in pot over medium heat. Add cattail, green onions and garlic. Sauté for about 5 minutes. Stir in crawfish, Creole seasoning and chicken stock. Cover. Cook on medium-low heat for approximately 15 minutes, stirring occasionally. Taste and adjust seasoning. Add rice and blend well. Cover. Cook about 5 minutes, stirring frequently to incorporate rice with mixture.

Serves 4

Cattails grow in the marshes and swamps of Louisiana. They are tasty, highly nutritious and easy to harvest. They were a major staple for the American Indians who used them for food and medicinal purposes.

How to season a "black iron pot" (cast iron cookware)
Use a charcoal barbecue pit or a propane grill. Coat the cast
iron pot with a light coating of shortening (DO NOT USE
MARGARINE OR BUTTER). Be sure to use good potholders or
heat resistant gloves when working with pots. Cast iron retains
heat for a very long time. Turn the pot, pan or skillet upside
down on the grill. Use high heat, around 450 to 500 degrees.
Cover the item loosely with foil or close the hood on the grill. This
process will take about 1 hour. Check the item to see if the oil has
been burned into the metal. It should be black in color. If it is not
black, allow to cool and again coat with shortening. Return to
fire and heat again 1 more hour. Allow to cool then clean with
hot water. Return to heat to dry properly. After using, scrape
off excess food particles before washing DO NOT SCOUR OR
PLACE IN DISHWASHER. DO NOT USE SOAP. ALWAYS
DRY OVER HEAT. Place a paper towel inside cookware when
storing. Do not store in open air.

CRÉOLE SEASONING MIX

2½ tablespoons salt

2½ tablespoons paprika

2 tablespoons garlic powder

1½ tablespoons onion powder

1 tablespoon Cayenne pepper

1 tablespoon dried oregano

1 tablespoon dried thyme

2 teaspoons coarse black pepper

1½ teaspoons white pepper

Combine all ingredients in a jar and shake until well blended.

Makes about 1 cup

Hint: *Makes great gifts.*

SPICY RUB

6	tablespoons paprika	2	tablespoons sugar
2	tablespoons black pepper	1	tablespoon garlic powder
2	tablespoons chili powder	1	tablespoon onion powder
2	tablespoons salt	1½	teaspoons Cayenne pepper

Mix all ingredients together and rub on meat.

ROUX

Stove Top Roux

1	cup oil	1	cup flour

Microwave Roux

2   cups flour

To make a roux on the stove, heat oil in a heavy saucepan. Stir in flour gradually. Stir constantly. Lower heat and cook until golden brown or the color of peanut butter. To make a microwave roux, place flour in a 4-cup microwave safe measuring cup. Microwave on high (100%) 6 to 7 minutes, stirring at least every minute. Once the flour turns light brown, it takes only 30 to 60 seconds more to reach dark brown. Stir often so that bottom and center will not burn. Roux freezes well.

Hint: *The color of a roux is a personal choice. These recipes can be adjusted by the length of time you brown the flour.*

BEEF AND BISCUIT CASSEROLE

1	pound ground beef	½	teaspoon basil
½	pound ground turkey	1	teaspoon oregano
1	small onion, chopped	1	(26-ounce) jar spaghetti sauce
3	cloves garlic, minced		
1	(6-ounce) package pepperoni, chopped	1	(12-ounce) can biscuits, quartered
1	(2-ounce) can sliced black olives	1¼	cups shredded mozzarella cheese
1	(4-ounce) can sliced mushrooms		

Preheat oven to 350 degrees. Grease a 9x13-inch baking dish. Brown beef and turkey on medium high heat. Stir in onion, garlic and pepperoni. Simmer until onion is tender. Add olives, mushrooms, basil, oregano and spaghetti sauce. Heat until bubbly, add biscuits. Stir until completely coated. Spoon into prepared dish. Bake 25 minutes. Sprinkle with cheese and bake an additional 10 minutes. Let stand 5 minutes before serving.

"We delight in the beauty of the butterfly, but rarely admit the changes it has gone through to achieve that beauty."

Maya Angelou

Beef Stew

1	cup vegetable oil	2	tablespoons hot sauce
1	cup flour	2	tablespoons salt
2	medium onions, chopped	2	quarts water
1	bell pepper, chopped	2	tablespoons parsley flakes
2	cloves garlic, minced		
1½	pounds beef stew meat		Salt and pepper to taste

In a large saucepan, heat oil on medium heat. Add flour and stir until golden brown (roux). Add onion, bell pepper and garlic. Sauté until clear. Season meat with hot sauce and salt. Add to roux mixture. Stir constantly, until meat is no longer pink. Pour 1 quart of water into the roux and meat mixture. Stir until mixture is thin. Add the remaining water as needed to maintain a creamy texture. Cook 1½ hours or until meat is tender. Add parsley. Season to taste with salt and pepper. Serve over hot rice.

Hint: *May add potatoes, carrots or halved hard boiled eggs.*

*"A butterfly with transparent wings is rare and beautiful.
All things beautiful do not have to be full of color to be noticed: in
life that which is unnoticed has the most power."*

Author Unknown

CAPPED BELL PEPPERS

8	large bell peppers	2	cups rice
1	pound ground beef	¼	cup vegetable oil
½	pound ground pork		Créole seasoning to taste
2	medium onions, chopped		Salt to taste
1½	(8-ounce) cans tomato sauce		

Cut tops off peppers to make a cap. Clean inside peppers. Make sure cap and pepper are kept together. Set aside. In large bowl, mix meats, onion, 1 can tomato sauce, rice and oil. Season mixture liberally with Créole seasoning and salt. Mix well. Fill each pepper with mixture and place cap on pepper. Place peppers standing up in a large pot, very close together. Add water to the rim of peppers, not over cap. Pour remaining tomato sauce over peppers. Cover and cook on medium high 1 hour 15 minutes. If needed, add more water.

Make 8 servings

Hint: *Any mixture left can be put on top of peppers before cooking.*

"Look through eyes of hope and see a butterfly inside the caterpillar, hope knows that beauty is waiting to be born in the unlikeliest places."

Miller Ryan

STUFFED BELL PEPPERS

6	medium green bell peppers	2	ribs celery, chopped
1½	pounds ground beef	¼	cup chopped green onions
1	medium onion, chopped	2	cloves garlic, minced
1	green bell pepper, chopped	¼	cup chopped parsley
1	red bell pepper, chopped	1	cup cooked rice
			Créole seasoning to taste

Preheat oven to 350 degrees. Clean and boil green bell peppers for about 10 minutes and drain. Brown beef and add onion, bell peppers, celery, green onions, garlic and parsley. Simmer for about 30 minutes. Add rice to meat mixture and season to taste. Spoon rice mixture into green bell peppers. Place in greased casserole dish. Bake 45 minutes or until bell peppers are tender.

Hint: *For more festive dishes you may stuff red or yellow bell peppers.*

Roasting brings out the natural sweetness of bell peppers and imparts a slight smoky taste. Halve bell peppers lengthwise, discard stems and seeds. Put peppers, cut sides down, on an oiled shallow baking pan. Broil 2 inches from heat until charred and softened, 15 to 18 minutes.

UPSIDE-DOWN BELL PEPPERS

6 large bell peppers
1 onion, chopped
1 bell pepper, chopped
3 ribs celery, chopped
2 cloves garlic, minced
1 tablespoon vegetable oil
1 pound ground beef
1 (10-ounce) can French onion soup
1 (10-ounce) can cream of mushroom soup
¾ cup water
1½ cups rice
Salt, red and black pepper to taste

Preheat oven to 350 degrees. Grease a 9x13-inch casserole dish. Cut off the stem end of each bell pepper, remove seeds, rinse and drain. Sauté onion, bell pepper, celery and garlic in hot oil until wilted. Add ground beef and brown well. Add soups, water and rice. Add salt, red and black pepper to taste. Mix well and cook until thoroughly heated. Spoon rice mixture into each bell pepper, about ¾ full. Invert each one, rice side down, into the prepared casserole dish. Put the remaining rice mixture around the bell peppers. Cover the dish. Bake 1 hour and 10 minutes. Do not uncover until baking is complete.

Celery, along with onions and bell pepper, make up the "holy trinity" of Cajun and Créole cooking. It is also one of the three vegetables (together with onions and carrots) that constitute (French) mirepoix. Mirepoix is used as a base for sauces and soups, as well as a bed on which to braise foods, usually meats and fish. Celery seeds can be used as flavoring as whole seeds or ground and mixed with salt, as celery salt.

MEATBALL STEW

"Fricasseé de boullette"

Meatballs

2 pounds ground beef
⅓ cup chopped green onions
1 teaspoon salt
1 teaspoon black pepper
1 teaspoon garlic powder
1 egg, beaten
¼ cup seasoned bread crumbs

Coating

½ cup flour
⅛ teaspoon salt
⅛ teaspoon black pepper
⅛ teaspoon garlic powder
1 cup oil for browning meatballs

Gravy

1 tablespoon oil and pan drippings
1 tablespoon flour
1 medium onion, diced
2 teaspoons Créole seasoning
2 cups water
2 tablespoons parsley
Salt and pepper to taste
Garlic powder to taste

To make meatballs, in a large bowl mix ground beef, green onions, salt, black pepper and garlic powder. Add egg and bread crumbs. Mix well. Shape into 2-inch balls. Set aside. To make coating, mix flour, salt, black pepper and garlic powder. Lightly coat meatballs with the flour mixture. Set aside. Heat oil. Add meatballs to hot oil and brown on all sides. Remove from pan. To make the gravy, remove all but 1 tablespoon of oil and pan drippings. Add flour and cook, stirring until golden brown. Stir in onion and cook until wilted. Add Créole seasoning and water. Mix well. Return meatballs to gravy. Cover and cook approximately ½ hour. Add more water if needed to keep the gravy from sticking. During the last 15 minutes of cooking, add the parsley. Season with salt, pepper and garlic powder to taste. Serve over rice.

CAJUN BRISKET

1 (15-pound) beef brisket
1 tablespoon Créole
   seasoning
2 teaspoons garlic powder
2 teaspoons black pepper
1 (16-ounce) bottle Italian
   dressing

1 (12-ounce) can beer
1 cup water
1 (14-ounce) can beef
   broth
1 (16-ounce) bottle
   barbecue sauce

Trim brisket and place brisket in a large container. Pierce brisket so that seasoning can penetrate. Sprinkle with Créole seasoning, garlic powder and pepper. Rub into the brisket. Pour salad dressing and beer over brisket, cover and refrigerate overnight. Preheat oven to 325 degrees. Pour water, beef broth and barbecue sauce into a roasting pan. Stir to mix. Place brisket into the roasting pan and spoon barbecue mixture over brisket. Cover with aluminum foil. Bake 4 to 5 hours, checking after 3 hours for tenderness and color. Baste brisket with sauce and finish baking.

Brisket is a cut of meat from the breast or lower chest of the animal. This is normally a tough cut of meat. Cooking it slowly, covered with the fat part up and basting will turn this toughness into juiciness and tenderness rivaling all other meats.

OVEN BARBECUED BRISKET

Brisket

1 (6-pound) beef brisket
1 tablespoon liquid smoke
2 teaspoons Worcestershire
    sauce

2 teaspoons garlic powder
2 teaspoons onion salt
2 teaspoons celery salt
2 teaspoons black pepper

Sauce

1 cup ketchup
1 teaspoon salt
1 teaspoon celery seed
¼ cup brown sugar

¼ cup Worcestershire sauce
2 cups water
1 onion, minced
¼ cup vinegar

Preheat oven to 275 degrees. Sprinkle brisket with liquid smoke, Worcestershire sauce, garlic powder, onion salt, celery salt and black pepper. Place in a large baking pan. Cover and bake 5 to 6 hours or until tender. Remove brisket. Drain excess oil reserving some of the liquid. To make the sauce, add ketchup, salt, celery seed, sugar, Worcestershire sauce, water, onion and vinegar to the reserved liquid. Mix well. Return brisket to pan with sauce. Bake uncovered 1 hour.

"If nothing ever changed, there would be no butterflies."

Author unknown

CABBAGE ROLLS

1	large cabbage	2	teaspoons Créole seasoning
2	cups shredded cabbage	1	large onion, minced
1	pound ground beef	1	teaspoon minced garlic
1	pound ground pork	1	cup cooked rice
2	tablespoons butter	1	(15-ounce) can seasoned diced tomatoes
½	teaspoon salt		

Preheat oven to 350 degrees. Grease a large casserole. Remove 8 to 10 large leaves from cabbage. Simmer in boiling water for 5 minutes. Drain and spread out to be filled. Boil shredded cabbage until tender, drain and set aside. Brown ground beef and pork, Remove excess oil. Add butter, salt, Créole seasoning, onion, garlic, shredded cabbage and rice. Fill each leaf with equal amounts of mixture. Roll up starting with part of leaf attached to stem. Fold ends to center, secure with toothpicks. Place in casserole with end of leaf facing down. Add tomatoes, cover and bake 45 minutes. Remove toothpicks before serving.

LAYERED CABBAGE ROLLS

1½	pounds lean ground beef		Salt, red and black pepper to taste
1	large onion, chopped		
½	bell pepper, chopped	½	cup rice
2	ribs celery, chopped	1	head cabbage, chopped
		1	(12-ounce) can V-8 juice

Preheat oven to 350 degrees. In a large skillet, brown meat. Add onion, bell pepper and celery. Cook until vegetables are tender. Drain fat. Season with salt, red and black pepper to taste. Add rice and mix well. In a large baking dish, layer cabbage and spread meat mixture evenly over cabbage. Pour V-8 juice over entire mixture. Cover and bake 1½ hours.

EASY CHILI

1½ pounds ground beef
2 tablespoons chili powder
1 teaspoon sugar
1 teaspoon salt
1 (15-ounce) can tomato sauce
1 (6-ounce) can tomato paste
1 cup water
1 bell pepper, chopped
1 (16-ounce) can kidney beans (optional)

Brown ground beef in a large skillet. Add chili powder, sugar and salt. Stir. Add tomato sauce, tomato paste, water, bell pepper and kidney beans. Cover and cook on low heat 30 minutes, stirring frequently.

EGGPLANT CASSEROLE

4 eggplants
1 stick butter
2 tablespoons water
1 medium onion, chopped
1 bell pepper, chopped
½ cup chopped green onions
1 teaspoon minced garlic
1 teaspoon Créole seasoning
1 pound ground beef
16 soda crackers, crushed

Preheat oven to 350 degrees. Grease casserole dish and set aside. Peel and dice eggplant. In a heavy saucepan, melt ½ stick butter and add water. Add eggplant, onion, bell pepper, green onions, garlic and Créole seasoning. Cover and cook until soft. Brown ground meat and add to vegetable mixture. Stir in ⅔ of the crushed crackers. Melt remaining ½ stick butter in a saucepan, add remaining crackers. Stir until lightly toasted. Place eggplant mixture in prepared casserole and top with toasted crackers. Bake 30 minutes or until light brown.

GREEN BEAN AND MUSHROOM MEDLEY

1 pound ground beef	½ cup chopped bell pepper
1 medium onion, chopped	½ cup chopped celery
1 (15-ounce) can green beans	1 cup milk
1 (15-ounce) can cream of mushroom soup	1 tablespoon Worcestershire sauce
1 (6-ounce) can mushroom pieces, drained	1 teaspoon salt
	1 (5-ounce) package noodles, uncooked

In a large skillet, cook and stir meat and onion until meat is brown and onion is tender, but not brown. Stir in beans with liquid. Add soup, mushrooms, bell pepper, celery, milk, Worcestershire sauce, salt and noodles. Heat to boiling, reduce heat, cover and simmer about 25 to 30 minutes or until the noodles are cooked. Stir frequently to avoid sticking.

SMOTHERED BEEF LIVER

1½ pounds beef liver	1 cup flour
1 teaspoon Créole seasoning	⅓ cup vegetable oil
	1 medium onion, sliced

Rinse and drain liver cutting off tough parts. Sprinkle with Créole seasoning. Sprinkle generously with flour. Heat oil in a large skillet over medium heat. Place each piece of liver in hot oil and cook to medium brown. Remove from skillet. Put onion in skillet and stir until onion is clear. Add enough water to make a thin gravy. Place cooked liver in gravy. Cover and simmer on low 5 minutes. Do not overcook. This makes the liver tough.

BEST OF THE BEST LASAGNA

¼	cup olive oil	2	ribs celery, chopped fine
1	stick butter	1	small carrot, minced
1	onion, minced		Salt and pepper to taste
1	pound ground beef	1	(8-ounce) package lasagna noodles
4	cloves garlic, minced		
3	tablespoons minced parsley	1	tablespoon olive oil
¼	cup red wine	1	pound mozzarella cheese slices
1	(15-ounce) can diced tomatoes	1	pound Ricotta cheese
1	(6-ounce) can tomato paste		

In a large saucepan, heat ¼ cup olive oil and butter, add onion and ground beef. Sauté until brown. Add garlic and parsley. Cook over low heat 10 minutes. Stir in wine, cover and simmer 5 minutes. Add tomatoes and tomato paste, bring to a boil. Add celery, carrot, salt and pepper. Cover and cook over low heat 1 hour, stirring occasionally. Boil noodles according to package directions. Add one tablespoon of olive oil to water. Drain. Cover the bottom of a rectangular baking dish with ½ of the lasagna noodles. Add ½ of the meat mixture and place ½ of the cheese slices over meat mixture. Top with ½ of the Ricotta cheese. Add the other half of the lasagna noodles. Cover with remaining meat mixture and cheeses. Bake 30 minutes in a 375 degree oven.

MEATBALLS AND SPAGHETTI

Sauce

1	cup vegetable oil
3	cups chopped onion
1	bell pepper, chopped
⅓	cup chopped celery
3	cloves garlic, minced
6	(6-ounce) cans tomato paste
2	(28-ounce) cans tomato sauce

1 (10-ounce) can diced tomatoes with green chilies
¾ cup sugar
1 quart water
Salt and pepper to taste

Meatballs

3 pounds ground beef
1 cup chopped onion
3 cloves garlic, minced
2 eggs, slightly beaten

¼ cup seasoned bread crumbs
¼ cup water
Salt, pepper and Créole seasoning to taste

Heat oil, add onion, bell pepper, celery and garlic. Sauté until vegetables are clear. Add tomato paste, tomato sauce, diced tomatoes, sugar, water, salt and pepper. Simmer 3 to 4 hours on low heat, stirring often to prevent sticking. Preheat oven to 350 degrees. Line pan with aluminum foil and set aside. To make meatballs, mix ground beef, onion and garlic. Add eggs, bread crumbs, water, salt, pepper and Créole seasoning. Shape into balls about 3-inches in diameter. Bake 10 minutes in prepared pan. Add to sauce and simmer 1 to 1½ hours.

Hint: *Meatballs may be added to sauce after sauce has been cooking 2½ to 3 hours.*

MEAT LOAF AND GRAVY

Loaf

1 pound ground beef	1 tablespoon bread crumbs
1 pound bulk pork sausage	Salt and pepper to taste
½ cup chopped green onions	Garlic powder to taste
	½ cup vegetable oil, for browning loaves

Coating

¼ cup flour	Garlic powder to taste
Salt and pepper to taste	

Gravy

⅓ cup oil	½ teaspoon salt
⅓ cup flour	¼ teaspoon pepper
12 ounces vegetable seasoning blend	½ teaspoon garlic powder
	Water

To make loaf, in a large bowl combine beef, sausage, green onions, bread crumbs, salt, pepper and garlic powder. Mix thoroughly. Divide in half and shape into loaves. Set aside. For coating mix flour, salt, pepper and garlic powder on a plate. Roll each loaf in flour mixture, coating all sides. Heat oil in large saucepan and brown loaves on all sides. Remove loaves and set aside. To make gravy, heat oil on medium high. Stir in flour. Stir constantly, until the color of peanut butter (roux). Add vegetable seasoning blend, salt, pepper and garlic powder. Cook until vegetables are wilted. Stir constantly. Add enough water to make a thin gravy and reduce heat. Return loaves to saucepan and cook on low 1 hour.

Makes 2 loaves

Hint: *If gravy thickens too much add water as needed until loaves are cooked. Gravy is great over creamed potatoes.*

Monday Meat Loaf

2 pounds ground beef
1 (1-ounce) envelope
   onion soup mix
2 eggs, slightly beaten

¾ cup water
⅓ cup ketchup
¼ cup Italian bread crumbs
   Salt and pepper to taste

Preheat oven to 350 degrees. In a large bowl, combine beef, soup mix, eggs, water, ketchup, bread crumbs, salt and pepper. Mix well. Shape into a loaf. Place in a 9x13-inch baking dish and bake 1 to 1½ hours. Let stand 10 minutes before slicing.

Meat Pies

⅓ cup oil
⅓ cup flour
2 onions, chopped
2 pounds ground beef
1 pound bulk pork sausage,
   hot

1 teaspoon minced garlic
1 (10-ounce) can cream of
   mushroom soup
1 teaspoon Créole
   seasoning
4 (9-inch) pie shells

Preheat oven to 350 degrees. Heat oil in a large skillet. Add flour and cook over medium heat, stirring constantly until color of peanut butter, (roux). Add onion and sauté over medium heat until clear. Add ground beef and sausage. Cook 10 minutes. Add garlic. Cover and cook over low heat 1 hour. Remove excess oil. Add soup and Créole seasoning. Mix well. Allow to cool. Spoon mixture into pie shells. Cover each pie with a second shell. Seal and crimp edges. Bake 1 hour or until golden brown.

Makes 2 pies

GROUND MEAT DELIGHT

1 (8-ounce) package egg noodles
1½ pounds ground beef
1 medium onion, chopped
1 medium bell pepper, chopped
1 rib celery, chopped
1 teaspoon garlic powder
1 (4-ounce) can sliced mushrooms
1 (8-ounce) can tomato sauce
1 (16-ounce) can stewed tomatoes
1 (15-ounce) can cream style corn
Salt and pepper to taste
4 slices cheese

Preheat oven to 375 degrees. Grease casserole dish and set aside. Cook noodles according to package directions. Drain and set aside. Brown beef in a large saucepan. Add onion, bell pepper, celery and garlic powder. Cook 25 minutes. Add mushrooms, tomato sauce, stewed tomatoes, corn, noodles, salt and pepper to taste. Mix well. Pour into prepared casserole and top with cheese slices. Bake 10 minutes or until cheese is melted.

EASY BEEF ROAST

1 (6-8 pound) roast
Créole seasoning
3 cloves garlic
2 (10-ounce) cans cream of mushroom soup
1 (1-ounce) package dry onion soup mix
2 cups water

Preheat oven to 350 degrees. Lightly season roast and stuff with garlic. Brown roast on stove. In baking pan, mix soups together. Add 2 cups water. Mix well. Put roast in pan and cover. Bake about 3 hours.

Hint: *Carrots and potatoes may be added about 1 hour before roast is cooked.*

Prime Rib Roast

1   (3-5 pound) prime rib
    roast
    Hot sauce to taste

Créole seasoning to taste
Garlic powder to taste
Mushrooms (optional)

Preheat oven to 500 degrees. Trim roast. Cover with hot sauce. Rub Créole seasoning and garlic powder over entire roast. Place in an aluminum baking pan. Bake 15 minutes. Reduce heat to 350 degrees. Bake 2 to 4 hours, according to the size of the roast. You may use a meat thermometer to check for degree of doneness. Remove from oven. Let stand 30 minutes before cutting to allow juices to redistribute. Pour drippings into a saucepan. Add mushrooms and sauté.

Hint: *1 pound beef for every 3 people when cooking for a mixed crowd. 1 pound of beef for every 2 people when cooking for men only.*

Swiss Steak

2   pounds of rump, round or
    chuck steak
    Salt and pepper, to taste
6   tablespoons flour
¼   cup vegetable oil

2   cups stewed tomatoes
    Diced bell pepper, to
    taste
    Sliced onions, to taste
    Mushrooms, to taste

Season meat with salt and pepper. Place under plastic wrap and pound with mallet to tenderize. Sprinkle with flour. In a heavy skillet, heat oil and brown meat. Add tomatoes, bell pepper, onion and mushrooms. Cover and cook slowly until meat is fork tender, about 2 hours. Add water if needed to keep meat from sticking.

APPLE ROASTED DUCKS

6	(½ pound) teals	1	cup diced onions
2	gallons water, simmering	⅓	cup diced celery
1	cup red wine vinegar	½	cup diced bell pepper
	Créole seasoning to taste	¼	cup minced garlic
4	apples, quartered	1	tablespoon minced parsley
3	onions, quartered		
3	ribs celery, quartered	1	orange, sliced
2	bell peppers, quartered	1	quart chicken broth
1	cup flour	¼	cup orange juice
4	strips bacon	½	cup red wine
½	cup vegetable oil	1	teaspoon Créole seasoning

Preheat oven to 350 degrees. Clean ducks under cold water, being careful to check for shots. Place ducks in heat proof pan and cover with hot water and vinegar. Allow ducks to soak 30 to 45 minutes or until plump. Drain well and pat dry. Season the ducks inside and out with Créole seasoning. Stuff the cavities with quartered apples, onion, celery and bell pepper. Dust ducks with the flour, shaking off excess. In a 12-quart Dutch oven (cast iron if available), fry bacon until crisp. Remove, crumble and set aside. Add oil and brown ducks, two or three at a time, until golden brown. After all are browned, return them to the pot, breast side down. Add diced onion, celery, bell pepper, garlic and parsley. Arrange orange slices over the ducks. Add chicken broth, orange juice, red wine, crumbled bacon and Créole seasoning. Bring liquids to a rolling boil. Remove pan from heat. Cover and bake 2 to 2½ hours. Gently turn ducks over and check for doneness by piercing breasts with a fork. When done, uncover pan and allow birds to brown evenly ½ hour longer.

Serves 6 to 12

BACON WRAPPED DUCK BREASTS

2	pounds deboned duck breasts (3 large ducks)	1	large bell pepper
	Créole seasoning to taste	2	pounds bacon
1	large onion	45	jalapeño pepper slices

Cut deboned duck breast into 1½ x 1½-inch cubes (approximately 45 cubes). Season ducks with Créole seasoning. Cut onion and bell pepper into ½ to ¾-inch squares. Cut bacon strips in half. Place 2 layers of onion on one side of duck cube. On the other side, place one slice jalapeño pepper and one square of bell pepper. Wrap layers in bacon using a toothpick to hold together (refrigerate overnight for tastier results). Preheat barbecue grill. Place wraps on baking pan sprayed with cooking spray. Grill on medium fire approximately 20 minutes turning frequently. Remove wraps from pan and place directly on grill. Turn frequently, cooking another 5 minutes.

SMOTHERED RABBIT

1	medium rabbit	1	small bell pepper, diced
	Salt and pepper to taste	3	large onions, diced
	Flour to coat each piece	½	cup water
2	tablespoons vegetable oil		

Cut, wash and season rabbit to taste. Lightly flour each piece. Heat oil in large pot (black cast iron if available). Add rabbit to hot oil and brown on both sides. Remove rabbit. Add bell pepper and onion, cook until wilted. Return rabbit to the pot. Add water. Cook covered on medium heat approximately 1 hour or until rabbit is tender. Cornstarch may be added if thicker gravy is desired. Serve over hot rice.

Serves 6

GRILLED SQUIRREL SUPREME

¼	cup cooking sherry		¼	cup molasses or honey
1	tablespoon liquid smoke			Garlic salt to taste
1	stick butter		4	squirrels, quartered
½	cup meat marinade			

Place sherry, liquid smoke, butter, marinade, molasses or honey and garlic salt in saucepan. Stir over low heat until thoroughly mixed (about 5 minutes). Place squirrels in mixture and allow to marinate at least two hours. Place on grill and cook over hickory chips until squirrels are tender.

VENISON APPETIZER

12	pieces venison, from back strap		12	pieces jalapeño pepper
1	large onion, sliced		1	pound bacon
				Toothpicks

Preheat oven to 375 degrees. This recipe will vary in size according to number of slices of bacon in your package. One appetizer can be made with each slice of bacon. This recipe is based on 12 slices. Place a piece of venison, a slice of onion and a slice of jalapeño pepper on a slice of bacon. Roll up and hold together with toothpicks. Place on a sheet pan. Bake 35 to 40 minutes.

Yields 12 appetizers

ITALIAN BARBECUED VENISON

1	(3-pound)venison roast	1	onion, chopped
½	cup Italian salad dressing	1	cup barbecue sauce
½	cup chopped bell pepper		

Place venison in large plastic self-sealing storage bag with Italian dressing, bell pepper and onion. Seal and marinate overnight. In the morning put contents of bag including liquid into slow cooker and add 1 cup barbecue sauce. Cook on low 8 to 10 hours. Remove roast and slice to serve.

GRILLED VENISON BACK STRAP ROLLS

½	venison back strap	30	(3-inch long) pieces
	Italian dressing		bacon
	Hot sauce	30	slices onion sliced thin
	Garlic powder		Seasoned salt

Cut back strap into 30 ¼-inch slices. Marinate in refrigerator in mixture of Italian dressing, hot sauce and garlic powder 1 to 2 days. Remove slices from marinate. Place each slice on a piece of bacon. Top each slice with a slice of onion. Roll up bacon and secure with a toothpick. Season rolls with seasoned salt. Cook on grill over hot coals 30 to 45 minutes or until bacon is cooked. Serve hot.

Makes 30 rolls

VENISON GROUND MEAT STUFFED FRENCH BREAD

Cooking spray
1 onion, chopped
1 bell pepper, chopped
1 pound ground venison
¼ cup chopped green onions
1 tablespoon garlic powder

Salt and pepper to taste
Hot sauce to taste
1 cup water
1 large French bread
1 (8-ounce) package mozzarella cheese

Spray cookie sheet with cooking spray. Sauté onion and bell pepper until wilted. Add ground venison and brown. Add green onions and garlic powder. Mix well. Season to taste with salt, pepper and hot sauce. Add water. Cook over medium heat until all ingredients are well done. Allow liquid to reduce. Cool mixture. The mixture should be free of all liquid. Cut French bread in half. Remove some of the soft white inside of the bread. Make a shallow section down the middle of each side. Place bread on prepared cookie sheet. Place cooked meat mixture into cut out section down the middle of the loaf. Cover with cheese. Place under broiler until cheese is melted and edges of the bread begin to brown. Cut into strips and serve hot.

Venison can describe any meat from the family of deer, elk, moose, caribou, wild boar, and brown, artic or blue hare. Venison may be eaten as steaks, roasts, sausages and ground meat. Venison is lower in fat content than beef, pork or lamb.

VENISON SAUCE PIQUANTE

4 tablespoons vegetable oil
4 tablespoons flour
3 medium onions, chopped
1 bell pepper, chopped
4 ribs celery, chopped
1 (8-ounce) can tomato
   paste
1 tablespoon sugar
3 (10-ounce) cans
   tomatoes with green
   chilies
4 cloves garlic, minced
4 pounds venison, cubed
2 cups chicken stock

1 (8-ounce) can
   mushrooms
1½ cups chopped green
   onions
4 bay leaves
½ teaspoon allspice
   Salt and black pepper to
   taste
   Red pepper to taste
¼ cup chopped parsley
1 stick butter
1 slice lemon, thin
½ cup cooking sherry

Heat oil in a heavy saucepan. Add flour and cook until the color of peanut butter, stirring constantly (roux). Add onion, bell pepper and celery. Simmer 3 minutes. Add tomato paste, sugar and tomatoes. Simmer 30 minutes. Add garlic, venison and chicken stock. Simmer 25 minutes. Add mushrooms, green onions, bay leaf, allspice, salt, black pepper and red pepper to taste. Cook 20 minutes. Add parsley, butter, lemon slice and cooking sherry. Simmer 20 minutes. Serve over rice.

Soaking venison, for approximately 1 hour, in a mixture of vinegar and water before preparing can remove some of the wild game taste. Since venison lacks a lot of fat it may be dry when cooking. Adding bacon wraps to the cooking meat or blending it with pork will help in the texture and taste

VENISON STEW

3 pounds venison, cubed
Créole seasoning
2 tablespoons olive oil
3 large onions, chopped
1 large bell pepper, chopped
3 ribs celery, chopped
4 cloves garlic, minced
1½ quarts water
2 tablespoons hot sauce
4 tablespoons Worcestershire sauce
1 tablespoon garlic powder
1 tablespoon onion powder
1 tablespoon paprika
Browning liquid to desired color
½ pound baby carrots
2 (5-ounce) bottles pearl onions, rinsed
6-8 small potatoes
2 tablespoons cornstarch
Water
1 cup chopped green onions
½ cup chopped parsley

Remove all skin from venison roast. Season with Créole seasoning. Brown all sides in oil (heavy iron pot if available). Remove meat with slotted spoon. Add onion, bell pepper and celery. Stir to prevent sticking. When onion is clear, add garlic. Continue to stir for a couple of minutes. Add water to make gravy. Add hot sauce, Worcestershire sauce, garlic powder, onion powder, paprika and browning liquid as desired. Cook 15 to 20 minutes on high heat. Stir occasionally. Add meat, cover and reduce heat. Cook 30 to 45 minutes. Stir as needed. Add more water if needed. Add carrots, pearl onions and potatoes. Cook covered 30 minutes, stirring as needed. You may use cornstarch mixed with water to thicken gravy. Cook 5 minutes. Add green onions and parsley. Serve over rice.

Serves 10 to 12

Pastalaya

2	tablespoons olive oil	2	teaspoons minced garlic
2	pounds pork, cubed	½	gallon water
1	cup chopped onion	2	teaspoons Créole
½	cup chopped bell pepper		seasoning
¼	cup chopped celery	2	(12-ounce) packages
1	pound smoked sausage, chopped		egg noodles

In a large, heavy pot, heat oil and brown pork. Add onion, bell pepper and celery. Sauté until clear. Add smoked sausage. Cook until brown. Add garlic, water and Créole seasoning. Cook over medium heat 30 minutes. Add noodles. Stir once and cook about 30 to 40 minutes until water is reduced and noodles are cooked. Cover until ready to serve.

Pork Chop Casserole

3	tablespoons olive oil	½	teaspoon browning liquid
6-8	pork chops	½	cup chopped green onions
1½	cups rice		
1	(10-ounce) can French onion soup		Salt and pepper to taste
			Garlic powder to taste
2	cups beef broth	1	tablespoon butter

Preheat oven to 350 degrees. In skillet heat oil and brown pork chops on both sides. Set aside. Layer rice in casserole dish. Mix soup, broth, browning liquid, green onions, salt, pepper and garlic powder. Pour this mixture over the rice. Place pork chops over rice and liquid mixture. Dab pork chops with butter. Cover with foil and bake 50 minutes.

Serves 6

PORK TENDERLOIN WITH PEACH GLAZE

1   (3-4 pound) pork
      tenderloin
    Créole seasoning to taste

Garlic powder to taste
½-1 cup water

Peach Glaze

1   (18-ounce) jar peach
      preserves
3   tablespoons soy sauce
2   tablespoons Créole
      mustard

1   tablespoon minced garlic
    Salt and pepper to taste

Preheat oven to 350 degrees. Season the tenderloin with
Créole seasoning and garlic powder. Place in a roasting pan.
Add water. Bake 20 minutes. To make glaze, mix preserves,
soy sauce, mustard and garlic. Add salt and pepper to taste.
Spoon glaze over the tenderloin and bake 1 to 1½ hours. Baste
tenderloin as it bakes.

*A chochon de lait, is basically a Cajun pig roast of a whole young
pig. The pig is slowly roasted for 8 to 12 hours outdoors. This
makes a chochon de lait an event rather than cooking a meal. It's
an extended family gathering, story telling, and fire tending day.*

Pork and Turnip Stew

8	medium turnips	1	tablespoon minced garlic
½	cup vegetable oil	4	cups water
½	cup flour	1	cup chopped green onions
2½	pounds pork, cubed		
1	cup chopped onions	½	cup chopped parsley
1	cup chopped celery		Salt and pepper to taste
½	cup chopped bell pepper		

Peel and chop turnips. Set aside. Make a roux by heating the oil and flour in a heavy pot, stirring constantly. Cook until color of peanut butter. Add pork and mix well with roux. Stir in onion, celery, bell pepper and garlic. Cook until vegetables are wilted, about 3 to 5 minutes. Add turnips and mix well. Add water, a little at a time, stirring constantly. Bring to a soft boil. Cover. Reduce heat and simmer 45 minutes. Add green onions, parsley, salt and pepper to taste. Cook until pork is tender. Serve hot over rice.

Sweet Pork Chops

4	(¾-inch thick) pork chops	4	lemon slices
½	teaspoon salt	¼	cup brown sugar, packed
4	(¼-inch thick) onion slices	¼	cup ketchup

Preheat oven to 350 degrees. Season pork chops with salt. Place in a large greased casserole dish. Top each pork chop with a slice of onion and lemon and a tablespoon each of brown sugar and ketchup. Cover and bake 1 hour. Uncover and bake 30 minutes more, basting occasionally.

CANDY CHICKEN

8 chicken thighs
1 (1-ounce) envelope onion soup
1 (16-ounce) bottle Thousand Island dressing

1 (16-ounce) jar apricot preserves

Preheat oven to 350 degrees. Place chicken in a casserole dish. Mix the soup, dressing and preserves in a food processor. Pour over chicken. Bake uncovered about 1 hour. When chicken starts to brown on top, place foil over it for the remainder of the cooking time (approximately 30 minutes).

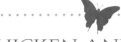

CHICKEN AND PASTA

1 (16-ounce) package angel hair pasta
4 boneless chicken breasts
1 teaspoon Créole seasoning
½ cup flour
2 tablespoons olive oil

1 (4-ounce) can sliced mushrooms
1 cup chopped green onions
2 tablespoons chopped parsley
1 (14-ounce) can chicken broth

Cook pasta according to package directions. Set aside. Season chicken with Créole seasoning and coat with flour. Pan fry in olive oil until golden brown. Cover and simmer 10 to 15 minutes or until completely cooked. Remove chicken, drain and set aside. Add mushrooms, green onions and parsley. Sauté until onions are wilted. Add chicken broth and bring to a boil. Lower heat and simmer 10 to 15 minutes, stirring occasionally. Add pasta to chicken broth mixture and heat thoroughly. Pour into a casserole. Top with chicken breasts.

CHICKEN BREASTS STUFFED WITH MUSHROOMS

6 whole chicken breasts	1⅓ cups bread crumbs
1½ teaspoons salt	3 tablespoons chopped parsley
1 teaspoon lemon juice	⅔ cup dry sherry or vermouth
½ pound Italian sausage, chopped	3 tablespoons melted butter
3 tablespoons chopped celery	1 cup chicken broth
2 tablespoons chopped onion	1 (4-ounce) can sliced mushrooms
1 (4-ounce) can mushrooms, chopped	

Preheat oven to 350 degrees. Debone breasts and cut a pocket in the thick portion. Sprinkle both sides with ½ teaspoon salt and lemon juice. Set aside. Brown sausage. Add celery and onion and sauté until vegetables are clear. Add chopped mushrooms, ⅓ cup bread crumbs, parsley, remaining salt and ⅓ cup sherry. Mix well. Place heaping tablespoonfuls of mixture in pocket and secure with toothpick. Brush with butter and roll in remaining bread crumbs. Place in a buttered casserole dish and bake 30 minutes. Combine broth with remaining sherry and pour over chicken. Place sliced mushrooms on top. Bake 20 to 25 minutes longer. Baste frequently. Reserve pan drippings to serve over chicken.

CHICKEN AND SHRIMP WITH CREAM SAUCE

1	(16-ounce) package angel hair pasta	¾	cup white wine
1	cup flour	1	tablespoon lemon juice
4	boneless, skinless chicken breasts	¼	teaspoon white pepper
5	tablespoons butter	¼	teaspoon Cayenne pepper
12	jumbo shrimp, butterflied	¾	cup whipping cream
1	chicken bouillon cube	2	tablespoons cold butter, cut into chips

Cook pasta according to directions on package. Set aside. Lightly flour chicken and set aside. Melt butter in a large skillet. Place chicken in butter and brown lightly on both sides. Add shrimp to chicken mixture. Cook until shrimp are pink. Remove chicken and shrimp. Add bouillon cube, wine, lemon juice, white pepper and Cayenne pepper. Cook mixture until slightly thickened. Add whipping cream, chicken and shrimp and simmer until creamy. Remove from heat and add butter chips. Pour over pasta.

Makes 4 servings

 Cayenne pepper is a hot red chili pepper used to flavor dishes and also for medicinal purposes. It is named for the city of Cayenne in French Guiana.

CHICKEN CASSEROLE

1 (10-ounce) can cream of
chicken soup
¾ cup milk
1 (1-ounce) envelope
onion soup mix

¾ cup rice
1½ cups cooked, diced
chicken or turkey

Preheat oven to 375 degrees. Spray 1½-quart casserole with nonstick spray. Mix soup, milk, onion soup and rice until onion soup is dissolved. Add chicken, or turkey and mix well. Cover with foil. Bake 35 to 40 minutes or until rice is tender.

Hint: *Cream of mushroom soup may be used instead of the chicken soup. ½ cup of peas or carrots can be added with the chicken.*

CHICKEN MOZZARELLA

1 (14-ounce) can cream of
mushroom soup
½ cup white wine
8 boneless, skinless chicken
breasts

2 cups grated mozzarella
cheese
1 (6-ounce) package
chicken-flavored
stuffing mix
1 stick butter, melted

Preheat oven to 350 degrees. Mix soup and wine. Spread on bottom of 9x13-inch baking pan. Place chicken breasts on top of soup and wine mixture. Sprinkle cheese over chicken. Sprinkle stuffing mix and then flavor packet from stuffing mix on top. Pour butter evenly over the stuffing. Bake uncovered 40 minutes.

CHICKEN PILLOWS

8	boneless chicken breasts	8	slices ham
1	teaspoon onion powder	8	slices pepper Jack cheese
1	teaspoon garlic powder		
1	teaspoon Créole seasoning	2	tablespoons bread crumbs
½	stick butter, melted		

Preheat oven to 350 degrees. Grease a baking dish. Set aside. Cover chicken breasts with plastic wrap and pound with mallet until flat. Mix onion powder, garlic powder and Créole seasoning with ½ of the butter. Coat chicken breasts with mixture. Place 1 slice of ham and cheese on each breast. Start at larger end and roll each breast. Secure with a toothpick. Place in a prepared baking dish. Pour remaining butter on pillows and sprinkle with bread crumbs. Bake 25 to 30 minutes.

CHICKEN WITH BRIE

4	boneless skinless chicken breasts, halved	½	pound mushrooms, quartered
	Salt and pepper to taste	1	cup walnut halves
½	cup flour	1	cup dry white wine
½	cup vegetable oil	10	ounces Brie
1	stick butter		

Rinse chicken and pat dry. Cover chicken with plastic wrap and pound gently with mallet until flat. Sprinkle with salt and pepper. Dredge in flour to coat all sides. Shake off excess. In a large skillet, heat oil over medium heat. Sauté chicken until light golden brown. Cover and cook 15 to 20 minutes or until tender. Remove from skillet. Drain and keep warm. Pour out oil and melt butter in skillet. Sauté mushrooms and walnuts for 2 minutes. Stir in wine and Brie (remove rind). Simmer over low heat until slightly thickened. Pour sauce over chicken breasts.

CRÉOLE STYLE CHICKEN

2 teaspoons Créole seasoning	1 clove garlic, minced
¾ cup flour	1 (14-ounce) can chicken broth
1 (4-5 pound) chicken, cut up	1½ cups water
⅓ cup vegetable oil	1 teaspoon browning liquid
1 medium onion, chopped	¼ cup chopped green onions
½ bell pepper, chopped	1 tablespoon chopped parsley
1 rib celery, chopped	

Add 1 teaspoon Créole seasoning to flour. Dredge chicken in flour until well coated. Heat oil in large skillet and brown chicken. Remove chicken. Add remaining flour and cook until golden brown (roux). Add onion, bell pepper, celery and garlic and sauté until tender. Stir in chicken broth, water, browning liquid and remaining Créole seasoning. Stir until well blended and almost boiling. Return chicken to skillet and reduce heat. Cover and simmer about 45 minutes to 1 hour or until chicken is tender. Add green onions and parsley. Cook another 5 minutes. Serve over rice.

"You want to fly so much you are willing to give up being a caterpillar."

Author unknown

EASY CHICKEN STEW

1 chicken, cut up
Salt and pepper to taste
2 tablespoons olive oil
2 onions, chopped
1 (10-ounce) can French onion soup
2 (10-ounce) cans cream of mushroom soup

1 teaspoon browning liquid
1 (4-ounce) can sliced mushrooms
¼ cup chopped green onions
2 tablespoons parsley

Preheat oven to 350 degrees. Salt and pepper chicken. Heat oil in a large pot with a cover that can be placed in the oven. Brown chicken. Add onion and sauté 5 minutes. Mix soups and browning liquid and stir until well blended. Add mushrooms, green onions and parsley. Pour over chicken. Cover and bake 1 to 1½ hours or until chicken is cooked.

MAYONNAISE CHICKEN

1 (4-5 pound) chicken, whole
Salt to taste
Cayenne pepper to taste
Garlic powder to taste

2 tablespoons mayonnaise
½ onion
1 rib celery
¼ bell pepper

Preheat oven to 375 degrees. Grease a casserole dish. Set aside. Rinse and dry chicken thoroughly. Season with salt, pepper and garlic powder. Rub chicken inside and out with mayonnaise. Put onion, celery and bell pepper into chicken cavity. Place in prepared casserole and bake 1 to 1½ hours. Baste 15 minutes before removing from oven. Chicken should be golden brown.

CAJUN JAMBALAYA (CHICKEN AND SAUSAGE)

1	(3-4 pound) chicken, cut up	1	cup chopped green onions
1	teaspoon salt	3	teaspoons minced garlic
1	quart chicken broth	3	tablespoons Créole seasoning
1	pound smoked sausage		
3	medium onions, chopped	1	teaspoon red pepper
1	bell pepper, chopped	2¼	cups long grain rice

Boil chicken in salted water. Debone and set aside. Save 1 quart of the chicken broth. Cut sausage into ½-inch slices. Place in Dutch oven and cook approximately 7 minutes or until brown. Remove from pot and set aside. Add chicken. Cook approximately 5 minutes or until brown. Remove from pot and set aside. Drain grease from pot, leaving 1 tablespoon. Add onion and bell pepper. Sauté until vegetables are clear. Add chicken, sausage, green onions, garlic, Créole seasoning and red pepper. Cook 20 minutes. Stirring occasionally. Add broth and rice and stir well. Bring to a boil. Cook until 90% of the liquid is absorbed. Stir mixture gently. Lower heat and cover. Cook over low heat approximately 15 minutes without lifting cover. Rice should be tender and fluffy.

Cajun Jambalaya originated from rural Louisiana's low lying swamp country where crawfish, shrimp and other seafood was readily available. Cajun Jambalaya is sometimes referred to as "brown jambalaya."

OVEN CHICKEN AND SAUSAGE JAMBALAYA

1	chicken	1	(10-ounce) can French onion soup
1	stick butter		
2	onions, chopped	1	(10-ounce) can water
2	ribs celery, chopped	1	(10-ounce) can tomatoes with green chilies
½	bell pepper, chopped		
1	pound smoked sausage	2	cups rice
1	(10-ounce) can golden mushroom soup	1	(4-ounce) can sliced mushrooms

Boil chicken, debone and set aside. Preheat oven to 350 degrees. Melt butter in a large saucepan. Add onion, celery and bell pepper. Sauté until vegetables are clear. Cut sausage into ½-inch slices. Add sausage and chicken to vegetable mixture. Cook until lightly brown. Add soups, water and tomatoes. Mix well. Remove from heat and add rice. Pour into a greased casserole. Cover and bake 30 minutes or until rice is tender. Let stand 5 minutes before serving.

Hint: *Chicken broth may be used in place of water.*

Créole Jambalaya originated from the French Quarter in New Orleans. It was an attempt by the Spanish to make Paella. The French spices changed this dish into what is now known as Créole Jambalaya. Créole Jambalaya uses tomatoes and is known in Louisiana as "red jambalaya".

ONE-DISH CHICKEN PIE

1	(16-ounce) package frozen mixed vegetables	2½	cups milk
1	(10-ounce) can cream of mushroom soup	3	cups cooked, diced chicken
1	(10-ounce) can Cheddar cheese soup	2	cups baking mix
		2	teaspoons parsley (optional)

Preheat oven to 350 degrees. Mix vegetables, soups, 1 cup milk and chicken in 9x13-inch baking dish. Mix baking mix and remaining milk. Pour evenly over chicken mixture. Sprinkle with parsley. Bake 25 to 30 minutes or until golden brown. Let stand 5 to 10 minutes before serving.

Makes 8 to 10 servings

Hint: *Freezes well.*

STICKY CHICKEN

1	(3-4 pound) chicken, cut up	¼	cup olive oil
2	teaspoons Créole seasoning		

Season chicken with Créole seasoning. Heat oil in large skillet and brown chicken pieces well on all sides. Cover and reduce heat to very low. Let simmer about 1 hour. Check occasionally. Add a small amount of water if chicken sticks too much. Cook until very tender.

PECAN CHICKEN CASSEROLE

Crumb Mixture

1 cup flour
½ teaspoon salt
⅓ cup vegetable oil
1 cup finely shredded
    Cheddar cheese

¾ cup finely chopped
    pecans
¼ teaspoon paprika

Filling

4 eggs
¼ cup mayonnaise
⅛ teaspoon hot sauce
1 cup sour cream
½ cup finely shredded
    Cheddar cheese
1 teaspoon Créole
    seasoning

1 cup chicken broth
¼ cup minced onion
4 cups diced, cooked
    chicken
4 slices fried bacon,
    crumbled
2 teaspoons chopped
    parsley

Preheat oven to 350 degrees. Grease a 9x13-inch casserole dish. In a bowl, combine flour, salt, oil, cheese, pecans and paprika. Set aside ½ cup of this mixture for topping. Press the remaining mixture into prepared dish and bake 10 minutes or until light golden brown. To make filling, beat eggs in a bowl. Add mayonnaise, hot sauce, sour cream, cheese, Créole seasoning and chicken broth and stir well. Add onion, chicken and bacon. Stir until blended and pour over baked crust. Sprinkle with the remaining crumb mixture. Bake 25 to 30 minutes or until a knife inserted in center comes out clean. Sprinkle with parsley. Let stand 10 minutes before serving.

PENNE PASTA CHICKEN

1 (16-ounce) package penne pasta

¼ cup chopped green onions

1 teaspoon minced garlic

½ cup olive oil

1 pound cooked chicken, chopped

1 (10-ounce) can tomato soup

1 (10-ounce) can cream of chicken soup

1 (10-ounce) can tomatoes with green chilies

1 teaspoon Italian seasoning

2 cups chicken broth

1 (16-ounce) package shredded Monterey Jack cheese

Preheat oven to 350 degrees. Prepare pasta according to directions on package. Set aside. Grease a 4-quart casserole dish. Set aside. Sauté onions and garlic in oil. Mix chicken, soups, tomatoes, seasoning, chicken broth and cooked pasta in prepared casserole. Top with cheese and bake 30 minutes or until bubbly.

SUGARED CHICKEN

1 (4-5 pound) chicken, cut up

Salt and pepper to taste

Hot sauce to taste

1 cup vegetable oil

1 cup sugar

3 medium onions, chopped

1 medium bell pepper, chopped

Season chicken with salt, pepper and hot sauce. Set aside. Heat oil on high. Add sugar and stir until sugar turns golden brown, about 10 minutes. Add chicken. Stir until all pieces are coated with sugar mixture. Cook on high 10 minutes. Add onion and bell pepper. Cook another 10 minutes on high. Reduce heat. Cover and cook 30 minutes. Stir frequently. To avoid sticking add small amounts of water as needed.

Southern Chicken Spaghetti Sauce

4 tablespoons Créole seasoning	¾ cup chopped green onions
1 teaspoon garlic powder	1 (15-ounce) can Italian style tomatoes, chopped
1 (3-4 pound) chicken, cut up	
⅓ cup vegetable oil	1 (8-ounce) can tomato sauce
½ cup flour	
1 large onion, chopped	1 quart water
1 bell pepper, chopped	

Mix 3 tablespoons Créole seasoning and ½ teaspoon garlic powder. Season chicken. Set aside. Heat oil. Add flour and brown stirring constantly until the color of peanut butter (roux). Add onion, bell pepper and green onions. Sauté, cover and reduce heat to simmer. Cook 25 to 30 minutes stirring often. Add tomatoes, tomato sauce, water, remaining Créole seasoning and garlic powder. Stir until thoroughly mixed. Cook on high until gravy begins to boil. Cover, reduce heat and cook 1½ hours. Stir often to prevent sticking. Add chicken and cook for another 40 to 45 minutes. Place lid on pot with space to allow steam to escape. Stir often. Uncover and cook 20 minutes. Serve over spaghetti.

Garlic is a species of the onion family. It is used for its pungent flavor as a seasoning or condiment. Garlic should be stored in a warm and dry place. Garlic is traditionally hung by long braided strands called "plaits" or short plaits called "gapers".

CORNISH HENS WITH LEMON BUTTER SAUCE

1 stick unsalted butter, softened	4 (1½ pound) Cornish hens
1 tablespoon garlic powder	1 teaspoon Créole seasoning
2 tablespoons lemon zest	1 tablespoon vegetable oil
1 teaspoon salt	1 tablespoon butter

Preheat oven to 450 degrees. In a small bowl, cream unsalted butter, garlic powder, lemon zest and salt. Inject some of the butter mixture under the skin of each hen and rub thoroughly on outside. Sprinkle each with Créole seasoning. Tie the legs of each hen with kitchen twine. Tuck the wings under each one. In a roasting pan heat oil and butter. Brown the hens on all sides. Place on rack and bake for 35 to 40 minutes. Baste the hens every 10 to 15 minutes. Remove from oven and allow to sit 10 minutes before serving.

PEACH-GLAZED CORNISH HENS

4 Cornish hens Créole seasoning to taste	1 (12-ounce) jar peach preserves
1 onion, quartered	1 cup Italian salad dressing
1 stalk celery cut in 4	2 tablespoons chopped green onions
1 tablespoon olive oil	
2 (1-ounce) envelopes onion soup mix	

Preheat oven to 350 degrees. Season hens inside and out with Créole seasoning. Place ¼ onion and celery in each hen cavity. Put oil and hens in a roaster and cover. Mix soup mix, preserves and salad dressing. Mixture will be thick. Spoon over hens. Bake about 1½ hours or until tender. Remove cover, baste with sauce and allow to brown. Add green onions after sauce is cooked.

Louisiana is the international leader in freshwater crawfish production.

HUSHPUPPIES

2	eggs, slightly beaten	½	cup chopped green onions
1½	cups evaporated milk	¼	cup minced bell pepper
1½	cups sugar	2½	cups yellow cornmeal
1	tablespoon salt	1	cup self-rising flour
2	teaspoons Cayenne		Vegetable oil for frying
½	teaspoon black pepper		
1½	cups minced onion		

In a large bowl, combine eggs, milk, sugar, salt, Cayenne and black pepper and mix well. Add onions, bell pepper and stir well. Add cornmeal and flour. Blend mixture thoroughly. Heat oil to 350 degrees. Drop mixture by tablespoonfuls into hot oil. Fry about 5 minutes or until golden brown. Place on paper towels to drain.

COCKTAIL SAUCE

1½	cups ketchup	¼	teaspoon sugar
1½	teaspoons prepared horseradish	¼	teaspoon garlic powder
1½	teaspoons Worcestershire sauce	¼	teaspoon salt
		¾	teaspoon black pepper
1	teaspoon hot sauce	¼	teaspoon fresh lemon juice

Mix all ingredients together until well blended. Chill and serve.

RÉMOULADE SAUCE

2 cups mayonnaise
¼ cup Créole mustard
1 tablespoon salad mustard
1 tablespoon ketchup
1 tablespoon horseradish
1 teaspoon Worcestershire sauce
Juice of ½ lemon
1 teaspoon minced garlic
¼ teaspoon hot pepper sauce
¼ cup minced onion (optional)
¼ cup sweet pickle relish (optional)

Mix all the above ingredients together until well blended. Chill before using. Store in airtight container in refrigerator.

SEAFOOD DIPPING SAUCE

1 onion, minced
2 cups sandwich spread
1 cup mayonnaise
1 tablespoon ketchup
1 teaspoon Worcestershire sauce
Dash of hot sauce

Mix all of the ingredients until well blended.

Hint: *Serve with hot boiled crawfish or shrimp and potatoes.*

SIMPLE SEAFOOD SAUCE

1 cup mayonnaise
½ cup ketchup
1 tablespoon prepared horseradish
½ teaspoon hot sauce

Mix all of the ingredients together until well blended.

TARTAR SAUCE

1 quart mayonnaise
1 tablespoon lemon juice, freshly squeezed
1 teaspoon white Worcestershire sauce

1 large onion, minced
1 rib celery, finely chopped
1 (8-ounce) jar sweet pickle relish

Mix mayonnaise, lemon juice and Worcestershire sauce until smooth. Add onion, celery and relish. Stir well. Store in refrigerator until ready to use.

Makes 5 pints

COLD WATER BATTER

1 cup flour
½ teaspoon sugar
½ teaspoon salt
1 egg, beaten

Red pepper to taste
2 teaspoons vegetable oil
½-¾ cup cold water

Mix flour, sugar, salt, egg, pepper and oil together in large mixing bowl. Add water until batter is consistency of cake mix. Dip shrimp into the mixture.

Makes enough mix to fry 75 shrimp

Note: *Can also be used to fry frog legs and crawfish.*

Regular Batter

1	cup flour	¼	teaspoon black pepper
1	teaspoon salt	¼	teaspoon red pepper
1	teaspoon garlic powder	⅓	cup evaporated milk

Mix flour, salt, garlic powder, black and red pepper in a bag. Dip shrimp in milk. Drain off excess milk. Place in the bag and shake bag to coat. Fry.

Choupic Patties

3	pounds Choupic	1½	cups bread crumbs
3	medium onions	3	eggs
1	large bell pepper		Hot sauce to taste
1	large potato		Salt and pepper to taste
1	cup chopped green onions		Vegetable oil (for deep frying)
½	cup parsley flakes	½	cup water

Grind Choupic, onion, bell pepper and potato in food processor or with meat grinder. Add green onions, parsley, bread crumbs, eggs and hot sauce. Salt and pepper to taste. Mix well with hands. Form into balls. Flatten somewhat and deep-fry until brown. Remove from oil. Remove excess oil from pot and add ½ cup water. Return patties to pot. Steam on low heat about ½ hour.

Makes 15 to 20 patties

Choupic is one of the many names for the bowfin fish. It has been around for 150,000,000 years.

BAKED CRAB CAKES

1 tablespoon butter
1 tablespoon olive oil
1 small onion, finely chopped
½ large bell pepper, finely chopped
2 ribs celery, finely chopped
2 cloves garlic, finely minced
2 teaspoons Créole seasoning
¾ teaspoon salt

¾ teaspoon pepper
½ cup Parmesan cheese
1 pound lump crabmeat
1 tablespoon mayonnaise
1 tablespoon Worcestershire sauce
1 teaspoon dry mustard
2 eggs, beaten
½ cup seasoned bread crumbs
Olive oil spray or cooking spray

Preheat oven to 350 degrees. Spray baking sheet and set aside. Heat butter and olive oil in a sauté pan. Add onion, bell pepper, celery, garlic, 1 teaspoon of Créole seasoning, ¼ teaspoon salt and ¼ teaspoon pepper. Sauté until vegetables are clear. Remove from heat. Cool. Place in a large mixing bowl. To the vegetables add cheese, 1 teaspoon of Créole seasoning, crabmeat, mayonnaise, Worcestershire sauce, mustard, eggs, and remaining salt and pepper. Mix well with a large spoon. Don't over mix. Form the mixture into cakes. Roll in bread crumbs. Place on prepared baking sheet. Spray top surface of cakes with olive oil or cooking spray. Place the sheet in the top rack of the oven. Bake 20 minutes or until the cakes start to brown. For the last 3 minutes broiler may be used to finish the browning. Remove and cool.

 Crabs can communicate by drumming or waving their pinchers.

CRABMEAT AU GRATIN

½ cup chopped green onions
1 stick butter
2 tablespoons flour
1 (12 ounce) can evaporated milk

1 pound fresh crabmeat
1-2 drops crab boil
4 slices cheese

Preheat oven to 350 degrees. Sauté green onions in butter until wilted. Add flour and evaporated milk. Stir constantly. Add crabmeat and crab boil. Mix well. Place crab mixture in a casserole dish. Top with cheese. Bake 10 minutes or until cheese is melted.

CRAB QUICHE

½ cup mayonnaise
½ teaspoon salt
2 eggs, beaten
½ cup milk
4 ounces grated Swiss cheese
4 ounces grated Munster cheese

2 tablespoons flour
1 pound white crabmeat, flaked
½ cup chopped celery
¼ cup chopped green onions
1 unbaked pie shell
Paprika

Preheat oven to 350 degrees. Combine mayonnaise, salt, eggs and milk in blender. Mix well. Toss cheeses with flour. Add cheese mixture, crabmeat, celery and green onions to mayonnaise mixture. Mix well. Pour into pie shell. Bake 40 to 50 minutes. Top will be brown. Sprinkle with paprika.

STUFFED CRABS

¼ stick butter, softened
½ cup finely chopped onion
½ cup finely chopped celery
½ cup finely chopped green onions
½ cup finely chopped parsley
¼ teaspoon black pepper
½ teaspoon salt
2¼ cups soft bread crumbs
1 pound white or dark crabmeat
Seasoned bread crumbs
Crab shells

Preheat oven to 350 degrees. Mix butter, onion, celery, green onions, parsley, pepper and salt in a large bowl. Add soft bread crumbs, mix well. Add crabmeat and mix. Place in crab shells. Sprinkle with seasoned bread crumbs. Bake 25 to 30 minutes or until edges start to turn light golden brown.

"Tomatoes and oregano make it Italian.
Wine and tarragon makes it French.
Sour cream makes it Russian.
Lemon and cinnamon makes it Greek.
Soy sauce makes it Chinese.
Garlic makes it 'GOOD'."

Alice May Brock

CRAWFISH BISQUE

Crawfish Balls

2 pounds Louisiana crawfish tails, peeled
1 (12-ounce) bag frozen vegetable seasoning blend
1 cup bread crumbs

2 eggs, lightly beaten
2 teaspoons Créole seasoning
1 teaspoon onion powder
1 teaspoon garlic powder

Gravy

½ cup flour
½ cup vegetable oil
1 (12-ounce) bag frozen vegetable seasoning blend
1 (8-ounce) can tomato sauce
4 cups water

1 pound Louisiana crawfish tails, peeled
¼ teaspoon liquid crab boil
1 tablespoon Créole seasoning
1 teaspoon onion powder
1 teaspoon garlic powder

Grease cookie sheet and set aside. Preheat oven to 350 degrees. To make crawfish balls grind crawfish tails and seasoning blend in a meat grinder. Mix in bread crumbs and eggs. Add Créole seasoning, onion and garlic powder. Form into small balls. Place on prepared cookie sheet. Bake 20 minutes. To make gravy heat oil in a large pot. Add flour and cook until flour is the color of a penny, stirring constantly. Add seasoning blend and tomato sauce. Continue stirring. Cook approximately 15 minutes. Add water, crawfish tails, crab boil, Créole seasoning, onion powder and garlic powder. Bring to a boil. Lower heat and simmer 20 minutes. Add crawfish balls. Simmer an additional 40 minutes. Serve over rice.

Hint: *Crawfish balls may be served alone as an appetizer.*

CRAWFISH CASSEROLE

1 (10-ounce) can cream of celery soup

1 (10-ounce) can cream of onion soup

1 (10-ounce) can tomatoes with chili peppers

2 cups cooked rice

1 onion, chopped

1 pound Louisiana crawfish tails, peeled

½ cup seasoned bread crumbs

2 tablespoons parsley flakes

Créole seasoning to taste

Preheat oven to 350 degrees. Grease a 9x13-inch baking dish. Mix soups, tomatoes, rice, onion and crawfish tails in a large bowl. Place in prepared baking dish. Sprinkle bread crumbs, parsley flakes and Créole seasoning over mixture. Bake 1 hour.

CRAWFISH EXTRAORDINAIRE

3 tablespoons margarine

1 cup chopped green onions

½ cup chopped parsley

3 tablespoons flour

1 (12-ounce) can evaporated milk

3 tablespoons sherry (optional)

1 pound Louisiana crawfish tails, peeled

⅛ teaspoon Cayenne pepper

8 ounces Monterey Jack jalapeño cheese, cubed

Salt and pepper to taste

In a skillet, melt margarine, sauté green onions and parsley. Blend in flour. Gradually add evaporated milk, stirring constantly until sauce thickens. Add sherry and crawfish tails, stirring gently. Cook approximately 15 to 20 minutes. Add Cayenne pepper and cheese. Cook until cheese is melted. Season to taste with salt and pepper. Serve with garlic toast.

To prepare seafood stock, keep the heads and shells of the shrimp. Place them in a saucepan and cover with water. Add a few drops of liquid crab boil. Bring to a boil and simmer for 5 minutes. Strain and throw away solids. Keep refrigerated.

CRAWFISH JAMBALAYA

3-4 pounds Louisiana crawfish tails, peeled
Salt to taste
½ teaspoon red pepper
3 tablespoons peanut oil
1 large onion, chopped
¾ cup chopped celery
½ cup chopped bell pepper
5 cups water
5 chicken bouillon cubes
2 cloves garlic, chopped
½ cup chopped green onions
½ cup chopped parsley
2 cups rice

Preheat oven to 350 degrees. Season crawfish with salt and red pepper. Brown in 2 tablespoons of oil. In another saucepan sauté onion, celery and bell pepper in remaining oil until wilted. Add water, crawfish, bouillon cubes and garlic. Bring to a boil. Boil 15 minutes, add green onions, parsley and rice, mixing well. Pour into a 3-quart casserole dish. Cover tightly. Bake 2 hours.

Serves 6 to 8

Hint: *Can also use chicken or shrimp for this recipe.*

CRAWFISH OMELET

2	tablespoons butter	1	teaspoon salt
1	pound Louisiana crawfish tails, peeled		Pepper to taste
1	large onion, chopped	4	eggs, beaten
½	cup chopped green onions	½	teaspoon cornstarch

Melt butter in saucepan. Add crawfish and onions. Simmer until onions are soft. If necessary add water to prevent sticking. Stir occasionally. Add salt and pepper. Cook 15 minutes. Mix eggs and cornstarch. Add egg mixture to crawfish. Cook 15 minutes on medium heat.

Serves approximately 3 people

CRAWFISH PIE

1	large onion, chopped fine	1	pound Louisiana crawfish tails, peeled and chopped
1	tablespoon minced garlic		
¼	cup minced bell pepper	¼	cup minced parsley
¼	cup minced celery		Salt and pepper to taste
1	stick butter	1	cup milk
1	(10-ounce) can cream of celery soup	½	cup seasoned bread crumbs
1	(4-ounce) can tomato sauce	1	egg, beaten
		2	(9-inch) pie shells

Preheat oven to 350 degrees. Sauté onion, garlic, bell pepper and celery in butter 15 minutes. Add soup, tomato sauce, crawfish, parsley, salt and pepper. Cook 10 minutes. Turn off heat. Add milk, bread crumbs, egg and mix well. Pour into pie shell. Top with other pie shell. Seal edges and slit top of shell. Bake 40 minutes or until brown.

QUICK CRAWFISH PIE

1	cup chopped onion	1	(10-ounce) can cream of mushroom soup
1	stick butter		
1	pound Louisiana crawfish tails, peeled	1	tablespoon cornstarch
¼	cup chopped green onions	1	(5-ounce) can evaporated milk
		2	(9-inch) pie shells

Preheat oven to 350 degrees. Sauté chopped onion in butter until clear. Wash crawfish tails. Add green onions and crawfish tails to sautéed onion. Cover. Cook 20 to 25 minutes. Add cream of mushroom soup. Dilute cornstarch in evaporated milk. Add to crawfish mixture. Allow mixture to come to a full boil. Stir to prevent sticking. Cool. Fill pie shells with mixture. Bake 25 to 30 minutes or until crusts are brown.

Hint: *These freeze well before or after being baked.*

Even though Louisiana is the international leader in freshwater crawfish production, Louisiana crawfish farmers have difficulty meeting market demands. They have even cultivated a new rice variety just to generate food for their crawfish ponds.

CRAWFISH STEW

2 cups oil
2 cups flour
4 medium onions, chopped fine
2 ribs celery, chopped fine
1 medium bell pepper, chopped fine
1 cup chopped green onion whites

1 (10-ounce) can tomatoes with chili peppers
Water as needed
Salt and red pepper to taste
6 pounds Louisiana crawfish tails, peeled
1 cup chopped green onion tops
Boiled eggs (optional)

Heat oil and add flour. Cook over medium heat until flour is the color of peanut butter (roux). Stir constantly. Add onion, celery, bell pepper and white part of the green onions. Cook until onions are wilted. Add tomatoes and water. Cook 30 minutes. Season with salt and red pepper. Cook 20 minutes. Add 1 pound of crawfish tails. Cook 45 minutes. Add the remaining crawfish, green onion tops and boiled eggs. Cook 40 minutes.

OVEN-FRIED CATFISH PARMESAN

½ cup grated Parmesan cheese
½ cup flour
¼ teaspoon pepper
1 teaspoon paprika

¼ cup skim milk
1 egg, plus 2 egg whites, beaten
6 (4-ounce) catfish fillets
Nonstick cooking spray

Preheat oven to 350 degrees. Spray baking sheet with cooking spray and set aside. Combine cheese, flour, pepper and paprika on a platter. Set aside. Combine milk and eggs in a shallow bowl. Dip fillets in egg mixture. Dredge in flour mixture. Arrange fillets on prepared baking sheet. Lightly spray each fillet with cooking spray. Bake 35 to 40 minutes.

Serves 6

TROUT ALMONDINE

6	fillets of trout	½	cup flour
1	cup milk	½	stick butter
1	teaspoon salt	½	cup slivered almonds
½	teaspoon pepper	6	lemon wedges

Dip each fillet in milk. Season with salt and pepper. Roll in flour so entire fillet is well coated. Melt butter in skillet and cook fillet, browning evenly on both sides. Remove fish. In same skillet, add almonds and sauté. Sprinkle evenly over fish. Serve with lemon wedges.

SAUCY FISH

1	tablespoon vegetable oil	¼	cup Italian dressing
1	large onion, chopped	½	stick butter, melted
1	tablespoon ketchup		Créole seasoning to taste
1	tablespoon mustard		Fish fillets to cover bottom
1½	tablespoons mayonnaise		of 9x13-inch pan
1	tablespoon red wine vinegar	1	can mushrooms, drained
1	tablespoon Worcestershire sauce	1	garlic bread

Preheat oven to 350 degrees. Grease a 9x13-inch pan. Set aside. Heat oil and sauté onion. In a bowl mix ketchup, mustard, mayonnaise, vinegar, Worcestershire sauce, Italian dressing and butter. Season fish to taste and put in prepared pan. Place mushrooms on top of fish. Add sautéed onion on top of mushrooms. Pour in mayonnaise mixture. Bake 30 to 40 minutes. Serve with garlic bread for dipping in sauce.

Serves 6

FISH STEW

"Poisson court-bouillon"

3-4 pounds catfish
    Salt and pepper to taste
¼ cup lemon juice
1 cup oil
1 cup flour
3 onions, chopped
1 bell pepper, chopped
6 pods garlic, chopped
3 ribs celery, chopped

1 (8-ounce) can tomato sauce
1 (10-ounce) can tomatoes with green chilies
3 cups water
    Salt and pepper to taste
½ cup chopped green onions

Cut fish into bite-size pieces. Season with salt, pepper and lemon juice. Marinate in refrigerator until needed. Heat oil in a 5-quart Dutch oven. Add flour and cook until the color of peanut butter, stirring constantly (roux). Add onion, bell pepper, garlic and celery. Cook on low heat until vegetables are wilted. Add tomato sauce and tomatoes. Cook on high heat for several minutes. Lower heat and cook 1 hour. Add water, salt and pepper to taste. Bring to a boil, lower fire and cook 30 minutes. Add green onions. Add fish (stirring will break the fish). If you must stir, do so very gently with a spatula. Cook 30 minutes. Serve over rice.

When buying fresh fish the flesh should be firm and elastic. To remove any surface bacteria, rinse fish in cold water for several seconds before seasoning. Thaw frozen fish in milk. The milk draws out the frozen taste and provides a fresh-caught flavor.

FROG SAUCE PIQUANTE

2	tablespoons vegetable oil	1	(16-ounce) can diced tomatoes
4	tablespoons flour	4	cups chicken broth
3	tablespoons unsalted butter	1	teaspoon hot sauce
1	large onion, chopped	1	teaspoon Worcestershire sauce
1	rib celery, diced	½	teaspoon black pepper
1	small bell pepper, chopped	3	pounds frog meat (15 to 20 legs or 8 to 10 backs)
3	cloves garlic, minced		Salt and Cayenne pepper to taste
1	(6-ounce) can tomato paste		

In a black iron skillet over high heat, heat oil. Add 2
tablespoons flour and cook until the color of peanut butter,
stirring constantly (roux). Add butter, onion, celery, bell
pepper and garlic. Cook until wilted. Add tomato paste.
Cook over medium heat about 10 minutes, stirring frequently.
Add the tomatoes with the liquid, chicken broth, hot sauce,
Worcestershire sauce and black pepper. Cover and simmer
over low heat 45 minutes. Season the frog legs or backs with
salt and Cayenne pepper. Lightly coat the frog legs with
remaining 2 tablespoons flour. In a separate lightly oiled skillet,
sauté the frog legs 3 minutes on each side until golden brown.
Add the frog to the sauce. Simmer about 20 minutes, or until
meat separates from the bones. Serve over rice.

FRIED OYSTERS

1	gallon peanut oil	3	pounds seasoned fish fry
1	gallon oysters	½	cup Créole seasoning

Heat oil in a large deep fryer to 350 degrees. Wash oysters, drain. Mix seasoned fish fry and Créole seasoning. Coat oysters evenly with mixture, a few at a time. Fry until golden brown (approximately 3 minutes). Do not overcook. Drain on paper towels.

Serves 15 to 20

OVEN SHRIMP

5	pounds large shrimp, unpeeled	2	lemons, juiced
6	tablespoons seasoned salt	6	tablespoons Worcestershire sauce
2	tablespoons red pepper	2	sticks butter
1	tablespoon paprika	¾	cup chopped green onions
2	tablespoons salt	¼	cup chopped parsley
8	cloves garlic, chopped		

Preheat oven to 425 degrees. Wash shrimp and drain. Put shrimp into a large baking pan. Season with seasoned salt, pepper, paprika, salt, garlic, lemon juice and Worcestershire sauce. Stir together. Cut butter into pieces and place over shrimp. Add green onions and parsley. Cook 25 minutes, stirring occasionally.

Serves 6 to 8

Hint: *Serve with hot French bread and salad.*

BUTTERFLY SHRIMP

4-5 pounds shrimp
1 large onion
2 (12-ounce) cans evaporated milk
4 large cloves garlic, cubed
¼ teaspoon hot sauce

1 teaspoon sugar
Black pepper to taste
1½ teaspoons salt
Flour
¾ teaspoon baking powder
Oil for frying

Peel shrimp, but leave the last segment of the tail intact. Slit each shrimp lengthwise through the body down to the last segment of shell. Remove vein. This slitting allows the crispy coating to cover more of the shrimp than if the shrimp were fried without slitting. In a medium bowl scrape the onion into the evaporated milk to make a marinade. Add cubed garlic (garlic cubes should not cling to the shrimp) hot sauce, sugar, pepper and salt. Place shrimp in mixture and let marinate at least 1 hour. Mix flour and baking powder in a paper bag. Drop a few shrimp at a time into the paper bag. Change the bag often as the flour becomes damp. Fry the shrimp in deep hot oil. Serve hot.

Shrimp Size	Count (per pound)	Average number of Shrimp (per pound)	(per 4-oz. serving)	Shrimp (per 5 pound box)
Jumbo	21/25	23	6	98-120
Extra Large	26/30	28	7	121-145
Large	31/35	33	8	146-173
Medium Large	36/40	38	10	174-190
Medium	41/50	45	12	191-240
Small	51/60	55	14	241-290
Extra Small	61/70	65	16	291-340

SHRIMP ÉTOUFFÉE

2-3 medium onions, chopped	1 teaspoon chopped parsley
4 ribs celery, chopped	
1 (10-ounce) can tomatoes with chili peppers	2 cloves garlic, minced
	½ (10-ounce) can cream of mushroom soup
1 bell pepper, chopped	
1½ sticks butter	1½ quarts peeled shrimp
½ lemon, juiced	Sherry (optional)
½ teaspoon Worcestershire sauce	

Sauté onion, celery, tomatoes and bell pepper in butter. Add lemon juice, Worcestershire sauce, parsley and garlic. Stir together. Add cream of mushroom soup and shrimp. A little sherry can also be added. Cook 20 to 25 minutes.

Hint: *Crawfish may be used instead of shrimp for this recipe.*

SHRIMP SCAMPI

4 cloves garlic, minced	¼ teaspoon minced parsley
½ stick butter	½ cup grated Parmesan cheese
¼ cup olive oil	
1 pound shrimp, cleaned	¼ teaspoon dried oregano (optional)
¼ cup lemon juice	
½ teaspoon pepper	¼ cup bread crumbs

In a 10-inch ovenproof skillet, sauté garlic in butter and oil until wilted. Stir in shrimp, lemon juice and pepper. Cook and stir 2 to 3 minutes or until shrimp turn pink. Sprinkle with parsley, cheese, oregano and bread crumbs. Place in oven. Broil 6-inches from heat 2 to 3 minutes or until top is brown. Serve over angel hair pasta.

Serves 4

Shrimp Fettuccini

1 pound Velveeta	3 pounds shrimp, cleaned
3 sticks butter	1 quart half-and-half
3 medium onions, chopped	3 cloves garlic, crushed
3 ribs celery, chopped	Salt and pepper to taste
2 bell peppers, chopped	1 pound package fettuccini
¼ cup flour	noodles
4 tablespoons chopped parsley	Parmesan cheese to taste

Preheat oven to 350 degrees. Cut Velveeta into ½-inch thick cubes. Set aside. Melt butter in a large saucepan. Add onion, celery and bell pepper. Cook 10 minutes until clear. Add flour, blend well. Cover and cook 15 minutes, stirring occasionally. Add parsley and shrimp. Cover and cook 20 minutes, stirring often. Add half-and-half, Velveeta and garlic. Mix well. Add salt and pepper to taste. Cover and cook on low heat 20 minutes, stirring occasionally. Cook noodles according to package directions. Add sauce to cooked noodles and mix. Pour into a casserole dish. Sprinkle with Parmesan cheese to your taste. Bake 20 to 25 minutes.

Hint: *Spice up, add 3 tablespoons chopped jalapeño peppers.*

Shrimp and Rice Casserole

1 onion, chopped	1 (12-ounce) can cream of
1 bell pepper, chopped	celery soup
1 stick butter	8 ounces Velveeta
1 pound peeled shrimp	2 cups cooked rice

Preheat oven to 350 degrees. Sauté onion and bell pepper in butter until wilted. Add shrimp, soup and Velveeta. Reduce heat to low. Let simmer about 10 minutes. Add rice, stir until well mixed. Transfer to casserole dish and bake until lightly browned.

TURTLE SAUCE PIQUANTE

"Tortue sauce piquante"

10 pounds turtle meat
1 quart cooking oil
2 pounds flour
10 pounds onions, chopped
1 (10-ounce) package frozen seasoning blend
1 (10-ounce) package frozen bell peppers
1 (10-ounce) can tomatoes with chili peppers
4 (15-ounce) cans tomato sauce

1 (2-ounce) bottle hot sauce
1 (3-ounce) bottle garlic powder
1 (14-ounce) bottle ketchup
1 cup green onions, chopped
Salt and pepper to taste
5 cups stock

Place meat in a large pot and add enough water to cover meat and bring to a boil. Boil 45 minutes. Drain and reserve 5 cups of stock. Heat oil over medium heat. Add flour and cook until a peanut butter color (roux). Stir constantly. Add onion. Sauté until soft. Add seasoning blend and bell pepper. Sauté until soft. Add tomatoes, tomato sauce, hot sauce, garlic powder, ketchup, green onions, salt, pepper and 2 cups stock. Cover and cook approximately 10 minutes or until all ingredients are mixed well and are hot. Add turtle and cook approximately 4 to 4½ hours or until the meat begins to separate from the bones. Add stock as needed. Serve over hot rice.

Hint: *Chicken, rabbit, venison, alligator or any meat you choose can be used in place of the turtle meat. Turkey necks make a great mock turtle sauce piquante.*

Serves approximately 30

Desserts

WESTFIELD

Butz Suarez

Sugar Cane

Of all the United States sugar producing areas, Louisiana is the oldest and most historic. Sugar cane was brought to Louisiana in 1751. It was used primarily for chewing purposes, for making taffia (a distilled drink) and syrup until 1795. That year Etienne de Bore developed a way to produce sugar from sugar cane on a commercial basis. During the Civil War the sugar industry was almost destroyed.

Today if you visit a sugarhouse in Louisiana, you will see in operation one of Louisiana's largest, oldest and most fascinating industries. Although the crop takes almost a year to mature, it is harvested only in October, November and December.

It is the main industry in Assumption Parish and much of the area is under cultivation year around. At present there are only eleven sugarhouses operating in Louisiana and two are in Assumption Parish.

To frost 12 cupcakes you will need 1 cup of frosting.

Almond Frosting

1½ cups chopped pecans	1 (8-ounce) container whipped topping
1 stick butter	2 teaspoons almond extract
1 (8-ounce) package cream cheese	
1 (16-ounce) package confectioners' sugar	

Preheat oven to 350 degrees. Spread pecans on a cookie sheet. Melt ½ stick of butter and pour over pecans. Toast in oven 15 minutes. Set aside to cool. In a medium bowl, cream the other ½ stick of butter, cream cheese and sugar and mix well. Add whipped topping, almond extract and cooled pecans. Mix well. Refrigerate.

Hint: *½ cup cocoa powder can be added to the confectioners' sugar.*

Birthday Cake Icing

1⅔ cups solid shortening	½ teaspoon salt
2 teaspoons clear vanilla	½ cup hot water
1 teaspoon butter flavoring	2 (16-ounce) packages confectioners' sugar
1 teaspoon almond extract	

Cream shortening, vanilla, butter flavoring and almond extract until creamy. Add salt to water, stir to dissolve. Slowly add sugar to shortening mixture. Add as much of the salt water mixture as needed to make the icing fluffy.

Hint: *2 sticks of butter can be substituted for shortening.*

BUTTERFLY FROSTING

1   stick butter
4   ounces cream cheese
1   (16-ounce) package
    confectioners' sugar

1½ teaspoons vanilla
3   tablespoons evaporated
    milk

Cream butter and cream cheese and add about half of the
confectioners' sugar. Beat in vanilla. Then alternate sugar and
milk until desired consistency is reached. All the sugar should
be used.

PINEAPPLE ICING

1   (4-ounce) box vanilla
    instant pudding
1   (15-ounce) can crushed
    pineapple

1   envelope dream whip

Stir dry pudding into pineapple. Prepare dream whip
according to package. Fold pineapple mixture into dream
whip topping. Keep refrigerated.

PECAN FUDGE ICING

1   (16-ounce) package
    confectioners' sugar
2   tablespoons cocoa
1   stick butter

1   teaspoon vanilla
¼   cup evaporated milk
½   cup chopped pecans

Mix sugar, cocoa and butter and beat until creamy. Add
vanilla and evaporated milk and mix thoroughly. Add pecans
and stir until all pecans are incorporated.

CREAMED ICING

3½ tablespoons flour

1 cup sugar

½ cup milk

1 cup solid shortening

⅓ cup butter

2 cups confectioners' sugar

¼ teaspoon salt

1 teaspoon vanilla

½ teaspoon almond extract

In a medium saucepan, mix flour, sugar and milk. Cook over medium heat, stirring constantly until mixture thickens. Set aside to cool. Cream together shortening, butter, ½ cup confectioners' sugar and salt. Add flour mixture to shortening mixture and beat well. Stir in vanilla and almond extract. Add the remaining confectioners' sugar and adjust the spreading consistency with additional milk or confectioners' sugar. Beat until light and fluffy.

CREAM CHEESE FROSTING

1 (16-ounce) package confectioners' sugar

1 (8-ounce) package cream cheese

1 stick butter, softened

2 teaspoons vanilla

⅛ teaspoon salt

Sift confectioners' sugar into a large bowl. In another large bowl beat together cream cheese and butter until fluffy. Beat in vanilla and salt. Add confectioners' sugar a little at a time until frosting is smooth.

LEMON GLAZE

1 stick butter

1 cup lemon juice

1½ cups confectioners' sugar

In a heavy pot, combine butter, lemon juice and sugar. Cook on medium heat until mixture is light and creamy and starts to thicken and coat the back of the spoon. Remove from heat. The mixture will be clear but should be thick. Do not over cook.

FRESH APPLE CAKE

2	medium apples	½	teaspoon allspice
1	cup sugar	1	stick butter, melted
1½	cups flour	1	egg, beaten
1	teaspoon baking soda	½	cup raisins
½	teaspoon salt	½	cup nuts
½	teaspoon cinnamon		Confectioners' sugar, to sprinkle
½	teaspoon nutmeg		

Preheat oven to 350 degrees. Grease and flour a Bundt pan. Pare and core apples. Coarsely chop and measure 1½ cups into a large bowl. Add sugar and let stand 10 minutes. Sift flour, baking soda and salt. Add cinnamon, nutmeg and allspice and sift again. Mix butter and egg and add to apple mixture. Add flour mixture. Stir in raisins and nuts. Stir until well mixed. Pour into prepared pan. Bake 40 minutes. Cool and sprinkle with confectioners' sugar.

Nutmeg is the actual seed of the tree. It has a sweet delicate flavor. It is best if it is ground fresh.

BABA CAKE

Cake

1 (18-ounce) box butter
   cake mix

Filling

1 (15-ounce) can   1 stick butter, melted
   sweetened coconut

Custard

1 (12-ounce) can   1 cup sugar
   evaporated milk   4 egg yolks, slightly beaten
2 cups milk   1 teaspoon vanilla
3 tablespoons cornstarch   ½ stick butter

Meringue

4 egg whites   ⅔ cup sugar
½ teaspoon cream of tartar

Preheat oven to 350 degrees. Grease and flour 9x13-inch baking dish. Prepare cake mix according to directions on box. Make holes with the handle of a wooden spoon in the cake while it is hot. To make filling, mix coconut and butter. Pour over warm cake. To make the custard, heat milks together to scalding, do not boil. Blend cornstarch and sugar with hot milk. Cook over medium heat until thick. Temper eggs by stirring a small amount of hot mixture into the egg yolks, being careful not to add too much as it will curdle the eggs. Continue until the eggs and milk mixture are completely incorporated. Return to heat and cook 5 minutes. Remove from heat. Add vanilla and butter. Return to heat and cook a few more minutes. Pour over cake. To make meringue, beat egg whites until foamy. Add cream of tartar and continue beating. Gradually add sugar until stiff peaks form. Spoon meringue over pudding and bake 15 to 20 minutes or until golden brown.

BANANA NUT CAKE

1 cup solid shortening	2 teaspoons baking soda
3 cups sugar	¼ teaspoon salt
4 eggs	½ cup buttermilk
2 teaspoons vanilla	1½ cups ripe mashed
½ teaspoon banana extract	bananas
1 teaspoon butter flavoring	1 cup chopped nuts
3½ cups flour	

Preheat oven to 325 degrees. Grease and flour a 10-inch tube pan. Cream together shortening and sugar. Add eggs, one at a time mixing well after each. Add vanilla, banana extract and butter flavoring. Sift flour, baking soda and salt together. Add to egg mixture alternating with milk. Add bananas and nuts. Mix well. Pour into prepared pan. Bake 1 hour and 15 minutes. Insert toothpick in center to test if cake is done.

BANANA SPLIT CAKE

2 cups graham cracker crumbs	1 (15-ounce) can crushed pineapple, drained
2 sticks butter, melted	1 (12-ounce) container whipped topping
3 cups confectioners' sugar	Cherries (optional)
4 large bananas	Pecans (optional)
2 egg whites	

Mix together graham cracker crumbs, 1 stick of butter and 1 cup confectioners' sugar. Press mixture into 9x13-inch pan. Slice bananas over crust. Combine egg whites, with remaining butter and confectioners' sugar. Beat for 10 minutes and pour over bananas. Spread pineapple on top. Spread whipped topping over pineapple. Garnish with cherries and pecans. Refrigerate overnight.

BLACK RUSSIAN CAKE

Cake

4	eggs
1	box yellow cake mix (no pudding in mix)
½	cup sugar
1	(5-ounce) box instant chocolate pudding

1	cup vegetable oil
¼	cup vodka
¼	cup coffee liqueur
¾	cup water

Glaze

½	cup confectioners' sugar
2	tablespoons coffee liqueur

Hot water as needed

Preheat oven to 350 degrees. Grease and flour Bundt pan. In a large mixing bowl beat eggs thoroughly. Add cake mix, sugar, pudding, oil, vodka, coffee liqueur and water. Mix on low speed 1 minute then on medium 3 minutes. Pour mix into prepared Bundt pan. Bake 1 hour or until cake is firm. Cool a few minutes then place on a cake plate. Pierce the cake all over with a fork. To make glaze, with a whisk blend confectioners' sugar and coffee liqueur. Hot water is added to get the consistency needed. Pour over warm cake. Place under cake cover so the cake will remain moist.

A liqueur is a sweet alcoholic beverage, often flavored with fruits, herbs, spices and sometimes cream. The word liqueur comes from Latin meaning "to dissolve." Liqueur can be used to flavor coffee and is used in baking.

BUTTERFLY CAKE

Cake

1	box yellow cake mix	4	large eggs
1	(3-ounce) box vanilla instant pudding	¾	cup vegetable oil
		10	ounces lemon lime soda

Preheat oven to 350 degrees. Grease and flour two 9-inch cake pans. Mix cake and pudding mix. Add eggs, oil and lemon lime soda. Mix 3 minutes on medium speed or until smooth. Pour into prepared pans. Bake 30 minutes. Set aside to cool.

Frosting recipe on page 190 (sprinkle with toasted pecans) or **bake** *and frost as shown below.*

Preheat oven to 350 degrees. Grease and flour a 9x13-inch pan. Pour Butterfly Cake mix into prepared pan. Bake 30 minutes. Set aside to cool.	Cut 1-inch strip from short side of cake. Cut diagonally to form four triangles for wings. Place pieces as shown above. Tint frosting a pale yellow and spread on cake.	Tint angel flake coconut yellow and sprinkle over butterfly. Slice gumdrops, gumdrop strips and licorice and decorate cake. Strips of licorice make the antennas.

CAJUN CAKE

Cake

2 cups cake flour
1½ cups sugar
1½ teaspoons baking soda
⅛ teaspoon salt

2 eggs, slightly beaten
1 (15-ounce) can crushed
   pineapple

Icing

1 cup sugar
1 stick butter
1 (5-ounce) can
   evaporated milk

1 cup flaked coconut
1 cup chopped pecans

Preheat oven to 325 degrees. Grease and flour 9x13-inch baking pan. Sift flour, sugar, baking soda and salt into a large mixing bowl. Stir in eggs and pineapple and mix well. Pour into prepared pan and bake 30 to 35 minutes. To make icing, combine sugar, butter and milk in a small saucepan. Bring to a boil. Cook 5 minutes, stirring constantly. Remove from heat and stir in coconut and pecans. Pour over warm cake.

Serves 20

Hint: *Cake can be frozen. Defrost and prepare icing.*

To open a coconut, the softest "eye" should be pierced with a skewer. The water should be drained. Wrap the coconut in a towel and hit it with a hammer. It will break into several pieces. To prepare the coconut for peeling place these pieces in a 350-degree oven for 15 minutes. Let cool and then peel. The white, fleshy part is edible and is used fresh or dried in cooking.

CARROT CAKE

Cake

1½ cups vegetable oil
2 cups sugar
4 eggs
2 cups flour
2 teaspoons baking powder
2 teaspoons cinnamon

1 teaspoon salt
2 teaspoons baking soda
3 cups grated carrots
½ teaspoon vanilla
1 cup chopped pecans

Icing

¾ cup butter, softened
1 (8-ounce) package cream cheese
1 (16-ounce) package confectioners' sugar

1 teaspoon vanilla
1 tablespoon evaporated milk

Preheat oven to 375 degrees. Grease and flour three 9-inch pans. Blend oil and sugar in a large bowl. Add eggs, one at a time, beating well after each addition. Sift flour, baking powder, cinnamon, salt and baking soda. Stir in carrots. Add flour mixture to sugar mixture. Add vanilla and pecans and mix well. Pour into prepared pans. Bake 45 to 60 minutes or until a toothpick inserted in center comes out clean. Set cake aside to cool. To make icing, beat butter, cream cheese, confectioners' sugar, vanilla and evaporated milk together. Spread icing on cake after it is cool.

For baking it is best to use medium to large eggs, extra large eggs may cause cakes to fall when cooled.

FAMILY FAVORITE CHEESECAKE

Crust

1 ¼ cups graham cracker
    crumbs

¼ cup sugar
½ stick butter, melted

Filling

5 (8-ounce) packages
    cream cheese, softened

1 cup sugar

3 tablespoons flour

1 tablespoon vanilla

1 cup sour cream

4 eggs

Preheat oven to 325 degrees. Mix graham cracker crumbs, sugar and butter. Press into the bottom of a 9-inch spring form pan. Bake 10 minutes. Remove and cool. To make filling, mix cream cheese, sugar, flour and vanilla with mixer until well blended. Add sour cream and mix well. Add eggs, 1 at a time, mixing after each addition until well blended. Pour over crust and bake 1 hour or until center is almost set. Loosen cake from side of pan and cool before removing. Refrigerate at least four hours before serving.

Makes 16 servings

Helpful Hints

3 teaspoons = 1 tablespoon
4 tablespoons = ¼ cup
1 tablespoon = ½ fluid ounce
1 cup = 8 ounces

2 cups = 1 pint
4 cups = 1 quart
4 quarts = 1 gallon

A dash is the amount of spice that comes out of a shaker when shaken once. Approximately ⅛ of a teaspoon.

BEST CHOCOLATE CAKE

Cake

1   box chocolate cake mix
1   cup vegetable oil
1   (3-ounce) box chocolate
     instant pudding
4   eggs
1   teaspoon vanilla

½   cup water
1   (8-ounce) package sour
     cream
1   (6-ounce) bag semisweet
     chocolate chips

Icing

1   stick butter, melted
1   (16-ounce) package
     confectioners' sugar
2   (1-ounce) squares
     unsweetened
     chocolate, melted

     Evaporated milk
     (spreading consistency)
½   cup chopped pecans

Preheat oven to 350 degrees. Grease Bundt pan. Mix together cake mix, oil, pudding, eggs, vanilla, water and sour cream. Mix 3 to 4 minutes on medium speed of mixer. Add chocolate chips. Pour into prepared pan and bake 45 minutes. Remove and set aside. To make icing, mix butter, sugar and chocolate. Add enough milk to bring mixture to spreading consistency. Spread on cooled cake and sprinkle with pecans.

Pecan trees grow wild in Louisiana. The nuts are edible, with a rich, buttery flavor. They can be eaten fresh or used in cooking. Some of the most famous desserts made with pecans are associated with Louisiana, one being the praline candy.

COCONUT DREAM CAKE

Cake

½ cup solid shortening
1 stick butter
2 cups sugar
4 eggs
3 cups cake flour

3 teaspoons baking powder
2 teaspoons vanilla
1 teaspoon almond extract
1 cup milk

Icing

3 cups sugar
1½ cups water
4 egg whites

1 teaspoon vanilla
1 fresh coconut, grated

Preheat oven to 350 degrees. Grease and flour three 9-inch cake pans. Cream shortening, butter and sugar until light and fluffy. Add eggs, one at a time, beating after each addition. Sift flour and baking powder. Stir vanilla and almond extract into milk and alternately add flour mixture and milk mixture into egg mixture. Pour into prepared pans and bake 20 to 25 minutes. To make icing, boil sugar and water until it spins a thread, (230 degrees). Beat egg whites until stiff and slowly add sugar water mixture. Add vanilla and stir. Spread on cake and sprinkle with coconut.

Hint: *1 (14-ounce) bag of flaked coconut can be used in the place of a fresh coconut.*

CUSTARD CAKE

"Gâteau à la bouillie"

Custard

⅔ **cup cornstarch**	1 **quart milk**
1¼ **cups sugar**	5 **egg yolks**
1 **(13-ounce) can evaporated milk**	1 **teaspoon vanilla**

Cake

1 **box yellow cake mix**

Preheat oven to 350 degrees. Grease and flour a 9x13-inch pan. To make custard, mix cornstarch and sugar in a heavy saucepan. Gradually add enough milk to dissolve the lumps. Add the rest of the milks and cook on low, stirring constantly, until thickened. Remove from heat, add a small amount of the hot milk mixture to the egg yolks to temper them. Return milk mixture to heat and gradually add the tempered egg yolks. Cook until thick. Add vanilla and stir well. Remove from heat and set aside. Prepare cake mix according to directions on box. Pour cake mix into prepared pan. Pour pudding over cake batter leaving a 1-inch border around the edges. Bake 30 to 40 minutes or until golden brown.

To temper egg yolks, put a small amount of the hot mixture into the egg yolks to warm them and then stir the warmed egg yolk mixture into the remaining hot mixture. This keeps the yolks from coagulating.

EGGNOG POUND CAKE

Cake

1 box yellow cake mix	¾ cup vegetable oil
1 (3-ounce) box vanilla instant pudding	4 eggs
¾ cup eggnog	½ teaspoon nutmeg

Butter Cream Frosting

2 tablespoons butter, melted	¾ cup confectioners' sugar
1 teaspoon eggnog	¼ teaspoon rum extract
	3-4 drops almond extract

Preheat oven to 350 degrees. Grease Bundt pan. Mix cake mix, pudding, eggnog and oil. Add eggs and nutmeg and mix well. Pour into prepared pan and bake 40 to 50 minutes or until golden brown. Remove and set aside. To make frosting, whisk butter, eggnog and confectioners' sugar together until smooth. Add rum and almond extracts. And mix well. Drizzle over warm cake.

Eggnog is a sweetened dairy-based beverage made with milk, cream, sugar, beaten eggs and flavored with cinnamon or nutmeg. Eggnog is associated with Christmas and New Year's celebrations. Usually fortified with rum, inexpensive liquor, this dairy product became very popular in America.

SIX FLAVORS POUND CAKE

Pound Cake

1	stick butter	1	teaspoon vanilla
½	cup solid shortening	1	teaspoon butter flavoring
3	cups sugar	1	teaspoon coconut extract
5	eggs, beaten	1	teaspoon rum extract
3	cups flour	1	teaspoon lemon extract
½	teaspoon baking powder	1	teaspoon almond extract
¾	cup milk		

Glaze

1	cup sugar	½	teaspoon coconut extract
½	cup water	½	teaspoon rum extract
½	teaspoon vanilla	½	teaspoon lemon extract
½	teaspoon butter flavoring	½	teaspoon almond extract

Preheat oven to 325 degrees. Grease and flour a 10-inch tube pan. Cream butter, shortening and sugar. Add eggs. Alternately add flour, baking powder and milk to mixture. Add vanilla, butter flavoring, coconut, rum, lemon and almond extracts. Pour into prepared pan and bake 1½ hours. Cool 20 minutes. Invert on plate to finish cooling. To make glaze, bring sugar and water to a boil. Add vanilla, butter flavoring, coconut, rum, lemon and almond extracts. Boil 1 minute longer. Make holes in cake with fork and pour glaze over cake.

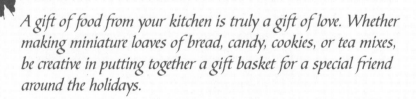

A gift of food from your kitchen is truly a gift of love. Whether making miniature loaves of bread, candy, cookies, or tea mixes, be creative in putting together a gift basket for a special friend around the holidays.

GERMAN CHOCOLATE CAKE

1   box German chocolate
      cake mix

Icing

1   cup sugar
1   cup evaporated milk
3   egg yolks
1   stick butter

1   teaspoon vanilla
1½ cups flaked coconut
1   cup chopped pecans

Preheat oven to 350 degrees. Bake cake according to directions on box. Set aside. To prepare icing, in a medium saucepan, combine sugar, milk, egg yolks and butter. Cook over medium heat, stirring constantly, until it comes to a boil. Lower heat and cook 10 minutes. Remove from heat and stir in vanilla, coconut and pecans. Let cool about 15 to 20 minutes. Spread icing between layers and outside of cake.

Chocolate is very sensitive to temperature and humidity. Chocolate should be stored away from other foods as it can absorb different aromas. It should be stored in a dark place and protected with a wrapping paper. A white discoloration to the chocolate can appear if refrigerated or frozen. Although unappealing, the chocolate is perfectly safe for consumption.

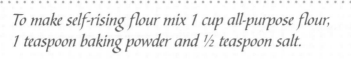

To make self-rising flour mix 1 cup all-purpose flour, 1 teaspoon baking powder and ½ teaspoon salt.

HEAVENLY HASH CAKE

Cake

4	eggs	2	sticks butter, melted
2	cups sugar	1	cup chopped pecans
1½	cups self-rising flour	2	teaspoons vanilla
½	teaspoon salt	1	(10-ounce) bag small marshmallows
¼	cup cocoa		

Icing

1	(16-ounce) package confectioners' sugar	½	cup evaporated milk
		⅛	teaspoon salt
½	stick butter	1	teaspoon vanilla
3	tablespoons cocoa	1	cup chopped pecans

Preheat oven to 350 degrees. Grease and flour a 9x13-inch baking pan. Beat eggs, adding sugar gradually. Sift flour, salt and cocoa. Add flour mixture, butter, pecans and vanilla to egg mixture. Mix well. Pour into prepared pan. Bake 40 to 50 minutes. Remove from oven and let stand 10 minutes. Invert on dish and spread marshmallows over hot cake. To make icing sift sugar. Set aside. In a medium saucepan melt butter and add cocoa. Stir in milk and salt. Over a low heat bring to a boil. Remove from heat and gradually beat in sugar. Add vanilla and pecans. If icing is too thick add more milk one tablespoon at a time until right consistency is reached. Pour on hot cake.

ITALIAN CREAM CAKE

Cake

1	stick butter	1	cup buttermilk
½	cup solid shortening	1	(7-ounce) can coconut flakes
2	cups sugar	1	cup chopped pecans
5	egg yolks	1	teaspoon vanilla
2	cups flour	5	egg whites
1	teaspoon baking soda		

Cream Cheese Frosting

1	(8-ounce) package cream cheese	1	teaspoon vanilla
½	stick butter		Chopped pecans
1	(16-ounce) package confectioners' sugar		

Preheat oven to 350 degrees. Grease and flour three 9-inch cake pans. Cream butter, shortening and sugar beating until light and fluffy. Add egg yolks and beat well. Combine flour and baking soda and add to sugar mixture. Add buttermilk and mix thoroughly. Stir in coconut, pecans and vanilla. Beat egg whites until peaks form and fold into mixture. Pour into prepared pans. Bake 25 minutes. To prepare frosting, beat cream cheese and butter until smooth. Add sugar and mix well. Add vanilla. Spread between layers and on top of cake. Sprinkle with pecans.

Vanilla is a flavoring derived from orchids. The name comes from the Spanish word "vanilla," meaning "little pod." Vanilla is used in many dishes and drinks to enhance the flavor of the recipe.

LEMON BUNDT CAKE

Cake

1	box lemon cake mix	4	large eggs
1	(3-ounce) box instant lemon pudding	¾	cup vegetable oil
		10	ounces lemon lime soda

Glaze

2	tablespoons fresh lemon juice	1	cup confectioners' sugar

Preheat oven to 350 degrees. Grease and flour Bundt pan. Place cake mix and pudding in large mixing bowl. Add eggs, oil and lemon lime soda. Mix at medium speed 3 minutes or until smooth. Pour into prepared pan and bake 40 minutes. Invert on plate. To make glaze, mix lemon juice and sugar until smooth. Drizzle over cake while cake is hot.

The Bundt pan (a registered trademark) was created in 1950. In early 2007 some of the original Bundt pans were taken into the Smithsonian Institution's collection.

MANDARIN CAKE

Cake

1 box yellow cake mix	1 cup vegetable oil
1½ teaspoons baking powder	2 (11-ounce) cans
4 eggs	Mandarins

Frosting

1 (15-ounce) can crushed pineapple	1 (12-ounce) container whipped topping
1 (3-ounce) box vanilla instant pudding	

Preheat oven to 350 degrees. Grease and flour three 8-inch cake pans. Mix cake mix, baking powder, eggs and vegetable oil until thoroughly blended. Fold in Mandarins and juice. Do not mash. Pour into prepared pans. Bake 30 minutes or until golden brown. Set aside and cool. To prepare frosting, drain pineapple, reserving juice. Mix pineapple, pudding and whipped topping. Add enough of the pineapple juice to get the required consistency to spread the frosting. Spread frosting between layers and on outside and top of cake. Refrigerate at least 4 hours before serving.

The Mandarin orange or Mandarin is a small citrus fruit resembling the orange. The shape roughly resembles a pumpkin. They are usually eaten plain, in fruit salads, cakes and other desserts.

MAYONNAISE CAKE

Cake

2 cups flour
2 teaspoons baking soda
1 cup sugar
2 tablespoons cocoa

1 cup cold water
1 cup mayonnaise
1 teaspoon vanilla

Glaze

1½ cups sugar
3-4 tablespoons cocoa
1 tablespoon evaporated
    milk

1 stick butter
1 teaspoon vanilla

Preheat oven to 300 degrees. Grease 9x13-inch pan. Mix flour, baking soda, sugar and cocoa. Mix water and mayonnaise. Add to flour mixture. Mix well. Add vanilla. Pour into prepared pan. Bake 40 minutes. To make glaze, mix sugar and cocoa. Add evaporated milk and butter and cook over low heat until it comes to a boil. Cook 2 to 3 minutes more. Remove from heat and add vanilla. Make holes in cake with fork and pour on glaze.

"Cocoa" is the dry powder made by grinding cocoa seeds and removing the cocoa butter from the dark, bitter cocoa solids. Cocoa can be used in candy, drinks and various other food recipes.

OATMEAL CAKE

Cake

2¼ cups boiling water
1½ cups quick cooking
    oatmeal
¾ cup vegetable oil
3 eggs
1½ cups sugar

1½ cups brown sugar
2¼ cups flour
¾ teaspoon salt
1½ teaspoons cinnamon
1½ teaspoons baking soda
1¼ teaspoons baking powder

Icing

3 tablespoons butter
3 tablespoons milk

7 tablespoons brown sugar

Preheat oven to 350 degrees. Grease and flour Bundt pan.
Place water in a small bowl and add oatmeal and set aside.
Blend oil, eggs and sugars in a large bowl. Add oatmeal. Sift
flour, salt, cinnamon, baking soda and baking powder. Add
to oatmeal mixture. Pour into prepared pan. Bake 50 to 55
minutes. To make icing, melt butter and add milk. Remove from
heat and let set for 5 minutes. Add brown sugar and stir. Make
holes in top of warm cake with fork and pour on icing.

*Oatmeal means any crushed oats, rolled oats, or cut oats
used in recipes. Oatmeal is a by product made by processing
oats. There is instant oatmeal, quick cooking oatmeal and old
fashioned oatmeal.*

PINEAPPLE MERINGUE CAKE

Cake

1	stick butter	2	teaspoons baking powder
½	cup sugar	⅛	teaspoon salt
4	egg yolks	1	teaspoon vanilla
1	cup cake flour, sifted	5	tablespoons milk

Meringue

4	egg whites	1	teaspoon vanilla
1	cup sugar	¾	cup chopped pecans

Pineapple Filling

1	cup crushed pineapple	¼	teaspoon vanilla
1	cup whipping cream		
2	teaspoons confectioners' sugar		

Preheat oven to 350 degrees. Grease and flour two 8-inch cake pans. Cream butter and sugar. Add egg yolks and mix thoroughly. Mix flour, baking powder and salt. Mix vanilla and milk. Alternately add flour mixture and milk mixture to butter mixture. Mix well. Pour into prepared pans and set aside. To make meringue, beat egg whites until foamy. Gradually add sugar and beat until stiff peaks form. Stir in vanilla. Spread ½ mixture over each cake. Sprinkle with pecans. Bake 35 minutes. Allow to cool. To make filing, drain pineapple. Whip the cream. Mix together. Add confectioners' sugar and vanilla. Place one cake layer, meringue side down, on a cake plate and spread on filling. Place second layer on top of filling with meringue side up.

POPPY SEED CAKE

Cake

1 cup vegetable oil	1½ cups milk
3 eggs	1½ teaspoons almond extract
2¼ cups sugar	1½ teaspoons butter flavoring
3 cups flour	1 (2-ounce) can poppy
1½ teaspoons baking powder	seeds
1½ teaspoons salt	

Glaze

½ cup sugar	½ teaspoon almond extract
¼ cup orange juice	½ teaspoon butter flavoring
½ teaspoon vanilla	

Preheat oven to 350 degrees. Grease and flour Bundt pan. Combine oil, eggs and sugar in a large mixing bowl. Beat on medium speed 2 minutes. Combine flour, baking powder and salt. Add to egg mixture alternately with milk. Begin and end with flour mixture. Mix well after each addition. Stir in almond extract, butter flavoring and poppy seeds. Pour batter into prepared pan. Bake 1 hour or until toothpick inserted in center comes out clean. Cool in pan 10 minutes. Remove and place on serving plate. Make holes in top of warm cake with a fork and set aside. To make glaze, combine sugar, orange juice, vanilla, almond extract and butter flavoring. Beat on medium speed until well blended. Mixture will be grainy. Pour glaze over cake.

RED VELVET CAKE

Cake

½ cup solid shortening
1½ cups sugar
2 eggs
2 cups flour
1 teaspoon salt

1 teaspoon vanilla
1 cup buttermilk
2 ounces red food coloring
1 tablespoon baking soda
1 tablespoon vinegar

Frosting

¼ cup flour
1 cup milk
½ cup solid shortening
1 stick butter

1 cup sugar
1 tablespoon vanilla
1 (7-ounce) can sweetened flaked coconut

Preheat oven to 300 degrees. Grease two 8-inch pans. Cream shortening, sugar and eggs. Add flour, salt, vanilla, buttermilk and food coloring. Beat until smooth. Dissolve baking soda in vinegar and stir into batter. Pour into prepared pans. Bake 25 minutes. Set aside. To make frosting, cook flour and milk until the mixture reaches pudding consistency. Set aside. Cream shortening, butter, sugar and vanilla. Add to the cooled pudding mixture and mix well. Spread frosting between layers and outside of cake. Sprinkle with coconut. Keep refrigerated.

Emergency Substitution

If you don't have:
1 cup buttermilk

Substitute:
1 tablespoon lemon juice plus enough whole milk to make 1 cup. Let stand 5 minutes before using.

RUM CAKE

Cake

1 cup chopped pecans or walnuts	4 eggs
1 box yellow cake mix	½ cup cold water
1 (3-ounce) package vanilla instant pudding	½ cup vegetable oil
	½ cup dark rum

Glaze

1 stick butter	1 cup sugar
¼ cup water	½ cup dark rum

Preheat oven to 325 degrees. Grease and flour a 10-inch tube pan or a 12 cup Bundt pan. Sprinkle nuts over the bottom of the pan. Mix the cake mix, pudding mix, eggs, water, oil and rum. Pour batter over nuts. Bake 1 hour. Cool and invert on a cake plate. Make holes in the top with a fork. To make glaze, in a small saucepan melt butter and stir in water and sugar. Boil 5 minutes stirring constantly. Remove from heat and stir in rum. Drizzle the glaze slowly and evenly over the top and sides of the cake allowing it to absorb the glaze.

Rum is a distilled beverage made from sugar cane by products such as molasses and sugar cane juice. In the 1800s the colonies, instead of using the heavily-taxed brandy and wines, used rum.

SNOWBALL CAKE

2	envelopes unflavored gelatin	2	tablespoons lemon juice
¼	cup hot water	1	cup boiling water
1	cup sugar	2	(12-ounce) containers whipped topping
1	cup chopped nuts	1	large angel food cake
½	cup chopped cherries	1	(7-ounce) can coconut
1	(8-ounce) can crushed pineapple		

In a large bowl completely dissolve gelatin with hot water. Stir in sugar, nuts, cherries, pineapple and lemon juice. Add boiling water and mix well. Refrigerate until it reaches a soft gel (not completely set). Add 1 container of whipped topping. Mix and set aside. Break angel food cake into bite size pieces. Add cake pieces to the gelatin mixture. Pour in a greased round bottom bowl. Refrigerate overnight. Invert on a cake plate and spread on remaining whipped topping. Sprinkle coconut over entire cake.

Gelatin is best known as a gelling agent in cooking. It may be used as a stabilizer, thickener, or to add texture in foods such as ice cream, jams, yogurt, cream cheese and margarine. It is also used for the clarification of juice and vinegar. It is still being used as a fining agent in wine and beer.

SOUR CREAM COFFEE CAKE

Cake

1	stick butter	2	cups flour
1¾	cups sugar	1	teaspoon baking powder
1	teaspoon vanilla	1	teaspoon baking soda
3	eggs	1	cup sour cream

Filling

¾	cup butter	4	teaspoons cinnamon
1½	cups brown sugar	1	cup chopped pecans
2	teaspoons cocoa		

Preheat oven to 350 degrees. Grease Bundt pan. Cream butter, sugar and vanilla. Add eggs one at a time beating thoroughly after each addition. Sift flour, baking powder and baking soda and add to egg mixture. Mix in sour cream and set aside. To make filling, cream butter and brown sugar. Add cocoa, cinnamon and pecans and mix well. Pour a layer of the batter in the prepared pan. Place spoonfuls of filling over the batter. Continue this procedure until all the batter and filling is used. End with filling. Bake 50 minutes. Remove from pan and cool.

Sour cream is a dairy product rich in fats. Sour cream can usually be refrigerated in its container for more than a month after the date stamped on the bottom of the container. It can be used as a base for salad dressings, added to cake and cookie mixes and also as a condiment.

SQUASH CAKE

5 squash	5 eggs
1 stick butter	1 (12-ounce) can evaporated milk
2½ cups sugar	
1½ cups self-rising flour	1 teaspoon vanilla

Preheat oven to 350 degrees. Grease and flour two 9x13-inch baking pans. Peel and clean squash. Boil until tender and strain. In a large bowl mix squash and butter and let cool. Mash squash and add sugar. Mix in flour, eggs, milk and vanilla. Mix well. Pour into prepared pans. Bake 1 hour and 20 minutes.

SURPRISE CAKE

2 sticks butter	1 cup flaked coconut
2 cups sugar	2 tablespoons vanilla
6 eggs	1 cup chopped pecans
½ cup milk	
1 (12-ounce) bag vanilla wafers, crushed	

Preheat oven to 350 degrees. Grease tube pan. Cream butter and sugar. Add eggs, one at a time, beating well after each addition. Add milk alternately with vanilla wafers and coconut. Add vanilla and pecans. Mix well. Pour into prepared pan and bake 1 hour and 30 minutes. Invert on serving plate.

Cane syrup is a thick, amber-colored form of sugar syrup. In the process of refining sugar cane juice into sugar one of the by-products is cane syrup. It tastes similar to honey and can be used as a substitute for honey.

SYRUP CAKE

"Gâteau de sirop"

1	cup vegetable oil	4	eggs
2	cups sugar	2	cups cane syrup
1	teaspoon cinnamon	4	cups flour
1	teaspoon nutmeg	3	teaspoons baking soda
1	teaspoon vanilla	2	cups water, boiling

Preheat oven to 375 degrees. Grease four 8x8-inch pans and set aside. Pour oil into a large mixing bowl. Mix sugar, cinnamon, nutmeg and vanilla. Pour into bowl with oil and stir. Add eggs and mix until light and fluffy. Add syrup to egg mixture. Sift flour and baking soda and add to egg and syrup mixture. Add boiling water and mix thoroughly. Pour into prepared pans and bake 30 to 40 minutes.

"Love is like a butterfly, it goes where it pleases and pleases where it goes."

Author unknown

TURTLE CAKE

Cake

1   box German chocolate
       cake mix
1   stick butter
1   (14-ounce) can
       condensed milk

½   cup vegetable oil
3   eggs
1   (14-ounce) package
       caramels
1   cup pecans

Topping

1   stick butter
3   tablespoons cocoa
1   tablespoon vanilla

¼   cup evaporated milk
1   (16-ounce) package
       confectioners' sugar

Preheat oven to 350 degrees. Grease and flour a 9x13-inch pan. To the cake mix, add butter, ½ can of condensed milk, oil and eggs and mix well. Pour ½ of the batter into the prepared pan. Bake 15 minutes and set aside. Melt caramels with the remaining ½ can of condensed milk in the microwave, about 2 minutes. Stir in pecans and pour over partially baked cake. Add the rest of the cake batter and bake 35 minutes. To make the topping, melt butter and add cocoa, vanilla, evaporated milk and sugar. Mix well and spread over cake.

"Love is like a butterfly, hold it too tight, it'll crush, hold it too loose, it'll fly away."

Author unknown

CATHEDRAL ROLLS

1   stick butter
1   (14-ounce) bag silver
    bells

1   cup chopped pecans
1   (10-ounce) bag miniature
    marshmallows

Melt butter and silver bells in a large saucepan over low heat. Remove from heat. Add pecans and marshmallows. Pour onto a 3 foot sheet of heavy duty foil. Roll into a log shape. Wrap foil firmly around roll. Chill 12 hours. Cut into 1-inch slices.

DATE NUT BALLS

2   egg yolks
½   cup sugar
1   stick butter, melted
1   (8-ounce) package
    chopped dates

1½ cups crisped rice cereal
1   cup chopped pecans
    Confectioners' sugar

Mix egg yolks and sugar in a small bowl. Mix in butter and microwave on high 2 to 3 minutes. Add dates and microwave on high 2 to 3 more minutes. Mix well. Add crisped rice cereal and pecans. Mix well. Roll dough into small balls. Roll balls in confectioners' sugar.

Makes 3 dozens

BURNT SUGAR FUDGE

4 **cups sugar**	1 **stick butter**
1 **(12-ounce) can**	2 **tablespoons vanilla**
evaporated milk	2 **cups chopped pecans**

Butter a 9x13-inch pan. Put 1 cup of sugar in a large, heavy saucepan. Cook over medium high heat until it liquefies and is caramel colored. Remove from heat. Add milk. Return to heat. Bring to a boil, stirring constantly. Add remaining sugar, stir and add butter. Cook over medium heat until the soft-ball stage (240 degrees) or test by dropping a small amount into a cup of water to form a soft-ball. Remove from heat. Add vanilla and pecans. Stir until mixture becomes thick. Pour into prepared pan. Score when hot and cut when cool.

Makes to 4 to 5 dozen squares

 Cook fudge until it reaches soft-ball stage. This can be tested by dropping a small amount in a cup of tap water. When it forms a soft-ball the fudge is cooked.

DIVINITY FUDGE

2½ **cups sugar**	**Pinch of salt**
⅔ **cup light corn syrup**	2 **teaspoons vanilla**
½ **cup water**	1 **cup pecans, chopped**
2 **egg whites**	

Butter a shallow baking pan. Set aside. Mix sugar, corn syrup and water in a heavy saucepan. Cook over medium heat until it reaches hard-ball stage (260 degrees) or test by dropping a small amount into a cup of tap water to from a ball. Beat egg whites and salt until stiff. Combine sugar mixture and egg white mixture. Beat with large spoon until it becomes thick. Add vanilla and pecans and continue to stir. When mixture becomes hard to stir, pour in prepared baking pan. Roll out with buttered rolling pin. Cut when cool.

Candy, especially divinity fudge, should not be made in humid or rainy weather.

DREAM FUDGE

2¼ cups sugar
¾ cup evaporated milk
½ stick butter
1 (7-ounce) jar marshmallow creme

1 (6-ounce) bag semisweet chocolate chips
2 cups chopped pecans

Butter a 9x13-inch pan. Set aside. Combine sugar, evaporated milk, butter and marshmallow creme in a heavy saucepan. Bring to a quick boil stirring constantly. When bubbles appear over top, reduce heat to medium. Cook 5 minutes stirring continuously. Remove from heat and stir in chocolate chips and pecans. Pour into prepared pan. Score when hot. Cut into squares when cool.

GRANNY'S FUDGE

1 cup sugar
1 teaspoon cocoa
1 (14-ounce) can condensed milk

½ stick butter
⅛ teaspoon vanilla
1 cup chopped pecans

Butter an 8x8-inch pan. Set aside. Mix sugar and cocoa in a heavy saucepan. Add condensed milk. Cook over medium heat, stirring constantly until soft-ball stage (240 degrees) or test by dropping small amount in a cup of water to form a soft-ball. Add butter, vanilla and pecans. Beat well. Pour into prepared pan. Score when hot. Cut into squares when cool.

LIGHT OPERA FUDGE

2	cups sugar	1	tablespoon light corn syrup
⅛	teaspoon salt	1	teaspoon vanilla
¾	cup heavy cream		
½	cup milk		

Butter an 8x8-inch baking pan. Set aside. Combine sugar, salt, cream, milk and corn syrup in a heavy saucepan. Cook over medium heat until mixture begins to boil. Cook to soft-ball stage (240 degrees). Stir frequently to prevent scorching. Remove from heat. Cool mixture without stirring until lukewarm (110 degrees). Add vanilla and beat until fudge loses gloss. Pour in prepared pan. Score when warm, cut when cool.

PEANUT BUTTER MARSHMALLOW CREME FUDGE

3	cups sugar	1½	cups peanut butter
1	stick margarine	1	(7-ounce) jar marshmallow creme
⅔	cup evaporated milk		
2	tablespoons Nesquik	1	teaspoon vanilla

Butter a 9x13-inch pan. Set aside. In a 3-quart saucepan, combine sugar, margarine, milk and Nesquik. Bring to a rolling boil. Stir constantly. Boil 5 minutes on medium heat or until the soft-ball stage (240 degrees) or test by dropping a small amount of mixture in a cup of water to form a soft-ball. Remove from heat and add peanut butter, marshmallow creme and vanilla. Mix well. Pour into prepared pans. Score when hot. Cut into squares when cool.

PEANUT BUTTER FUDGE

6	cups sugar	2	tablespoons vanilla
2	cups evaporated milk	2	cups peanut butter
2	sticks margarine		

Spray 9x9-inch pan (larger pan if you want it thin). In a large saucepan bring sugar, evaporated milk and margarine to a boil, stirring constantly. Cook until the soft-ball stage (240 degrees) or test by dropping a small amount in a cup of water. Remove from heat. Mix in vanilla and peanut butter. Pour into prepared pan. Cut into squares when cooled.

Score candy when warm and cut when cool.

SWEET POTATO FUDGE

4	cups sugar	2	teaspoons vanilla
1	cup evaporated milk	2	cups chopped pecans
½	stick butter		
1	cup cooked, mashed sweet potatoes		

Butter a 9x13-inch pan and set aside. Combine sugar, milk, butter and potatoes in a heavy saucepan. Cook to firm-ball stage (250 degrees). Remove from heat and add vanilla and pecans. Beat until mixture looses its gloss. Pour into prepared pan. Score when hot, cut when cool.

TRADITIONAL FUDGE

3	cups sugar	1½	cups evaporated milk
⅔	cup unsweetened cocoa	½	stick butter
⅛	teaspoon salt	1	teaspoon vanilla

Butter 9x13-inch pan. Set aside. Mix sugar, cocoa and salt in a heavy saucepan. Add milk and stir well. Cook over medium heat, stirring occasionally, until it reaches the soft-ball stage (240 degrees) or test by dropping a small amount in a cup of water to form a soft-ball. Remove from heat, stir in butter and vanilla. Cool to lukewarm (110 degrees). Beat until fudge loses its gloss. Spread into prepared pan. Cut into squares.

HONEY ROASTED CLUSTERS

1	(11-ounce) package butterscotch morsels	2½	cups honey roasted peanuts
1	(6-ounce) package semisweet chocolate chip morsels		

Melt butterscotch and chocolate morsels in a heavy saucepan on low heat. Remove from heat, add peanuts. Mix well. Drop by teaspoonfuls onto wax paper.

NUTTY NOODLY CLUSTERS

1 (12-ounce) package
butterscotch morsels

1 (5-ounce) can Chow
Mein noodles

¾ cup cocktail peanuts

Melt butterscotch morsels in a heavy saucepan over low heat. Quickly stir in noodles and peanuts until they are evenly coated. Drop by teaspoonfuls onto wax paper. Let dry naturally until hardened.

Makes 24 clusters

Hint: *Can be prepared in the microwave. Watch carefully so as not to burn morsels*

PECAN BRITTLE

1 cup sugar

½ cup light corn syrup

½ cup water

2 cups pecans

1 tablespoon butter

1 teaspoon vanilla

1 heaping teaspoon baking
soda

Place buttered aluminum foil on the counter. In a heavy saucepan, mix sugar, syrup and water and cook to the soft-ball stage (240 degrees) or test by dropping a small amount in a cup of water to form a soft-ball. Add pecans and cook until brown. Remove from heat and add butter, vanilla and baking soda. Stir and pour onto aluminum foil. Roll with buttered jar. Break into pieces after cool.

CRÉOLE PRALINES

2 cups sugar
1 cup dark brown sugar
1 stick butter
1 cup evaporated milk

2 tablespoons light corn syrup
3 cups chopped pecans
½ teaspoon vanilla

Mix sugars, butter, evaporated milk and corn syrup in a saucepan. Cook on medium heat, stirring often, until it reaches soft-ball stage (240 degrees) or test by dropping a small amount in a cup of water to form a soft-ball. Remove from heat and add pecans and vanilla. Stir until it loses its gloss. Drop onto wax paper by tablespoonfuls. Let cool.

Makes 24 pralines

CREAMY PRALINES

3 cups sugar
2 sticks margarine
1 (15-ounce) can evaporated milk

10 large marshmallows
2 teaspoons vanilla
2 cups pecans

Mix sugar, margarine and evaporated milk in a saucepan. Bring to a boil. Cook at moderate heat until the mixture reaches a soft-ball stage (240 degrees) or test by dropping a small amount in a cup of water to form a soft-ball. Cook for 5 more minutes. Turn heat off. Add marshmallows, vanilla and pecans. Beat mixture well. Drop onto wax paper by tablespoonfuls and let cool.

PECAN PRALINES

1   (14-ounce) can
    condensed milk
1   cup sugar

½   stick butter
2   cups pecan halves

Cook milk and sugar in a heavy saucepan over medium heat stirring constantly. When mixture reaches 240 degrees (soft-ball stage) or test by dropping a small amount in a cup of water to form a soft-ball, add butter and stir until melted. Add pecans and stir until coated. Remove from heat. Drop by teaspoonfuls onto wax paper. Allow to cool before removing.

Makes 36 pralines

SPICED PECANS

4   cups sugar
¾   cup light corn syrup
1   cup water

2   teaspoons cinnamon
6   cups pecan halves

Combine sugar, corn syrup and water in a heavy saucepan. Stir until well blended. Cook over medium heat until mixture reaches soft-ball stage (240 degrees). Immediately remove from heat. Add cinnamon and stir until mixture stops bubbling. Add pecans and stir until all pecans are coated and begin to separate from each other. Pour on a cookie sheet and allow to cool completely.

Makes 3 pounds

SUGARED PECANS

| 1 | cup sugar | 2 | teaspoons vanilla |
| 1 | cup water | 2 | cups pecans |

Butter a cookie sheet. Set aside. Bring sugar, water and vanilla to a boil until it starts to crystallize (230 degrees) or test by dropping a small amount in a cup of water to form a soft-ball. Stir to prevent sticking. Add pecans and mix well. Spread on prepared cookie sheet. Break into pieces when cool. Store pecans in an airtight container.

Makes 2 cups

Toast nuts at 350 degrees.
Almonds (whole)   10 minutes
Almonds (slivered)   2 to 3 minutes
Pecans   5 minutes or until you smell them
Walnuts   10 minutes

TOFFEE

1	pound margarine	10	(1.5 ounce) milk chocolate candy bars
2	cups sugar		
½	cup ground pecans	1	cup ground toasted pecans

Butter a 9x13-inch pan. Melt margarine in a saucepan and add sugar and ½ cup pecans. Cook on medium heat until golden brown. Pour into prepared pan and spread out. Layer chocolate bars on the hot mixture. Spread chocolate with a knife. Sprinkle with toasted pecans and break into pieces when cool.

Brown Sugar Squares

2	large eggs	¼	teaspoon salt
2	cups light brown sugar	2	teaspoons vanilla
1	cup flour	2	cups chopped pecans
½	teaspoon baking soda		

Preheat oven to 350 degrees. Grease 9x13-inch pan. Beat eggs and sugar until light and fluffy. Sift flour, baking soda and salt. Add to egg mixture. Add vanilla and stir well. Add pecans and mix thoroughly. Pour into prepared pan. Bake 18 to 20 minutes.

Brownies with Icing

Brownies

2	sticks butter	⅛	teaspoon salt
⅓	cup cocoa	1½	cups pecans
2	cups sugar	2	teaspoons vanilla
1½	cups flour	4	eggs, beaten

Icing

1	stick butter	½	teaspoon almond extract
⅓	cup cocoa	1	(16-ounce) package
⅓	cup milk		confectioners' sugar

Preheat oven to 350 degrees. Grease 9x13-inch pan and set aside. Melt butter and add cocoa. Set aside. Mix sugar, flour, salt and pecans. Blend in vanilla, eggs and cocoa mixture. Pour in prepared pan. Bake 35 minutes. To prepare icing, melt butter, add cocoa. Stir in milk and almond extract. Slowly add sugar beating on low speed until well blended. Spread over cooled brownies.

HOLIDAY COOKIE EXCHANGE

Invite 11 friends and ask each to make 6 dozen cookies of the same kind and 11 copies of the recipe. Make 12 packages with 6 cookies in each package and take to the party. Supply sandwiches and beverages. Each person attending will have 11 packages of different cookies for the holidays and 11 new recipes.

BUTTERFINGER COOKIES

1⅓ **cups flour**
1 **teaspoon baking soda**
¼ **teaspoon salt**
¾ **cup sugar**

⅓ **cup shortening**
1 **egg**
2 **(2-ounce) Butterfinger bars**

Preheat oven to 350 degrees. Grease cookie sheet and set aside. Sift flour, baking soda and salt and set aside. Cream sugar and shortening, add egg and mix well. Add flour mixture to sugar mixture and mix well. Crush Butterfinger bars and stir into dough. Roll into balls and place on prepared cookie sheet, mash slightly with a fork. Bake 12 to 15 minutes until golden brown. Remove with a spatula and place on wire racks or paper towels to cool. Store the cookies in an airtight container.

Makes 2 dozen cookies

CARROT CAKE COOKIES

Cookies

1 stick butter, softened	2 cups flour
1 cup light brown sugar	1 cup chopped pecans
½ cup sugar	1 cup quick cooking oats
2 large eggs	1 teaspoon baking powder
½ cup buttermilk	1 teaspoon cinnamon
1 teaspoon vanilla	½ teaspoon nutmeg
1½ cups grated carrots	¼ teaspoon salt

Cream Cheese Glaze

1 (8-ounce) package cream cheese, softened	½ cup confectioners' sugar
	½ cup milk

Preheat oven to 400 degrees. Line 2 baking sheets with parchment paper. Set aside. In a medium bowl, combine butter and sugars. Beat at medium speed until fluffy. Add eggs, beating well. Add buttermilk and vanilla, beating until blended. Stir in carrots. In a separate bowl, combine flour, pecans, oats, baking powder, cinnamon, nutmeg and salt. Gradually add flour mixture to carrot mixture beating at low speed until blended. Drop by tablespoonfuls onto prepared baking sheets. Bake 10 to 12 minutes or until light brown. Transfer to wire racks and cool completely. To make glaze, combine cream cheese and confectioners' sugar in a medium bowl. Beat at low speed until creamy. Gradually add milk, beating well. Drizzle glaze on cookies.

Makes about 2½ dozen cookies

CHANGO BARS

1	stick butter	1	tablespoon baking powder
1	stick margarine		
2	cups light brown sugar	1	teaspoon salt
3	eggs	2	cups chocolate chips
2⅓	cups flour		

Preheat oven to 350 degrees. Grease a 9x13-inch pan and set aside. Melt butter and margarine. Cream brown sugar and eggs. Add butter and margarine mixture. Combine flour, baking powder and salt. Stir into sugar mixture. Fold in chocolate chips. Pour into prepared pan. Bake 45 to 50 minutes. Cut into bars.

CHEESECAKE COOKIES

Crust

1	cup flour	1	cup chopped pecans
¼	cup brown sugar	1	stick butter, softened

Filling

2	(8-ounce) packages cream cheese	1	teaspoon vanilla
		3	eggs
1	cup sugar		

Topping

2	cups sour cream	1	teaspoon vanilla
6	tablespoons sugar		

Preheat oven to 350 degrees. Grease 9x13-inch glass baking dish and set aside. Mix flour, brown sugar, pecans and butter. Press into prepared baking dish. Bake 10 to 15 minutes until brown. To make filling, mix cream cheese, sugar and vanilla. Add eggs and beat well. Pour over baked crust and bake 20 minutes more. To prepare topping, mix sour cream, sugar and vanilla. Pour over baked filling. Bake 5 minutes more. Cool and place in refrigerator before cutting into squares.

CHOCOLATE CHIP DROP COOKIES

1	stick butter	½	teaspoon salt
½	cup brown sugar	½	teaspoon baking soda
½	cup sugar	½	cup chopped nuts
1	egg	½	cup semisweet chocolate chips
½	teaspoon vanilla		
1	cup plus 2 tablespoons sifted flour		

Preheat oven to 375 degrees. Grease cookie sheet and set aside. Cream butter and sugars. Add egg and vanilla and mix well. Sift flour, salt and baking soda. Add to egg mixture. Mix in nuts and chocolate chips. Drop by teaspoonfuls 2 inches apart onto prepared cookie sheet. Bake approximately 10 minutes.

ULTIMATE CHOCOLATE CHIP COOKIE

¾	cup butter flavored solid shortening	1¾	cups flour
1¼	cups brown sugar	1	teaspoon salt
2	tablespoons milk	¾	teaspoon baking soda
1	tablespoon vanilla	1	cup chopped pecans
1	egg	1	cup semisweet chocolate chips

Preheat oven to 375 degrees. Butter cookie sheet and set aside. In a large bowl, cream shortening, sugar, milk and vanilla. Blend until creamy. Blend in egg. Combine flour, salt and baking soda. Add to creamed mixture gradually. Stir in pecans and chips. Drop by tablespoonfuls 2 to 3 inches apart on prepared cookie sheet. Bake 8 to 10 minutes.

Makes 3 dozen 3-inch cookies

DISH PAN COOKIES

2 cups brown sugar	2 teaspoons baking soda
2 cups sugar	1 teaspoon salt
1 pound butter or 2 cups vegetable oil	2 cups coconut
	1½ cups quick oatmeal
4 eggs	4 cups corn flakes
2 teaspoons vanilla	1 cup chopped pecans
4 cups flour	1 cup chocolate chips

Preheat oven to 325 degrees. Butter cookie sheet and set aside. Cream sugars and butter. Beat until creamy. Add eggs and mix well. Stir in vanilla. Combine flour, baking soda, salt, coconut, oatmeal, corn flakes, pecans and chocolate chips. Gradually stir mixture into butter and egg mixture until thoroughly blended. Drop by teaspoonfuls onto prepared cookie sheet. Bake 8 to 10 minutes.

Makes about 10 dozen cookies

FRENCH LACE COOKIES

1 stick butter	1 cup chopped pecans
1 cup sugar	1 tablespoon vanilla
1 egg	1 teaspoon flour
1 cup instant oatmeal	

Preheat oven to 325 degrees. Cover cookie sheet with aluminum foil and set aside. Beat butter, sugar and egg. Add oatmeal, pecans, vanilla and flour. Mix well. Drop by ½ teaspoonfuls onto cookie sheet. Bake 8 to 10 minutes or until golden brown. Allow cookies to cool completely before removing from cookie sheet.

Grease knife before cutting dried fruit. After cutting 1 cup of the fruit, grease the knife again.

FRUIT CAKE LIZZIES

1 stick butter	1 teaspoon nutmeg
1½ cups brown sugar	1 teaspoon allspice
4 eggs	½ teaspoon salt
2 tablespoons evaporated milk	1 pound candied cherries, chopped
½ cup whiskey	1 pound candied pineapple, chopped
3 teaspoons baking soda	1 pound golden raisins
3 cups flour	1 pound dark raisins
1 teaspoon cloves	2 quarts chopped pecans
1 teaspoon cinnamon	

Preheat oven to 325 degrees. Grease cookie sheet and set aside. Cream butter and sugar. Add eggs one at a time beating well. Add milk and whiskey. Sift baking soda, flour, cloves, cinnamon, nutmeg, allspice and salt into mixture. Add fruit and pecans and mix well. Drop by teaspoonfuls onto prepared cookie sheet. Bake 15 to 20 minutes.

NOTHING COOKIES

2   sticks butter
¼   cup confectioners' sugar
2   cups flour
1½ teaspoons baking powder
½   teaspoon salt
1   tablespoon vanilla
1   cup chopped toasted
    pecans

Preheat oven to 375 degrees. Grease cookie sheet and set aside. Cream butter and sugar. Sift flour, baking powder and salt. Add flour mixture slowly to butter mixture. Add vanilla and nuts. Chill dough slightly. Roll dough into 1-inch balls and place on prepared cookie sheet. Mash with fork. Bake until golden brown.

Makes 5 to 6 dozen cookies

Hint: *Sprinkle with confectioners' sugar, if desired.*

OATMEAL COOKIES

1   cup brown sugar
½   cup solid shortening
1   egg
½   teaspoon baking powder
½   teaspoon baking soda
¼   teaspoon salt
1   teaspoon vanilla
1   cup flour
1   cup oatmeal
½   cup chopped pecans

Preheat oven to 350 degrees. Butter cookie sheet and set aside. Beat sugar and shortening together until smooth. Continue beating and add egg, baking powder, soda, salt and vanilla. Mix in flour and oatmeal. Stir in pecans. Drop by teaspoonfuls onto prepared cookie sheet. Bake 12 to 15 minutes.

Makes 3 dozen cookies

SOUTHERN OATMEAL COOKIES

1	pound butter	2	teaspoons baking soda
2	(16-ounces) boxes dark brown sugar	2	teaspoons salt
4	eggs	1	(6-ounce) box golden raisins
2	teaspoons vanilla	4	cups chopped pecans
⅓	cup molasses	6	cups oatmeal
3	cups flour		

Cut butter into small pieces and place in a large bowl. Add brown sugar, eggs, vanilla and molasses and mix with an electric mixer. Sift flour, baking soda and salt into the bowl. Add in separately and mix raisins, pecans and oats. Mixture will be very thick. Divide into six equal balls, roll each ball into a shape similar to that of slice-and-bake cookies and wrap in plastic wrap. Store in zip lock bags in freezer until ready to bake. Cut each roll into exactly 12 cookies and bake (frozen) at 350 degrees 13 minutes. Cookies will not look done, but will harden when cool. Remove cookies from sheet promptly or cookies will stick.

Makes 72 large cookies

Use a 1 or 2-quart measuring cup to mix batters that you will need to pour into muffin tins, small cups or pans. This allows you to easily pour the ingredients into the small container from the same bowl in which you mixed the ingredients.

PEANUT BUTTER COOKIES

½ cup creamy peanut butter

1 stick butter

½ cup sugar

½ cup brown sugar

1 egg

½ teaspoon baking soda

½ teaspoon baking powder

½ teaspoon vanilla

1¼ cups flour

Preheat oven to 375 degrees. Butter baking sheet and set aside. In a large bowl beat peanut butter and butter until creamy. Add sugars, egg, baking soda, baking powder and vanilla. Beat until well blended. Stir in flour and mix thoroughly. Form mixture into 1-inch balls and place 2 inches apart on prepared baking sheet. Dip a fork into flour and flatten balls into a crisscross pattern. Bake 8 to 10 minutes or until light brown around edges. Remove and cool on wire rack.

Makes about 3 dozen cookies

PECAN COOKIES

3 egg whites

⅛ teaspoon salt

2 cups brown sugar

2 teaspoons flour

1 teaspoon vanilla

2 cups chopped pecans

Preheat oven to 350 degrees. Grease cookie sheet and set aside. Beat egg whites and salt until stiff. Add sugar, flour, vanilla and pecans. Mix well. Drop by teaspoonfuls onto prepared cookie sheet. Bake 10 to 12 minutes.

PECAN KISSES

1	egg white	¼	teaspoon salt
1	cup brown sugar	1½	cups chopped pecans

Preheat oven to 275 degrees. Grease and flour cookie sheet and set aside. Beat egg white until stiff but not dry. Add sugar and continue beating until well blended. Add salt and pecans. Drop by teaspoonfuls onto prepared cookie sheet. Bake 25 minutes until brown.

PECAN PIE FINGERS

Crust

2	cups flour	2	sticks butter, chilled
½	cup confectioners' sugar		

Pecan Filling

1	(14-ounce) can condensed milk	1	teaspoon vanilla
		1	cup almond brickle
1	egg	1	cup chopped pecans

Preheat oven to 350 degrees. Grease a 9x13-inch baking pan and set aside. Combine flour and sugar in bowl and mix well. Cut in butter until crumbly. Pat crumb mixture over the bottom of prepared baking pan and bake 15 minutes. Set aside. Maintain oven temperature. To make filling, beat condensed milk, egg and vanilla in a mixing bowl until blended. Stir in brickle and pecans. Spread the pecan mixture over the baked layer and bake 25 minutes. Cool in the pan 10 minutes. Chill covered in refrigerator. Cut into bars.

PECAN PRALINE COOKIES

Cookie

1   stick butter, softened
1½ cups light brown sugar
1   large egg
1   teaspoon vanilla

1⅔ cups flour
1½ teaspoons baking powder
½   teaspoon salt

Icing

1   cup light brown sugar
½   cup whipping cream

1   cup confectioners' sugar
1   cup whole pecans

Preheat oven to 350 degrees. Grease baking sheet and set aside. In a large bowl beat butter and sugar until fluffy. Beat in egg and vanilla. In separate bowl, mix flour, baking powder and salt. Mix into butter mixture and blend thoroughly. Form teaspoonfuls of dough into balls and place 2 inches apart on prepared baking sheet. Bake 10 to 12 minutes until lightly brown. Cool on baking sheet 10 minutes and remove to cool completely on wire rack. To prepare icing, in a small saucepan over medium heat, mix sugar and cream and bring to a boil. Cook and stir 2 minutes. Remove from heat and mix in confectioners' sugar and stir until smooth. Dip bottoms of pecans into icing and place 2 onto each cookie. Drizzle tops with icing.

Makes 3 dozen cookies

PRALINES 'N CRACKERS

4½ dozen club crackers
3 sticks butter

2 cups chopped pecans
1 cup sugar

Preheat oven to 350 degrees. Place the crackers on an 11x16-inch cookie pan. In a saucepan combine butter, pecans and sugar. Cook until it comes to a full boil. Pour mixture over crackers. Bake 10 minutes. Cool and separate.

PUMPKIN BARS

Cake

4 eggs
1⅔ cups sugar
1 cup vegetable oil
1 (16-ounce) can pumpkin
2 cups flour

2 teaspoons baking powder
2 teaspoons cinnamon
1 teaspoon salt
1 teaspoon baking soda

Cream Cheese Frosting

1 (3-ounce) package cream cheese
1 stick butter

1 teaspoon vanilla
2 cups sifted confectioners' sugar

Preheat oven to 350 degrees. In mixing bowl, beat together eggs, sugar, oil and pumpkin until light and fluffy. Mix flour, baking powder, cinnamon, salt and baking soda. Add to pumpkin mixture and mix thoroughly. Spread batter in 10x15-inch baking pan. Bake 25 to 30 minutes. Cool. To make frosting, mix cream cheese and butter. Stir in vanilla. Add confectioners' sugar and beat until smooth. Spread on cooled cake.

Hint: *Cover with chopped pecans if desired.*

TEA COOKIES

Cookies

¾ cup shortening
1 cup sugar
2 eggs
1 teaspoon almond extract

½ teaspoon salt
1 teaspoon baking powder
2½ cups flour

Frosting

3 tablespoons milk
3 cups confectioners' sugar

1 teaspoon almond extract
Food coloring

Lightly grease baking sheet and set aside. Cream shortening and add sugar. Beat until fluffy. Add eggs and almond extract, mix well. Combine salt, baking powder and flour in separate bowl. Add to sugar and egg mixture, mixing well. Divide dough in half and chill at least 1 hour. Roll half of dough to ¼-inch thickness on a lightly floured surface. Keep remaining dough chilled. Cut dough with cookie cutter. Place on prepared baking sheet. Bake in a 350 degree oven for 8 minutes or until edges are lightly browned. Cool cookies on a wire rack. Repeat with remaining dough. To make frosting, mix milk, sugar and almond extract until smooth and thin enough to spread. Add food coloring, blend together and use to frost cookies.

"The little caterpillar dreamed that it could fly and waking from a long, long sleep discovered it was a butterfly."

Author unknown

WHITE CHOCOLATE CHUNK COOKIES

1 stick butter	½ teaspoon salt
½ cup shortening	2 teaspoons vanilla
¾ cup sugar	10 ounces white chocolate, chopped
½ cup brown sugar	
1 egg	½ cup chopped macadamia nuts, lightly toasted
1 teaspoon baking soda	
1¾ cups flour	

Cream butter and shortening, gradually adding sugars. Beat well at medium speed. Add egg. Beat well. Combine soda, flour and salt and add to creamed mixture. Stir in vanilla. Stir in chocolate and nuts. Chill dough 1 hour. Lightly grease cookie sheet. Heat oven to 350 degrees. Drop by tablespoonfuls 3 inches apart onto prepared cookie sheet. Bake 12 to 14 minutes. Cookies will be soft. Cool slightly and remove to wire racks to cool completely.

Makes 1½ dozen cookies

Use a pizza cutter to cut fudge or any square candy or cookie. Butter the edges of the cutter before using and it will slide easily through the candy or cookies.

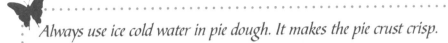

Always use ice cold water in pie dough. It makes the pie crust crisp.

BASIC PIE CRUST

3	cups flour	1	cup solid shortening
1	teaspoon salt	1	scant cup water, ice cold

Preheat oven to 400 degrees. Combine flour and salt. Cut shortening into flour mixture with pastry blender until the mixture resembles a coarse meal. Make a well in the center and pour water into the hole. Stir with a fork until mixture holds together. Do not over mix. Form into 2 balls and wrap in waxed paper. Refrigerate about 1 hour. Roll out on flour-covered surface and place in a pie pan. Press pie crust in pan and prick around sides and bottom of pie crust to prevent pie crust from rising up, causing crust to shrink. For single crust, flute with fingers or tines of fork and bake 15 to 20 minutes or according to pie directions. For a two crust pie, follow instructions for filled pie and seal second crust by tucking top crust under the rim of the bottom crust and flute. Pierce top of crust in several places to allow steam to escape while pie is baking. Bake according to instructions for each pie.

GRAHAM CRACKER PIE CRUST

3	tablespoons sugar	6	tablespoons butter, melted
1¼	cups graham cracker crumbs	1	egg yolk, beaten

Preheat oven to 350 degrees. Combine sugar and crumbs in a medium sized bowl. Stir in butter, mix thoroughly. Press firmly into 9-inch pie pan bringing crumbs evenly up to rim. Brush with egg yolk and bake 8 to 10 minutes. Cool, chill and fill.

SWEET DOUGH PIE SHELL

¾ **stick butter**
½ **cup sugar**
¼ **cup milk**
1 **egg, beaten**

½ **teaspoon vanilla**
2½ **cups flour**
1 **teaspoon baking powder**

Butter two 9-inch pie pans and set aside. Cream butter and sugar, stir in milk, egg and vanilla, and blend thoroughly. Sift flour and baking powder into a large bowl. Make a well in center of the flour and pour in sugar mixture. Working from the center, blend with a fork the sugar mixture into the flour until dough can be kneaded with hands. Cover and refrigerate at least 2 hours. Divide dough in half and roll on a floured pastry cloth. Place dough in two 9-inch pie pans. Trim and crimp edges.

Makes 2 pie shells

Hint: *Use for custard, blackberry or fruit pies*

MERINGUE

3 **egg whites**
½ **teaspoon cream of tartar**

⅔ **cup sugar**

Preheat oven to 350 degrees. Beat egg whites until foamy. Add cream of tartar and continue beating on high speed, gradually adding sugar until stiff peaks form. Spoon meringue over pie filling and bake until light golden brown.

WHIPPED CREAM

1   (8-ounce) container   2   tablespoons sugar
    whipping cream

Place bowl and beaters in freezer at least 1 hour. Be sure
that both are completely chilled. Whip cream at medium
speed until it becomes slightly thick. Gradually add sugar and
continue beating. Do not over beat or you will make butter.

*A teaspoon of sugar added to the pie crust ingredients makes
the pie crust darker.*

APPLE PIE

¾   cup sugar   6   cups sliced apples
¼   cup brown sugar   1   tablespoon lemon juice
1   tablespoon cornstarch   1   tablespoon butter
1   teaspoon cinnamon   2   (9-inch) pie shells

Preheat oven to 425 degrees. Mix sugars, cornstarch and
cinnamon, toss with apples and lemon juice. Place in pie shell
and dot with butter. Cover with top shell, seal and flute edges.
Cut slits in top. Bake 50 minutes until brown.

BANANA DREAM PIE

Crust

1	(12-ounce) box vanilla wafers
1	stick butter, melted

Filling

¾	cup sugar	2	cups milk
⅓	cup flour	2	teaspoons vanilla
2	eggs	3	bananas, sliced
4	egg yolks		

Meringue

4	egg whites	⅔	cup sugar
½	teaspoon cream of tartar	½	teaspoon vanilla

Preheat oven to 350 degrees. Crush half of the vanilla wafers to make crumbs. Stir the crumbs and butter until blended. Press into a 9-inch pie plate and up sides to form a pie crust. Bake 10 to 12 minutes or until light brown. Set aside to cool. In a heavy saucepan, beat sugar, flour, eggs, egg yolks and milk with a wire whisk. Cook over medium to low heat, stirring constantly, until mixture becomes thick. Remove from heat. Add vanilla. Arrange the bananas in the prepared pie crust and spread ½ of the filling over bananas. Spread remaining vanilla wafers over pudding then pour remaining pudding over vanilla wafers. For meringue beat egg whites until foamy, add cream of tartar. Continue beating while gradually adding sugar until stiff peaks form. Add vanilla and mix well. Spread over pie filling and bake 10 to 15 minutes until golden brown. Cool 1 hour before placing in refrigerator. Chill at least 4 hours before serving.

To patch a pie crust, brush area with water before rolling broken pieces of dough together.

BLACKBERRY PIE

1	cup sugar	4	cups blackberries
5	tablespoons flour	2	(9-inch) pie shells
½	teaspoon cinnamon	1½	tablespoons butter

Preheat oven to 425 degrees. Mix sugar, flour, cinnamon and blackberries in a bowl. Pour into pie shell. Dot the top of mixture with butter. Cover with the top shell, seal and flute the edges. Make slits in top shell. Bake 35 to 40 minutes.

BLUEBERRY PIE

4	cups blueberries, fresh	¼	cup flour
2	teaspoons lemon juice, fresh	½	teaspoon cinnamon
1½	cups sugar	2	(9-inch) pie shells
1	teaspoon grated lemon zest	2	tablespoons butter, unsalted

Preheat oven to 450 degrees. Place blueberries in a large bowl and sprinkle with lemon juice. In a separate bowl, combine sugar, lemon zest, flour and cinnamon. Sprinkle sugar mixture on the blueberries. Toss berries gently, until mixture is evenly distributed. Pour into pie shell. Dot mixture with butter. Cover with top shell, seal and flute edges. Cut slits in top shell. Bake 10 minutes, decrease the oven temperature to 350 degrees and bake 30 to 40 minutes until golden brown.

CHOCOLATE CREAM PIE

Pie

1 (9-inch) pie shell	2 tablespoons cocoa
4 egg yolks	⅛ teaspoon salt
1⅛ cups sugar	1 cup half-and-half
½ stick butter, melted	1 teaspoon vanilla

Meringue

4 egg whites	½ cup sugar

Preheat oven to 325 degrees. Bake pie shell according to directions on package and set aside. Beat egg yolks. Add sugar, butter, cocoa, salt and half-and-half. Cook in top of double boiler until thick. Cool and add vanilla. Pour in pie crust. For meringue beat egg whites until stiff, adding sugar while beating. Spread meringue over pie. Bake 12 to 18 minutes or until golden brown.

CRUSTY COCONUT PIE

1¼ cups flaked coconut	3 tablespoons flour
½ cup milk	3 eggs
½ stick butter	1 teaspoon vanilla
1 cup sugar	1 (9-inch) pie shell

Preheat oven to 350 degrees. Lightly toast coconut. Pour milk over coconut and blend. Set aside. Beat butter and sugar until light and fluffy. Add flour and mix thoroughly. Blend in eggs, vanilla and coconut mixture. Pour into pie shell. Bake 30 minutes until firm and golden brown.

COCONUT CREAM PIE

Pie

1	(9-inch) pie shell	3	egg yolks
¾	cup sugar	1	(3-ounce) can coconut
¼	cup cornstarch	1	teaspoon vanilla
⅛	teaspoon salt	1	teaspoon butter
2	cups milk		

Meringue

3	egg whites	⅔	cup sugar
¼	teaspoon cream of tartar		

Preheat oven to 325 degrees. Bake pie shell according to directions and set aside. Mix sugar, cornstarch and salt in a saucepan. Stir well. Add ½ cup milk. Add yolks one at a time beating after each one. Add remaining milk and coconut. Stir. Cook over medium heat until mixture thickens. Cook 5 minutes more, stirring constantly. Remove from heat, add vanilla and butter. Cool. Pour into pie crust. For meringue beat egg whites until foamy, add cream of tartar and gradually add sugar beating until soft peaks form. Spread on top of pie. Bake 15 to 20 minutes.

CRACKER PIE

6	egg whites	1½ cups chopped pecans	
2	cups sugar	Whipped topping	
2	sleeves Ritz crackers, crushed		

Preheat oven to 325 degrees. Grease 9x13-inch pan. Beat egg whites, add sugar and beat until thick. Fold in crackers and pecans. Spread in prepared pan. Bake 30 minutes. Cool, top with whipped topping and chill.

IMPOSSIBLE PIE

½	cup baking mix	1	(3-ounce) can coconut
½	cup sugar	1	teaspoon vanilla
4	eggs	3	tablespoons butter
2	cups milk		

Preheat oven to 400 degrees. Place all ingredients in mixing bowl and blend well. Pour into greased 9-inch pie pan. Bake 35 to 40 minutes or until knife inserted in center comes out clean.

LEMON PIE

Pie

1	(9-inch) pie shell	3	egg yolks, beaten
1⅓	cups sugar	⅓	cup lemon juice, fresh
6	tablespoons cornstarch	2	tablespoons butter
⅛	teaspoon salt	2	teaspoons grated lemon zest
1¼	cups boiling water		

Meringue

3	egg whites	1	(7-ounce) jar marshmallow crème
⅛	teaspoon salt		

Preheat oven to 350 degrees. Bake pie shell according to directions on package and set aside. Combine sugar, cornstarch and salt in saucepan, gradually add water. Bring to a boil, stirring constantly. Cook 1 minute or until mixture is clear and thickened. Stir small amount of hot mixture into beaten egg yolks, return this to hot mixture. Cook over medium heat 3 minutes, stirring constantly. Stir in lemon juice, butter and lemon zest. Pour into pie crust. For meringue beat egg whites and salt until soft peaks form. Gradually add marshmallow crème, beating until stiff peaks form. Spread over filling and to edge of crust to seal. Bake 12 to 15 minutes or until golden brown.

CREAMY LEMON PIE

3   egg yolks
1   (14-ounce) can
      condensed milk
½   cup lemon juice

1   (9-inch) graham cracker
      crust
1   (8-ounce) whipped
      topping

Preheat oven to 325 degrees. In a medium bowl, beat egg yolks with milk and lemon juice. Pour into pie crust. Bake 30 minutes, cool and refrigerate to chill. Top with whipped topping. Refrigerate leftovers

Hint: *Regular pie crust can be substituted.*

SOUR CREAM LEMON PIE

1   (9-inch) pie shell
1   cup sugar
3½ tablespoons cornstarch
1   tablespoon grated lemon
      zest
½   cup lemon juice, fresh

3   egg yolks, slightly beaten
1   cup milk
½   stick butter
1   cup sour cream
1   cup whipped topping
    Lemon twists for garnish

Preheat oven to 325 degrees. Bake pie shell according to directions on package and set aside. Combine sugar, cornstarch, lemon zest, lemon juice, egg yolks and milk in a heavy saucepan. Cook over medium heat until thick. Stir in butter and cool mixture to room temperature. Stir in sour cream and pour filling into pie crust. Cover with whipped topping and garnish with lemon twists. Refrigerate

MILLIONAIRE PIES

2 graham cracker pie crusts

1 (29-ounce) can sliced peaches

1 (20-ounce) can crushed pineapple

1 (12-ounce) container whipped topping

1 (14-ounce) can condensed milk

½ cup lemon juice, fresh

¼ cup chopped pecans (optional)

Preheat oven to 350 degrees. Toast crusts slightly. Thoroughly drain peaches and pineapple. Mix whipped topping, milk and lemon juice until thick. Add peaches and pineapple, mix well. Pour into crusts and top with chopped pecans. Chill before serving.

Makes 2 pies

ALL-IN-ONE PECAN PIE

¾ cup pecans

3 egg whites

1 cup sugar

11 graham crackers, 22 halves

1 teaspoon baking powder

1 (8-ounce) whipped topping

Preheat oven to 325 degrees. Grease the bottom only of a 9-inch pie pan and set aside. Toast and finely chop pecans, set aside. Beat egg whites stiff but not dry. Slowly fold in sugar. Roll crackers into fine crumbs and add baking powder. Fold the crackers into the egg mixture and add pecans. Pour this into the prepared pie pan. Bake 25 minutes or until golden brown. Cool and top with whipped topping.

Serves 8

BOURBON PECAN PIE

½ stick butter, melted
1 cup sugar
3 eggs, slightly beaten
¼ teaspoon salt
¾ cup corn syrup, light
2 tablespoons bourbon

1 teaspoon vanilla
1 cup chopped pecans
1 cup chocolate chips, semisweet
1 (9-inch) pie shell

Preheat oven to 375 degrees. Cream butter, sugar and eggs. Add salt, syrup, bourbon and vanilla. Mix until well blended. Spread pecans and chips on bottom of pie shell. Pour filling over pecans and chips. Bake 40 to 50 minutes.

LOUISIANA SWEET POTATO PIE

Pie

3 sweet potatoes
6 tablespoons sugar
⅛ teaspoon salt
⅛ teaspoon cinnamon

2 medium eggs
¾ cup evaporated milk
1 tablespoon butter, melted
1 (9-inch) pie shell

Pecan Topping

4 tablespoons brown sugar
2 tablespoons flour
3 tablespoons pecan pieces

2 tablespoons butter, melted

Preheat oven to 375 degrees. Peel potatoes and boil until tender. Drain and mix in sugar, salt and cinnamon until smooth. Blend eggs and milk and stir into the potato mixture. Stir in butter and pour into pie shell. For topping blend brown sugar, flour and pecan pieces. Add butter and rub ingredients together with hands. Sprinkle over top of pie filling. Bake 45 to 55 minutes.

HARVEST PECAN PIE

3 tablespoons butter	1 cup corn syrup, dark
1 cup sugar	1 cup pecans
3 eggs	1 teaspoon vanilla
1½ tablespoons flour	1 (9-inch) pie shell

Preheat oven to 450 degrees. Cream butter and sugar. Mix in eggs, flour, syrup, pecans and vanilla. Pour into pie shell. Bake 10 minutes, then lower temperature to 350 degrees and bake 1 hour.

SATIN PIE

Pie

1 cup peanut butter, creamy	2 teaspoons vanilla
2 cups sugar	1½ cups whipping cream, heavy
2 (8-ounce) packages cream cheese, softened	2 graham cracker pie crusts
2 tablespoons butter, melted	

Topping

3 (1.5-ounce) chocolate candy bars	2 tablespoons evaporated milk

Beat peanut butter, sugar, cream cheese, butter and vanilla in a large bowl with an electric mixer until smooth and creamy. In a separate bowl beat whipping cream until soft peaks form. Fold into peanut butter mixture. Spoon into the pie crusts. Refrigerate 6 hours. For topping melt chocolate bars with milk over low heat. Spread over fillings. Refrigerate until firm.

Makes 2 pies

STRAWBERRY PIE

1   deep pie shell
1½ cups water
2   cups sugar
¼   cup cornstarch
1   (3-ounce) box strawberry
      gelatin

½   teaspoon salt
1   quart fresh strawberries
1   cup whipped topping

Preheat oven to 325 degrees. Bake pie shell according to directions and set aside. Combine water, sugar, cornstarch and gelatin in a saucepan. Bring to a boil. Stir and cool. Add salt. Slice strawberries and place in the pie crust. Pour gelatin mixture over strawberries. Refrigerate to set. Top with whipped topping.

Serves 8

CUSTARD PIE

"Tarte à la bouillie"

⅔   cup cornstarch
1¼ cups sugar
1   quart milk
5   egg yolks, beaten

1   (12-ounce) can
      evaporated milk
1½ teaspoons vanilla
2   sweet dough pie shells

Preheat oven to 350 degrees. In a saucepan combine cornstarch, sugar and ½ cup of the milk. When mixture is dissolved stir in remaining milk, egg yolks and evaporated milk. Cook over medium to low heat, stirring constantly, until pudding consistency. Remove from heat. Add vanilla. Cool slightly. Pour equal amounts into pie shell. Crisscross top with narrow strips of dough. Bake 25 minutes or until brown.

Hint: *Sweet dough recipe preceding pie section. Use leftover dough to make crisscross strips.*

BANANAS FOSTER

6	tablespoons dark brown sugar	2	ounces banana liqueur
½	stick butter	¼	cup dark rum
3	ripe bananas, sliced	½	teaspoon cinnamon
			Vanilla ice cream

In a heavy skillet over low heat, melt sugar and butter. Add bananas and liqueur. Cook until bananas soften and are well glazed. Add rum and flame. Sprinkle with cinnamon and quickly spoon over hard ice cream.

CHESS SQUARES

1	box yellow cake mix	1	(8-ounce) package cream cheese
1	stick butter, melted	1	(16-ounce) box confectioners' sugar
3	eggs		

Preheat oven to 350 degrees. Grease 9x13-inch pan. Set aside. In a large bowl mix cake mix, melted butter and 1 egg. Spread mixture into prepared pan. In a large bowl blend 2 eggs, cream cheese and powdered sugar with electric mixer. Reserve a small amount of confectioners' sugar for the top of the dessert. Spread on top of first layer. Bake 35 to 40 minutes or until golden brown. Let cool. Sprinkle with extra confectioners' sugar. Cut into squares.

BLACKBERRY COBBLER

1	stick butter, melted	1	cup flour
2	tablespoons flour	1	cup sugar
1½	cups sugar	1¼	cups milk
½	cup water	1	teaspoon vanilla
3	cups blackberries		

Preheat oven to 400 degrees. Pour butter into a 1½-quart casserole dish. Mix 2 tablespoons flour, 1½ cups sugar and water. Add berries and pour over melted butter. Mix remaining flour and sugar. Add milk and vanilla. Mix thoroughly. Pour over berry mixture. Bake 25 to 30 minutes or until golden brown.

PEACH COBBLER

2	(29-ounce) cans sliced peaches	2	cups buttermilk baking mix
1	tablespoon cornstarch	1½	cups sugar
½	teaspoon cinnamon	1	cup milk
1	stick butter		

Preheat oven to 350 degrees. Drain peaches, reserving juice. Mix cornstarch and cinnamon. Add juice slowly and mix well to dissolve lumps. Cook over low heat until thickened. Set aside. Melt butter in a 9x13-inch baking dish. Pour peaches over butter. Put in cinnamon mixture. Combine baking mix, sugar and milk. Pour this mixture over cinnamon and peaches. Bake 35 to 40 minutes or until golden brown.

LEMON CURD

2	teaspoons grated lemon zest	½	cup fresh lemon juice
1½	cups sugar	¼	teaspoon salt
5	egg yolks	1	stick unsalted butter, melted

Combine zest and sugar in food processor. Pulse to mince and process until fine. Add egg yolks, lemon juice and salt. Process 10 seconds. Add butter while processor is running. Transfer mixture to double boiler. Cook over low heat until thickened. Cool and refrigerate.

Makes 3 cups

Hint: *Use as dip with cubed pound cake.*

COOKED CUSTARD ICE CREAM

4	eggs	½	pint cream
2	cups sugar	¼	teaspoon salt
1½	quarts milk	1	teaspoon vanilla
1	(12-ounce) can evaporated milk		

Beat eggs. Add sugar and milk. Heat to boiling, stirring constantly. Set aside to cool. When cool, add evaporated milk, cream, salt and vanilla. Mix well. Pour custard into an electric ice cream freezer or hand-crank freezer.

Makes 1 gallon

Hint: *For peach ice cream add extra sugar and 1 dozen peaches. You may also add bananas or strawberries.*

OLD-FASHIONED CUSTARD ICE CREAM

1 (14-ounce) can condensed milk	2 cups sugar
1½ cups evaporated milk	4 tablespoons flour
1 quart milk	½ teaspoon salt
8 eggs, separated	1 tablespoon vanilla

Combine all milks in a 3-quart saucepan. Heat to boiling. Remove from heat. Set aside. In a mixing bowl, combine egg yolks, sugar, flour, salt and vanilla. Cream well. Set aside. Stir in ½ cup milk mixture into egg mixture. Reheat remaining milk mixture. Slowly pour egg mixture into milk mixture and heat to boiling. Remove from heat. Set aside. Beat egg whites until stiff and fold into custard. Cool custard before placing into ice cream freezer. Follow recommended directions for freezing.

Makes 1 gallon

Hint: *Fruit can be added to cooked mixture after it cools.*

JELLY ROLLS

5 eggs, separated	1 cup flour
1 cup sugar	1 teaspoon vanilla
3 tablespoons milk	½ cup confectioners' sugar

Preheat oven to 350 degrees. Line cookie sheet with parchment paper or wax paper and grease. Beat egg yolks and sugar until light and clear. Add milk, flour and vanilla. Beat egg whites until stiff but not dry. Gently fold sugar mixture into egg whites. Pour into prepared cookie sheet. Bake 15 minutes. Spread with favorite filling. Roll up on pastry cloth that has been dusted with confectioners' sugar. Place seam side down and slice when cool.

CRACKER PUDDING

Pudding

1 sleeve unsalted crackers (40)	½ cup water
6 egg yolks	¼ cup cornstarch
1⅓ cups sugar	2 tablespoons vanilla
3 (10-ounce) cans evaporated milk	¾ cup butter

Meringue

6 egg whites	½ teaspoon cream of tartar
½ cup sugar	

Preheat oven to 350 degrees. Break crackers into large pieces and place in 9x13-inch casserole dish. Set aside. In a large saucepan, mix egg yolks with sugar and stir until creamy. Add milk and cook 5 minutes. Turn heat to medium. Cook until sugar is dissolved. Combine water and cornstarch and mix well. Pour into sugar mixture. Cook 10 to 15 minutes, stirring constantly, until mixture begins to thicken. Add vanilla and butter. Stir. Pour over crackers and allow to cool. To make meringue, beat egg whites, gradually adding sugar and cream of tartar. When egg whites form stiff peaks spoon over top of cracker mixture. Bake 10 to 12 minutes or until meringue is golden brown.

Hint: *Reserve some of the pudding (before adding crackers) to top pudding when serving.*

"Butterflies are like flowers thrown into the sky, lighting our world with wonder and color."

Author unknown

BREAD PUDDING

Bread Pudding

10 slices white bread, broken into pieces
4 egg yolks
2 cups milk

1 (12-ounce) can evaporated milk
1¼ cups sugar
1½ teaspoons vanilla
¼ cup butter, melted

Meringue

4 egg whites
½ teaspoon cream of tartar

¾ cup sugar
½ teaspoon vanilla

Custard

3 cups milk
1 (12-ounce) can evaporated milk
1 cup sugar

⅓ cup cornstarch
½ stick butter, not margarine
1 teaspoon vanilla

Preheat oven to 350 degrees. Grease 9x13-inch baking pan. Place bread in large bowl. In a separate bowl, combine egg yolks, milk and evaporated milk. Add sugar and stir well. Add vanilla and butter. Mix with wire whisk and pour over bread. Mix thoroughly making sure bread absorbs milk mixture. Pour into prepared baking pan and bake 1 hour or until firm. To make meringue, place egg whites in a clean, dry bowl (free from oil or water). Beat until fluffy, but not dry. Add cream of tartar and blend. Continue beating and gradually add sugar, beating until stiff peaks form. Add vanilla and blend well. Spread over baked bread pudding. Return to oven 15 to 20 minutes or until golden brown. To make custard, place milks in a heavy saucepan over medium heat. Heat until milk is almost scalded. Mix sugar and cornstarch. Pour some of the milk into the mixture to form a light

continued next page

Bread Pudding *continued*

paste, making sure all lumps are dissolved. Add more milk until watery and pour into hot milk. Stir constantly until thickened, making sure mixture does not stick to bottom of saucepan. Add butter and vanilla. Continue stirring until butter is melted. Custard is spooned over bread pudding when served.

Bread pudding makes 12 to 15 servings, and custard makes about 1 quart

CHOCOLATE PUDDING PIE

Pie

2 **(9-inch) pie shells**	3 **(12-ounce) cans**
4 **tablespoons flour**	**evaporated milk**
2 **tablespoons cornstarch**	2 **cups milk**
1½ **cups sugar**	8 **egg yolks, beaten**
4½ **tablespoons cocoa**	4 **teaspoons vanilla**
½ **teaspoon salt**	

Meringue

8 **egg whites**	1½ **cups sugar**
1 **teaspoon cream of tartar**	

Preheat oven to 350 degrees. Bake pie shells and set aside. Mix flour, cornstarch, sugar, cocoa and salt in a saucepan. Combine both milks and egg yolks. Mix well. Add to dry ingredients, stirring while adding. Cook on medium heat, stirring frequently until thick. Remove from heat, stir in vanilla. Pour into pie crusts and cool. To make meringue beat egg whites until soft peaks form. Add cream of tartar. Continue beating, gradually adding sugar. Beat until stiff peaks form. Spoon on pies. Bake until golden brown.

OLD-FASHIONED BANANA PUDDING

Pudding

¾ cup sugar	2 tablespoons butter
⅓ cup flour	½ teaspoon vanilla
Dash of salt	Vanilla wafers
2 cups whole milk	4-5 medium very ripe
4 large egg yolks, slightly beaten	bananas

Meringue

4 egg whites	½ teaspoon cream of tartar
½ teaspoon vanilla	¾ cup sugar

Preheat oven to 375 degrees. Combine sugar, flour and salt in the top of a double boiler. Mix well. Add milk and egg yolks. Stir until well blended. Cook, stirring constantly over boiling water until mixture is very thick. Remove from heat. Add butter and vanilla. Blend well. Cover the bottom of a 2-quart casserole dish with vanilla wafers. Slice half the bananas over wafers. Pour half custard over the bananas and wafers. Repeat with remaining wafers, bananas and custard. To make meringue, beat egg whites until foamy. Add vanilla and cream of tartar. Continue beating, gradually adding sugar. Beat until stiff peaks form. Spoon over custard. Bake until golden brown.

Cream of tartar is best known in our kitchens for helping stabilize and give more volume to beaten egg whites. It can also be used to clean brass and copper cookware.

Rice Pudding

"Riz au lait"

2	quarts milk	4	cups cooked rice
4	egg yolks	1½	cups sugar
2	tablespoons cornstarch	2	teaspoons vanilla

Scald milk in a saucepan. Set aside. Beat egg yolks and gradually stir in 1 cup of the hot milk. Mix in cornstarch stirring constantly. Slowly pour egg mixture into saucepan of milk. Add rice and sugar. Stir well. Cover, reduce heat to medium low. Cook 20 to 25 minutes, stirring frequently, until thickened. Remove from heat. Stir in vanilla. Pour into a serving bowl. Cool before refrigerating.

Fresh Peach Surprise

8	peaches	¼	teaspoon salt
1	cup flour	½	teaspoon cinnamon
1	cup sugar	1	stick butter

Preheat oven to 375 degrees. Generously butter an 8x8x2-inch baking dish. Peel and slice peaches and place in prepared dish. Sift flour, sugar, salt and cinnamon into a mixing bowl. Cut butter into flour mixture with a pastry blender or two knives. Mixture should be coarse. Sprinkle mixture evenly over peaches. Bake 45 to 50 minutes or until top is golden brown and peaches are tender.

LOUISIANA LAND SLIDE

Crust
1 cup flour
1 stick butter, melted

1 cup pecans, toasted and chopped

First Layer
1 cup sifted confectioners' sugar
1 (8-ounce) cream cheese, softened

1 (8-ounce) whipped topping

Second Layer
1 (3-ounce) chocolate pudding, instant
1 (3-ounce) vanilla pudding, instant

Additional whipped topping

Preheat oven to 350 degrees. Mix flour, butter and pecans. Press into a greased 9x13-inch pan. Bake 20 minutes. Cool. To prepare first layer, cream sugar and cream cheese. Fold in whipped topping. Spread over cooled crust. To prepare second layer, prepare chocolate pudding according to directions on box. Pour over cream cheese layer. Prepare vanilla pudding according to directions on box and pour over chocolate layer. Top with whipped topping.

"The butterfly counts not months but moments, and has time enough."

Damien Hirst

PEACH PECAN PRINCESS

2	(29-ounce) cans sliced peaches	1	teaspoon lemon juice
3	tablespoons cornstarch	1	(18-ounce) box butter cake mix
3	tablespoons sugar	1	stick butter, melted
½	cup water	1	cup chopped pecans
½	teaspoon cinnamon		

Preheat oven to 350 degrees. Drain peaches, reserving juice. Mix cornstarch, sugar, water and cinnamon in heavy saucepan. Make sure that all lumps are dissolved. Stir in juice from peaches. Cook over medium heat until thickened. Add lemon juice. Stir and add peaches. Pour into 9x13-inch baking dish. Shake cake mix over the peach mixture. Drizzle butter over the dry mix. Sprinkle pecans over casserole. Bake 45 to 50 minutes.

Cinnamon comes from the bark of a small evergreen tree. It is widely used as a spice and gets its flavor from the aromatic essential oil which is contained in the bark.

Blueberry Sauce

½ cup sugar	¼ teaspoon nutmeg
1 tablespoon cornstarch	½ cup water
½ teaspoon cinnamon	1 pint blueberries

In a medium saucepan, combine sugar, cornstarch, cinnamon, nutmeg and water. Cook over medium heat and stir until thick. Stir in blueberries and continue cooking until well heated.

Praline Sauce

¼ cup dark brown sugar	½ cup heavy cream
4 tablespoons butter	½ cup chopped pecans

Heat sugar and butter, stirring until smooth. Whisk in cream. Bring to a boil. While whisking boil about 5 minutes until sugar barely begins to caramelize. Add chopped pecans. If too thick add a little cream. Pour warm over ice cream or cake.

Strawberry Soup

1 cup strawberries, crushed	1 quart half-and-half
1 cup sugar	1 teaspoon fresh lemon juice
1 cup sour cream	

Beat strawberries, sugar and sour cream at low speed in a mixing bowl until well mixed. Stir in half-and-half and lemon juice. Chill covered until ready to serve.

Makes 4 to 6 servings

Chocolate Syrup

2   cups sugar
1   tablespoon light corn
    syrup
½   cup cocoa

1   cup whipping cream
1   teaspoon vanilla
2   tablespoons butter

Combine sugar, syrup, cocoa and cream in a medium saucepan. Bring to a boil and boil 2 minutes. Remove from heat, add vanilla and butter.

Strawberry Cheesecake Trifle

2   pints fresh strawberries,
    sliced
1   cup sugar, divided
2   (8-ounce) packages
    cream cheese, softened
3   tablespoons orange juice
3   cups whipping cream,
    whipped

1   (10-ounce) loaf pound
    cake
3   (1-ounce) squares
    semisweet chocolate,
    grated
Chocolate curls and
    additional strawberries,
    optional

In a bowl toss strawberries with ½ cup sugar and set aside. In a mixing bowl beat cream cheese, orange juice and remaining sugar until smooth. Gently fold in the whipped cream and set aside. Drain strawberries, reserving juice. Set aside. Cut cake into ½-inch cubes. Gently toss cake cubes with reserved juice. Place ½ of cake in a 4-quart trifle bowl. Top with ⅓ cream cheese mixture, ½ of strawberries and ½ of grated chocolate. Repeat layers. Top with remaining cream cheese mixture. Garnish with chocolate curls and strawberries if desired. Cover and refrigerate at least 4 hours.

Serves 14 to 16

SHOW PUDDING

Shell

½ pound cake cut in finger size strips

Meringue

2 envelopes (4 teaspoons) unflavored gelatin

½ cup cold water

4 egg whites

8 tablespoons sugar

1 tablespoon cream of tartar

Custard

½ cup sugar

Pinch salt

1 tablespoon cornstarch

4 egg yolks

2 cups milk

1 teaspoon vanilla

½ pint heavy cream

2 tablespoons sugar

½ cup chopped nuts, toasted

To make shell, line a deep dish pie plate with pound cake strips. To make meringue, dissolve gelatin in cold water. Set aside. Beat egg whites until soft peaks form. Add cream of tartar. Gradually add sugar. Beat until stiff peaks form. Add gelatin mixture and blend thoroughly. Let set about 5 minutes and pour over cake strips. To make custard, mix sugar, salt and cornstarch. Beat egg yolks until thick and lemon colored. Add to sugar mixture. Mix well. Heat milk until very hot, but not boiling. Add to sugar mixture gradually. Cook over medium heat, stirring constantly until thickness of heavy cream. Add vanilla. Cool. Pour over meringue. Whip heavy cream with sugar until light and fluffy. Spread over custard. Sprinkle with chopped pecans. Chill thoroughly before serving.

Company's Coming

Nolia Leblanc

Crawfish Boil

The ancestry of the people of South Louisiana is very diverse. Immigrants from many countries made their way to this beautiful area with its meandering bayous and mystic swamps. In the year 1775, approximately 5000 Acadians were deported from Nova Scotia, many settling in Louisiana.

There was so much vegetation and wildlife they had never seen or heard of before. The skies were filled with ducks and geese. Alligators glided silently through the swamps. A vast variety of fish and game was found in the bayous and marshes of South Louisiana. There was food and game for everyone.

Fishing, trapping and hunting remain a part of everyday life along these bayous and swamps. Many families still make a living off the land and the bayous. Crawfishing is a major industry in this area.

The word "crawfish" is magic in South Louisiana, bringing to mind "a good time for all." Crawfish boiling in a huge pot over an open fire...long tables covered with checkered cloths…potato salad…boiled corn…French bread…washtubs filled with drinks for all…and homemade ice cream for dessert. Invite family, friends, and neighbors, and "laissez les bon temps rouler" (let the good times roll).

Food to Feed 100 Guests

Baked Beans	5 gallons	Milk	6 gallons
Beef	40 pounds	Pies	18 whole
Beverages	6 gallons	Potatoes	40 pounds
Bread	10 loaves	Potato salad	12 quarts
Butter	3 pounds	Rice	8 pounds
Cakes	8 whole	Rolls	200
Chicken	40 pounds	Salad dressing	3 quarts
Coffee	3 pounds	Tomatoes	25 large
Doughnuts	200		
Grits	5 pounds		
Ham	40 pounds		
Ice cream	4 gallons		
Juice	3½ gallons		
Lettuce	20 heads		

Vegetables
canned, corn, beets, beans, etc.
5 (6.8 ounces average) cans
There are 24 (½ cup) servings per can

Buffet Table

Rule: Plates first.

Why: Common sense.

Rule: Main dish next to plate.

Why: You may place meat on the plate with two serving utensils, if necessary, while the plate is still on the table.

Rule: Vegetables and accompanying food follows the main dish.

Why: It's easier to serve with your right hand while holding the plate in your left.

Rule: Forks and napkins at the end of the food.

Why: The fork may be placed on the plate, and a napkin is easy to hold underneath the plate.

Rule: Beverage last.

Why: Your right hand is now free to pick up and carry the beverage.

BREAD PUDDING

Pudding

40	slices bread, broken into pieces
16	egg yolks
2	quarts milk

4	(12-ounce) cans evaporated milk
5	cups sugar
2	sticks butter, melted
1½	tablespoons vanilla

Meringue

16	egg whites, room temperature
2	teaspoons cream of tartar

2⅔	cups sugar
2	teaspoons vanilla

Custard

3	cups milk
1	(12-ounce) can evaporated milk
1	cup sugar

½	cup cornstarch
½	stick butter
1½	teaspoons vanilla

Preheat oven to 350 degrees. Grease roasting pan and set aside. To make pudding, place bread in a large bowl. Whisk together egg yolks, milk and evaporated milk. Add sugar and mix thoroughly. Add butter and vanilla. Stir well. Pour milk mixture over bread. Blend, making sure all of bread absorbs the milk mixture. Pour into prepared roasting pan. Bake 1 hour or until firm. For meringue place egg whites in a clean dry bowl (free of oil and water). Beat with mixer until fluffy, but not dry. Add cream of tartar and mix. Continue beating, gradually adding sugar, until stiff peaks form. Add vanilla and blend well. Spread over baked pudding. Bake 15 to 20 minutes or until golden brown. For custard, heat milk to scalding in a large saucepan. Do not boil. Add evaporated milk. Remove from heat. Mix sugar and cornstarch in bowl. Pour a small amount of hot milk into sugar mixture. Continue adding milk, stirring, until sugar mixture is thin. Stir sugar mixture into remaining hot milk. Cook over medium heat. Stir constantly, to prevent sticking, until desired consistency. Add butter and vanilla. Stir until melted. Serve over scoops of bread pudding.

Serves 50 to 60

Hint: *Custard makes about 1 quart.*

Coleslaw

12 pounds cabbage,
shredded
1 pound carrots, minced
1¼ cups sugar

¼ cup Créole seasoning
2 quarts mayonnaise
1¼ cups vinegar
3 onions, minced

Place cabbage in a large pan. Add carrots and toss thoroughly. Sprinkle with sugar and Créole seasoning. Stir well. Mix mayonnaise, vinegar and onion. Stir until well blended. Pour mayonnaise over cabbage mixture. Toss until completely coated.

Serves about 100

Hint: *Best when prepared ahead and allowed to chill.*

Salad

10 heads lettuce
12 large tomatoes, chopped
4 cucumbers, sliced

1½ quarts salad dressing of
choice

Wash lettuce, drain and break into bite size pieces. Add tomatoes and cucumbers. Toss with salad dressing.

Serves 50 to 60

BRISKET PO BOYS

Brisket

8 briskets
¼ cup Créole seasoning
¼ cup meat tenderizer
¼ cup garlic powder
1 tablespoon black pepper
8 (12-ounce) cans beer,
      room temperature

2 (24-ounce) bottles of
      Italian dressing
10 pounds charcoal
4 (14-ounce) cans beef
      broth

Gravy

8 pounds ground beef
6 pounds onions, chopped
1 bell pepper, chopped
1 rib celery, chopped
4 cloves garlic, minced
6 (8-ounce) cans tomato
      sauce
1 (10-ounce) can cream of
      celery soup

1 (2-ounce) bottle chili
      powder
   Reserved brisket liquid
   Pepper to taste
   Water, if needed
   Cornstarch, if needed
100 po boy breads

Trim fat from briskets. Sprinkle and rub both sides with Créole
seasoning, meat tenderizer, garlic powder and black pepper.
Prick briskets with a fork on both sides. Place in a large covered
plastic container. Pour beer and Italian dressing over briskets.
Cover. Refrigerate overnight. Start charcoal fire. Fire should
be low with lots of smoke. Place briskets on pit. Reserve brisket
liquid and set aside. Smoke slowly for about 3 hours checking
and turning frequently. Preheat oven 225 to 250 degrees.
Remove smoked briskets from pit and place in a large pan.
Pour reserved liquid and broth over briskets. Add enough
water to about ¾-inch from bottom of pan. Bake 2½ hours.
Turn briskets over. Cover. Bake 2 hours more or until tender.

continued next page

Brisket Po Boys *continued*

Remove briskets. Reserve liquid and set aside. For gravy, brown meat. Add onion, bell pepper, celery and garlic. Cover and simmer on low heat until vegetables are wilted. Add tomato sauce, soup, chili powder and reserved liquid. Add pepper to taste. Simmer uncovered 30 minutes. To thicken gravy dilute cornstarch in cold water and stir into gravy. Slice briskets and serve with gravy on po boy bread. Bon appétit.

Serves 100

The most widely accepted story about the "po-boy" is that the sandwich was invented by Benjamin and Clovis Martin, brothers and former streetcar drivers who went on strike in 1929. The brothers took up their cause and made an inexpensive sandwich of gravy and spare bits of roast beef on French bread that they would serve to unemployed workers out of the rear of their restaurant. When the workers would come by to get one, the cry would go up in the kitchen, "Here comes another poor boy!" The name was transferred to the sandwich, eventually becoming "po-boy" in common usage.

POTATO SALAD

"Salade aux pomme de terre"

25	pounds potatoes, peeled and diced	⅓	cup mustard
3	dozen eggs, boiled	1	cup vegetable oil
2	quarts mayonnaise		Salt and pepper to taste

Boil potatoes. Do not overcook. Drain and set aside. Separate the egg yolks from whites. Chop whites. Add to potatoes and stir. Mash yolks with mayonnaise and mustard. Slowly stir in oil. Blend well. Pour mayonnaise mixture over potatoes. Mix until potatoes are coated. Add salt and pepper to taste.

Serves 50

RED BEANS

4	pounds dried red beans	4	pounds smoked sausage, sliced
1	gallon water		
6	medium onions, chopped	1	cup chopped green onions
1	cup bacon drippings		
¼	cup minced garlic	1	cup chopped parsley
2	teaspoons black pepper	1½	tablespoons salt

In a large pot soak beans in water overnight. Drain. Return beans to pot and add water, onion, bacon drippings, garlic and pepper. Bring to a boil. Cook about 30 minutes. Add sausage and reduce heat to medium. Cook until beans are tender, approximately 45 minutes. Stir occasionally. 15 minutes before beans are completely cooked remove 2 cups of beans. Mash beans and return to pot. This makes beans creamy. Add green onions and parsley. Cook 10 minutes more. Salt to taste. Serve over cooked rice.

Serves about 40

WHITE BEANS

6	pounds dried navy beans	2	pounds ham, chopped
2	pounds onions, chopped	2	tablespoons salt
	Water for cooking	1	tablespoon garlic powder

Wash beans and place in a large pot. Add water 3 inches above beans. Bring to a boil. Boil 45 minutes and drain. Return beans to the pot. Add onion and water 1½ inches over beans. Cook 45 minutes. Remove 1 cup of beans. Mash beans and return to pot. This will make beans creamy. Add ham and cook on medium heat until beans are tender and creamy. Stir in salt and garlic powder. Stir often to prevent sticking.

Serves 50 to 60

BALL PARK CHILI

5	pounds ground beef	3	(10-ounce) cans tomatoes with green chilies
2	cups vegetable oil		
2	cups flour	1	(28-ounce) can whole tomatoes, chopped
10	onions, chopped		
1	bell pepper, chopped		Salt and pepper to taste
½	cup minced garlic	1	(5-ounce) jar chili powder
3	(12-ounce) cans tomato paste		
2	(15-ounce) cans tomato sauce		

Brown beef and set aside. Heat oil and add flour, cook over medium heat, stirring until golden brown (roux). Add beef, onion, bell pepper and garlic. Sauté until vegetables are wilted. Cool. Add tomato paste, tomato sauce, tomatoes with chilies and chopped tomatoes. Cook 15 to 20 minutes. Add salt, pepper and chili powder. Cook 3 to 4 hours.

Makes 3 gallons

RICE DRESSING

1	cup vegetable oil	2	bell peppers, chopped
5	pounds ground beef	1	(10-ounce) can diced seasoned tomatoes
2	pounds ground pork		
1	pound chicken gizzards, ground	1	(14-ounce) can chicken broth
	Salt, red pepper and garlic powder to taste	1	(10-ounce) can cream of mushroom soup
2	pounds onions, chopped	5	pounds rice, cooked

Heat oil in a large pot. Add beef, pork and gizzards. Cook until brown. Add salt, pepper and garlic powder. Simmer 20 to 30 minutes over low heat. Add onion, bell pepper and seasoned tomatoes. Simmer 30 minutes. Add broth and soup. Simmer 30 minutes. Remove from heat. Stir in cooked rice blending thoroughly.

Serves 50

Millions of shingle-like, overlapping scales give butterfly wings their color. The smallest butterfly has a wingspan of less than 2mm and the largest a wingspan of 32mm (slightly over 1 foot).

CRAWFISH STEW

1½ quarts canola oil
6 cups flour
6 pounds onions, chopped
2 bell peppers, chopped
½ bunch celery, chopped
1 bulb garlic, minced
2 lemons, rind only

3 bunches green onions, chopped
Water
Créole seasoning to taste
2 bunches parsley, chopped
12 pounds Louisiana crawfish tails

Heat oil. Add flour, cook over medium heat, stirring until dark brown (roux). Add onion, bell pepper and celery. Simmer 20 minutes. Add garlic. Cook 5 to 10 minutes. Add lemon rind and green onions. Cook 5 to 10 minutes. Add enough water to make gravy thick. Add Créole seasoning to taste. Cook 30 to 40 minutes. Add parsley and crawfish. Simmer until tails are tender, about 45 to 60 minutes. Remove lemon rind.

Makes 18 to 20 quarts

Stories handed down from generation to generation tell the history of the crawfish. It is said that when the Acadians left Novia Scotia to come to Louisiana the lobster followed them. The lobster lost its appetite on the long hard journey and shrunk in size. The Acadians named the smaller crustaceans "crawfish."

SHRIMP AND CRAB BISQUE

2 sticks butter
1 cup diced celery
1 cup diced onion
1 cup diced bell peppers
1 tablespoon chopped
    garlic
½ cup finely chopped green
    onions
½ cup parsley flakes
7-8 pounds shrimp, small to
    medium
1 (16-ounce) jar picante
    sauce

2 (14-ounce) cans chicken
    broth
6-8 (15-ounce) cans cream
    style corn
6 pints half-and-half
1 (24-ounce) package
    sliced American cheese
1 (3-ounce) container
    Parmesan cheese
2 pounds crabmeat
2 tablespoons sugar
    Créole seasoning to taste

In a large pot melt butter. Add celery, onion, bell pepper,
garlic, green onions and parsley. Cook until vegetables are
wilted. Add shrimp sautéing until incorporated. Stir in picante
sauce, broth and corn. Reduce heat to low. Gradually stir
in half-and-half. Add cheeses, crabmeat, sugar and Créole
seasoning. Stir. Cook 3 to 4 hours over low heat. Stir frequently.

Serves 30

*Butterfly fossils are rare. The earliest butterfly fossils are from about 130 million
years ago. There are approximately 24,000 species of butterflies.*

Shrimp and Crab Stew

1 gallon vegetable oil	2 (10-ounce) cans cream of mushroom soup
5 pounds flour	
25 pounds onions, diced	1 (14-ounce) bottle ketchup
2 ribs celery, diced	
6 bell peppers, diced	Hot sauce, red pepper and salt to taste
8 (8-ounce) cans tomato sauce	1 (8-ounce) bottle garlic powder
6 (6-ounce) cans mushroom steak sauce	1½ gallons water
4 (10-ounce) cans tomatoes with green chilies	25 pounds shrimp
	10 pounds crabmeat

Heat oil until hot. Add flour, cook over medium heat, and stir until the color of peanut butter (roux). Add onion, celery and bell pepper. Cook until vegetables are wilted. Add tomato sauce, steak sauce, tomatoes with chilies, soup, ketchup, hot sauce, pepper, salt and garlic powder. Mix thoroughly. Add water. Cook 2 hours stirring constantly. Add shrimp. Cook 15 to 20 minutes stirring constantly. Add crabmeat. Cook 15 to 20 minutes stirring constantly. Serve hot over rice.

Makes 14 gallons

"They seemed to come suddenly upon happiness as if they had surprised a butterfly in the winter woods."

Edith Wharton

SEAFOOD GUMBO

2 pints vegetable oil	10 pounds shrimp
2 pounds flour	4 pounds Louisiana crawfish
4 pounds onions, chopped	10 (15-ounce) cans cut okra
1 rib celery, chopped	4-5 quarts water
4 bell peppers, chopped	2 cups ketchup
2 (10-ounce) cans diced tomatoes with green chilies	Salt, garlic powder and red pepper to taste
	6 pounds crabmeat

Heat oil in large stock pot. Add flour, cook over medium heat, stirring until dark brown (roux). Cool 15 to 20 minutes. Add onion, celery, bell pepper and tomatoes with chilies. Cook 30 minutes. Add shrimp, crawfish and okra. Cook 20 minutes. Add water and bring to a boil. Reduce heat. Cook 20 minutes. Add ketchup, salt, garlic powder, pepper and crabmeat. Cook 5 minutes.

Serves 40 to 50

SHRIMP FETTUCCINI

10 sticks butter	7 (12-ounce) packages egg noodles, #43
6 pounds onions, chopped	2 small bunches green onions, chopped
4 bell peppers, chopped	
1 rib celery, chopped	2 tablespoons parsley flakes
10 pounds shrimp	
4 pints half-and-half	Salt, garlic powder and red pepper to taste
6 pounds Jalapeño cheese, cubed	

Melt butter. Add onion, bell pepper and celery. Cook 45 minutes to 1 hour. Add shrimp. Cook 30 minutes. Add half-and-half and bring to a boil. Add cheese and cook until melted. Boil noodles 8 minutes. Drain. Combine noodles with shrimp mixture. Blend thoroughly. Cook 10 minutes. Add green onions, parsley, salt, garlic powder and pepper. Stir.

Serves 60

PORK AND SAUSAGE JAMBALAYA

15 pounds pork, cubed
   Créole seasoning and
   steak seasoning
10 pounds smoked sausage,
   sliced
10 pounds onions, chopped
1 bunch celery, chopped
4 bell peppers, chopped
1 (4-ounce) jar garlic
2 (10-ounce) cans
   tomatoes with green
   chilies

5 ounces Worcestershire
   sauce
2 (2-ounce) boxes onion
   soup
7½ quarts water
   Browning liquid, for
   desired color
20 cups extra long grain rice
   Salt and red pepper to
   taste
   Parsley (optional)

Season pork with Créole and steak seasonings. Refrigerate overnight. In a large pot, cook pork with a little water and cook until very brown. Remove pork. Drain on a paper towel. Set aside. Add sausage with a little water and cook until grease is removed from sausage. Remove sausage and drain. Set aside. Remove excess oil leaving meat drippings. Add onion, celery, bell pepper, garlic and tomatoes with green chilies. Sauté until vegetables are wilted. Add pork, sausage, Worcestershire sauce, soup and water. Add browning liquid if darker color is desired. Bring to a boil. Boil 6 minutes. Add rice, salt and pepper. Stir mixture well to keep from sticking. Return to a boil. Reduce heat to low. Cover. Stir every 7 to 8 minutes. Cook about 40 minutes or until rice is cooked.

Serves 70

Hint: *Mixture must be salty and hot to taste in order to compensate for the rice. 1½ cups water per 1 cup rice. 2½ pounds of meat per 1 pound rice.*

PASTALAYA

5	pounds lean pork, cubed	2	bell peppers, chopped
	Salt, red pepper and garlic powder to taste	1	(10-ounce) can tomatoes with green chilies
1	pint vegetable oil	1	(8-ounce) can tomato sauce
4	pounds pork smoked sausage, sliced	1	cup ketchup
4	pounds boneless chicken, chopped	1	(10-ounce) can cream of mushroom soup
6	pounds onions, chopped	7	quarts water
6	ribs celery, chopped	7	pounds noodles

Season pork with salt, pepper and garlic powder. Heat oil in a large pot. Add pork. Cook 30 minutes. Remove pork. Set aside. Add sausage and chicken. Cook 30 minutes. Remove sausage and chicken. Set aside. Add onion, celery, bell pepper and tomatoes with green chilies. Cook 30 minutes. Add tomato sauce, ketchup and soup. Cook 20 minutes. Stir in pork, sausage and chicken. Cook 20 minutes. Pour water in meat and vegetable mixture. Bring to a boil. Add noodles. Cook 8 to 10 minutes or until noodles are cooked. Stir. Turn off heat.

Serve 50 to 60

Hint: *1 quart of water for every pound of noodles.*

"A butterfly hovers closely and then quickly moves away, swiftly going where so ever her heart may freely say."

Author unknown

FRIED TURKEY

1 (18-pound) turkey	2 gallons peanut oil
1 pint turkey marinade	

Defrost and clean turkey. Remove neck and loose parts from cavity. Discard. Inject all parts of turkey with marinade. Place turkey in a large plastic bag. Refrigerate 2 days. Heat oil in a turkey fryer to 330 degrees. Carefully place turkey in oil. Allow the temperature to drop to 280 degrees. Maintain this temperature for approximately 90 minutes. Cooking is complete when inside of turkey leg is cooked. This is the last place to cook completely.

Hint: *Most marinade comes with an injector. A large garbage bag cut to size can be used to marinate turkey. Cooking time is 5 minutes per pound.*

BOILED CRABS

4 dozen large crabs, washed and iced	5 onions, quartered
3 (1-ounce) bags crab boil	3 ounces hot sauce
1 (4-ounce) bottle liquid crab boil	2 bulbs garlic
2 medium bell peppers, quartered	1½ (26-ounce) boxes salt
	3 ounces red pepper
	6 lemons

Wash and ice crabs. Fill a 70-80 quart boiling pot to ⅓ water capacity. Add bags of crab boil, liquid crab boil, bell pepper, onion, hot sauce and garlic. Bring to a boil. Add crabs. Boil 5 minutes. Turn off heat. Add salt, pepper, juice of lemon and rind. Soak 10 to 15 minutes.

Hint: *Crabs should be iced with shells up and ice on top of crabs.*

BOILED CRAWFISH

1 (45-pound) sack Louisiana crawfish	1 cup Cayenne pepper
6 onions, quartered	2 (26-ounce) boxes salt
1 bell pepper, quartered	1 (2-pound) bag small potatoes
1 bunch celery	6 lemons
2 bulbs garlic, broken into pods	8 ears corn
3 (1-ounce) bags crab boil	2 (5-pound) bags smoked sausage (optional)
1 cup liquid crab boil	
1 (12-ounce) bottle hot sauce	

Wash crawfish. Fill 70-80 quart boiling pot to ⅓ capacity. Add onion, bell pepper, celery, garlic, crab boil bags, crab boil liquid, hot sauce, pepper, salt, sausage and potatoes. Bring to a rolling boil. Add crawfish. Cook 8 minutes. Add corn, lemon juice and rind. Boil 4 minutes. Remove from heat. Soak 20 minutes and taste test. Drain and serve.

"A butterfly lights beside us like a sunbeam and for a brief moment, its glory and beauty belong to our world. But then it flies again, and though we wish it could have stayed ... we feel lucky to have seen it."

Author unknown

CRAB PUPPIES

Oil for sautéing
1½ onions, minced
½ bell pepper, minced
½ cup minced green
   onions,
4 (8-ounce) boxes Jiffy
   cornbread mix
1 (14-ounce) can chicken
   broth

1 tablespoon minced
   garlic
2 pounds crabmeat
   Flour and water for batter
   Corn flour for coating
   Oil for deep frying

Sauté onion, bell pepper and green onions in vegetable oil. Mix cornbread mix and chicken broth together. Add sautéed ingredients and garlic. Add crabmeat. Make oval shapes. Place on cookie sheet and put in freezer for a couple hours. Take out and dredge in batter of flour and water. Coat with corn flour. Deep fry slowly. Pick with fork to check to see if cooked inside.

Makes about 100 puppies

Landry's Seafood Restaurant
Lloyd and Ceola Landry
Highway 70
Pierre Part, Louisiana

"The caterpillar does all the work but the butterfly gets all the publicity."

George Carlin

SHRIMP RÉMOULADE

¾ cup chopped celery

¾ cup chopped scallions (white and green parts)

½ cup chopped curly parsley

1 cup chopped yellow onion

½ cup ketchup

½ cup tomato puree

½ cup Créole mustard

2 tablespoons prepared horseradish

¼ cup red wine vinegar

2 tablespoons Spanish hot paprika

1 tablespoon Worcestershire sauce

½ cup salad oil

4 dozen jumbo (15 count) shrimp, boiled, peeled and chilled

1 small head of iceberg lettuce, washed, dried and cut into thin ribbons

Mince the celery, scallions, parsley and onion in a food processor. Add the ketchup, tomato puree, Créole mustard, horseradish, red wine vinegar, paprika and Worcestershire sauce. Begin processing again and add the oil in a slow drizzle to emulsify. Stop when the mixture is smooth. Chill for 6 to 8 hours or overnight. Correct the seasoning with additional horseradish, if desired, after the ingredients have had the opportunity to marry. In a large bowl, add the sauce to the shrimp and toss gently to coat. Divide the lettuce among 6 chilled salad plates. Divide the shrimp evenly atop the lettuce and serve.

Serves 6

Galatoire's Restaurant
New Orleans, Louisiana

Strawberry Salad

Vinaigrette

1 cup strawberries	2 cups olive oil
1 cup rice vinegar	⅛ teaspoon salt
½ cup honey	⅛ teaspoon pepper

Salad

1 pound fresh spinach	8 ounces goat cheese
Strawberry vinaigrette	32 whole strawberries
1 red onion, shaved	
4 teaspoons shaved almonds	

To make vinaigrette, puree strawberries, vinegar, honey, olive oil, salt and pepper in a blender. To make salad, gently toss 1 cup fresh spinach leaves with 1 teaspoon vinaigrette. Place spinach on a salad plate and top with 1 tablespoon onion, ½ teaspoon almonds, 2 tablespoons goat cheese and 4 strawberries. Drizzle vinaigrette around salad.

Makes 8 servings

Hint: *The vinaigrette will hold for a week. Any fruit can replace the strawberries. Any lettuce may be substituted for the spinach.*

Executive Chef Doyle Orlando
JACMEL INN
Hammond, Louisiana

"Butterflies are self propelled flowers."

R. H. Heinlein

CREAM OF BROCCOLI SOUP

2	quarts chicken broth	1	cup shredded Cheddar cheese
1	pound broccoli, cut into pieces	5	tablespoons Romano cheese
¼	cup prepared roux		Salt and pepper to taste
1	cup heavy cream		

Into a stock pot pour chicken broth and broccoli, and boil slowly 45 minutes. Then add roux and boil 5 minutes. Add cream and cheeses, and allow to melt. Add salt and pepper to taste and simmer for 5 minutes.

Chef Philippe Parolla
À la Cart Foods, Inc.
Paincourtville, Louisiana

BRACIOLINI

1	(⅜-inch thick) large round steak	¼	cup chopped bell pepper
	Pork chops, thin cut, boneless (to cover steak)	¼	cup Parmesan cheese
		¼	cup Italian bread crumbs
¼	cup olive oil	⅛	cup dried mint
¼	cup chopped celery	4	pods garlic, minced
¼	cup chopped onion		Enough olive oil to brown steak

Remove center bone from round steak. Season pork chops. Blend the ¼ cup olive oil, celery, onion, bell pepper, cheese, bread crumbs, mint and garlic. Rub round steak with paste. Layer pork chops over round steak. Rub paste on pork chops. Roll round steak up tightly. Tie with string in 4 places. Brown in olive oil. Cook in your favorite red sauce. Cook about 2 hours. Remove. Slice and serve over angel hair pasta.

Vince's
Vince and Vivian Sotile
Highway 70
Pierre Part, Louisiana

ANGIE'S BAYOU DELIGHT

Topping

Oil to sauté
¼ cup chopped green onions
¼ cup sliced mushrooms
1 clove garlic, minced
¼ cup diced tomatoes
2 ounces smoked sausage
2 ounces dry white wine or chicken broth
1 tablespoon lemon juice
½ pound Louisiana crawfish tails, peeled
1½ sticks melted butter
Créole seasoning to taste

Fish

1 pound catfish fillets

Oil for frying

Lightly oil pan. Add green onions, mushrooms, garlic, tomatoes and sausage. Sauté until tender. Add wine or chicken broth and lemon juice. Bring to a boil. Add crawfish. Cook until liquid is bubbly. Lower heat. Add melted butter. Stir until completely blended. Add Créole seasoning to taste. Keep warm. Fry fish until golden brown. Place warm topping on freshly fried fish. Serve and enjoy.

Angie's on the Bayou
Neal Dugas and Jeff Daigle
Angie Glaviana
Bayouside Golf Course
Napolenoville, Louisiana

BLACKENED CATFISH PAPPADEUX

Pappadeux Sauce

3 tablespoons butter, divided

2 tablespoons thinly sliced green onions, bottoms only

¼ cup thinly sliced button mushrooms

2 tablespoons thinly sliced green onions, tops only

2 tablespoons chopped parsley

¼ cup Louisiana crawfish tail meat, cooked

¼ pound small shrimp, peeled

1 teaspoon paprika

1 teaspoon finely minced garlic

¼ teaspoon white pepper

¼ teaspoon Cayenne pepper

¼ cup concentrated chicken stock

½ cup heavy cream

1 tablespoon all-purpose flour

Catfish

4 (6 to 8-ounce) catfish fillets

½ cup clarified butter

½ cup blackened seasoning

8 tablespoons butter

To make sauce, in a cast iron or other heavy skillet over medium to high heat, add 2 tablespoons butter and green onion bottoms. Sauté 3 minutes. Stir in mushrooms and cook 1 minute. Add green onion tops and parsley. Cook and stir 1 minute. Add crawfish and shrimp and cook 3 minutes. Add paprika, garlic, white pepper, and Cayenne and stir well. Cook 2 minutes. Add stock and cream. Stir well and bring to a boil. Reduce heat to a low simmer and cook 10 minutes, stirring attentively. Mix remaining 1 tablespoon butter with flour to make a blond butter roux. Slowly add flour, a little at a time, until all is blended and mixture begins to thicken. Continue cooking on low simmer 4 minutes, stirring occasionally. Set aside. To prepare catfish, place a cast iron pancake sheet

continued next page

Blackened Catfish *continued*

pan on high heat 10 minutes or until seasoning smokes when tested. Place fillets on a cookie sheet and pat dry. With a pastry brush, brush the top of fillets with clarified butter and sprinkle remaining seasoning on the other side of the fish. Place a dollop of butter onto hot pancake sheet, which will begin to smoke immediately over the heat. Spread butter in a small circle to quickly melt evenly. Place a seasoned fish fillet, skinned side down, onto smoking butter. Repeat the process with remaining butter and fish fillets, cooking each side. For extra crispness, finish fish under broiler 1 to 2 minutes, Serve with ½ cup Pappadeux Sauce.

Makes 4 servings

Prejean's Restaurant
Lafayette, Louisiana

Paprika is a spice made from the grinding of dried sweet red bell peppers. The seasoning is used in many dishes to add color and flavor. The name was derived from the Latin word "piper", for "pepper."

CATFISH ACADIAN

Topping

⅛ teaspoon kosher salt

⅛ teaspoon fresh ground black pepper

⅛ teaspoon granulated garlic

3 tablespoons unsalted butter

8-10 ounces Louisiana crawfish tails

8-10 ounces (60-70 count) Louisiana shrimp

5-8 ounces crab claw meat

2 tablespoons lemon juice

¼ cup heavy cream

Fish

4 (5-7-ounce) catfish fillets

Salt and pepper to taste

1 tablespoon olive oil

Parsley to garnish

To make topping first blend the salt, garlic and black pepper and set aside. In a large skillet melt the butter over medium heat. Add crawfish and shrimp. Stir. Add the blended seasoning. When the shrimp starts to turn pink add the crabmeat and lemon juice. Cook until shrimp are pink, add cream and cook until blended. Approximately 1 minute. Set aside and keep warm. To prepare the fillets, season with salt and pepper to taste. Heat oil. Place fillets in the pan and sauté on medium heat until brown on both sides. Place the cooked fillet in the center of the plate and top with the topping. Garnish with parsley. Enjoy the fruits of your labor.

Serves 4

Chef Nicholas Catlett
Pat's Family Restaurant
Highway 1
Brusly, Louisiana

CRABMEAT AU GRATIN

1 cup diced onion	1 teaspoon salt
1 stalk celery, chopped fine	½ teaspoon red pepper
¼ pound butter	¼ teaspoon black pepper
½ cup all-purpose flour	1 pound white crabmeat
1 can evaporated milk	½ pound Cheddar cheese, grated
2 egg yolks	

Preheat oven to 375 degrees. Grease a casserole dish and set aside. Sauté onion and celery in butter until onion is wilted. Blend flour in well with this mixture. Pour in the milk gradually, stirring constantly. Add egg yolks, salt, red and black pepper. Cook 5 minutes. Turn off heat. Add crabmeat, blend well. Transfer into prepared casserole dish and sprinkle with grated Cheddar cheese. Bake 10 to 15 minutes or until light brown.

Serves 6

Down"Da" Bayou Restaurant
Bryan and Michelle Blanchard
Highway 1
Labadieville, Louisiana

*"Just living is not enough," said the butterfly,"
one must have sunshine, freedom and a little flower."*

Hans Christian Anderson

CRABMEAT CHEESECAKE

Meunière Sauce

2 ounces demi-glace
1 tablespoon lemon juice
4 ounces white wine
1 pound butter, cut into pieces
Salt and pepper to taste

Crust

1 cup Parmesan cheese
1 cup bread crumbs
1 tablespoon Créole seasoning
½ cup melted butter

Cheesecake

1 cup chopped onion
1½ tablespoons minced garlic
1 tablespoon olive oil
1½ pounds cream cheese
4 eggs
½ cup heavy cream
½ cup sliced green onions
1 teaspoon kosher salt
1 teaspoon white pepper
1 cup shredded Fontina cheese
⅓ cup Parmesan cheese
⅓ cup Romano cheese
1 tablespoon lemon juice
1 pound jumbo lump crabmeat

Hollandaise Sauce

4 egg yolks
¼ cup white wine
2 tablespoons lemon juice
1½ teaspoons salt
Dash Cayenne
Dash Tabasco
1 pound butter, melted

To make meunière sauce, in a sauté pan over high heat combine the demi-glacé, lemon juice and white wine. Reduce by ½. Slowly incorporate the butter, one piece at a time, shaking the pan constantly until it is all incorporated. Remove from heat. Season to taste with salt and pepper. Keep warm.

continued on next page

Crabmeat Cheesecake *continued*

To make crust for cheesecake, in a mixing bowl, blend the Parmesan cheese, bread crumbs, Créole seasoning and butter. Line a spring form pan with film and press the crust mixture into the bottom. Set aside. To make the cheesecake filling, sauté the onion and garlic in olive oil until the onion is very soft and is beginning to turn light brown. Set aside. In the food processor, blend the cream cheese. Add the eggs, one at a time waiting until it is fully incorporated before you add the next one. Scrape down the sides and add the heavy cream. Blend 1 more minute. Scrape into a bowl and add the green onions and the remaining cheesecake ingredients. Pour into the prepared pan and bake 1 hour at 325 degrees. Refrigerate 2 hours before slicing. To prepare the hollandaise Sauce, in a small stainless steel bowl, combine the yolks, wine, lemon juice, salt, Cayenne and hot sauce. Place over a pot of boiling water and whisk vigorously. Be careful that your eggs don't scramble. The bowl should not get too hot too fast. Remove it from heat to control the temperature. When the mixture begins to get thick (the whisk pulls a ribbon through it) remove from heat. While whisking, add the melted butter a little at a time waiting until it is incorporated before adding more butter. If the mixture begins to break or gets too thick, add a little hot water. Pour into a squeeze bottle. To serve pour meunière sauce on plate, slice cheesecake and place one slice over meunière sauce. Pour hollandaise sauce over cheesecake.

Ruffino's Italian Restaurant
18811 Highland Road
Baton Rouge, Louisiana

PECAN CRUSTED SOFT-SHELL CRAB

Crab

1 cup ground pecans	½ cup cream or buttermilk
Créole seasoning to taste	10 whole cleaned soft shell crabs
½ cup flour	Oil for deep frying
4 eggs	

Meunière Sauce

2 tablespoons olive oil
2 pats whole butter
4 sweet yellow onions, diced
6 crimini mushrooms, sliced
¼ red bell pepper, roasted and diced
1 green onion, sliced

4 dashes Worcestershire sauce
Créole seasoning to taste
1½ lemons, juice only
½ teaspoon chopped fresh garlic
½ can jumbo lump crabmeat

Grits

4 cups grits, cook according to package
¼ pound grated smoked Dutch cheese, Gouda
1 package Tasso, diced and sautéed

Salt and pepper to taste
1 chicken bouillon cube, melted in 4 tablespoons hot water

In 3 separate bowls, add to bowl #1 the pecans and Créole seasoning, add to bowl #2 flour and Créole seasoning, add to bowl #3 eggs and cream and whisk. Place crab in the flour mixture then into the egg mixture and then into the pecan mixture. Deep fry until crabs float. About 4 minutes. Fry in batches of 2 or 3 and keep hot until needed for service. To prepare sauce, in a medium saucepan, add oil and butter.

continued next page

Pecan Crusted Soft-Shell Crab *continued*

Heat until butter begins to brown and then add the onion, mushrooms, red bell pepper and green onions. Sauté until tender. Add Worcestershire sauce, Créole seasoning, lemon juice, garlic and crabmeat and simmer to let the flavors meld. Keep hot until needed. To prepare grits follow instructions on package and add all other ingredients. On a hot serving plate, add grits. Place a soft-shell crab on top of the grits. Top with meunière sauce. Enjoy!

Chef Scott Varnedoe
Carriage House Restaurant
St Francisville, Louisiana

JUMBO LUMP CRAB CAKES

2 ounces butter	1 cup Panko bread crumbs (Japanese)
1 onion, minced	1 lemon, juice only
1 cup finely chopped celery	½ teaspoon salt
½ cup cream	⅛ teaspoon pepper
1 pound lump crabmeat	1 cup all-purpose flour

Melt butter, add onion and celery cook until translucent. Add cream and reduce mixture on low heat until thick. Fold in crabmeat, bread crumbs, lemon juice, salt and pepper and cool. Form into mini cakes, dust in flour and sauté on each side until lightly browned.

Executive Chef Doyle Orlando
JACMEL INN
Hammond, Louisiana

CRAWFISH AND TASSO ALFREDO

Alfredo Cream Sauce

1   pound butter
2   cups diced yellow onion
2   cups diced green bell peppers
2   cups diced celery
½   tablespoon black pepper
1   teaspoon Cayenne pepper
2   teaspoons granulated garlic

1   tablespoon Créole seasoning
2½ cups all-purpose flour
3   cups chicken stock or broth
5   cups half-and-half
5   cups heavy cream
1   pound shredded Cheddar or Gruyére cheese

Crawfish and Tasso

10 ounces olive or canola oil
1   pound finely shaved and diced tasso
2   pounds peeled Louisiana crawfish tails

20 ounces white wine
    Alfredo Cream Sauce
10 cups cooked pasta
    Grated Parmesan cheese
    Fresh parsley

To make cream sauce, melt butter over medium heat in a six-quart heavy bottom stock pot. Add onion, bell pepper and celery and cook until vegetables are clear. Add dry seasonings and simmer for 2 minutes. Add flour and mix thoroughly. Add chicken stock, half-and-half and heavy cream. Whisk frequently until sauce thickens. Add cheese and whisk until completely incorporated. To prepare crawfish and tasso, in a sauté skillet, heat 2 ounces of olive or canola oil on high heat. Add 2 ounces of tasso and render the tasso for 30 seconds, then add 6 ounces of crawfish to the sauté pan and cook

Crawfish and Tasso Alfredo *continued*

another 30 seconds. Deglaze the pan with 4 ounces of white wine and reduce for 30 seconds. Add 6 ounces of Alfredo Cream Sauce and lower the heat. Stir sauce to blend all the flavors in your skillet. Serve over 8 to 10 ounces of your favorite pasta. Garnish with grated Parmesan cheese and fresh parsley.

Makes 5 servings

Chef Bill Swanz
Blue Dog Café
1211 West Pinhook Rd.
Lafayette, Louisiana

Tasso is a specialty of Cajun cuisine. Tasso is cut from the shoulder butt of the pig. This cut is typically fatty and, because the muscle is constantly used by the animal, has a great deal of flavor. The meat is sliced across the grain and then dredged in a salt cure, which usually includes sugar. The meat is left to cure very briefly, only three or four hours. It is then rinsed, rubbed with a spice mixture which is sure to contain Cayenne pepper and garlic, and hot-smoked until cooked through. Tasso is not typically eaten on its own, but may be found in dishes ranging from pasta to crab cakes, soup to gravy. Appropriate to its roots, tasso is most often found in recipes of Cajun/Créole origin.

CATFISH NOCELLO

Sauce

⅔ cup butter
1 cup brown sugar
1 cup chopped pecans, toasted

3 ounces Nocello or Hazelnut Liqueur
¼ cup heavy whipping cream

Catfish

4 catfish fillets
  Créole seasoning

1 cup flour
2 tablespoons olive oil

To make sauce, combine butter and brown sugar in skillet cook over low heat until blended. Add toasted pecans; simmer on low 2 to 3 minutes. Add Nocello or Hazelnut liqueur carefully as alcohol may flame. Allow alcohol to burn off, this happens by cooking for a few minutes. Right before you are ready to top fish, add the whipping cream until blended and you have achieved a smooth creamy sauce. To prepare the catfish, lightly season four fillets of catfish with your favorite Créole seasoning, then gently dust the fillets in flour. Cover the bottom of a skillet with olive oil. When oil is hot, place fish top side down until golden brown. Flip and sauté about another 3 minutes. Time will vary according to the size of the fish, this time is for an 8-ounce fillet of fish. Place on serving dish or plate and ladle a spoonful of sauce over corner of fillet.

The Inn at Seventy and One
Jamelia Dugas, owner
Highway 1
Paincourtville, Louisiana

CHICKEN AND SAUSAGE JAMBALAYA

5 pounds lean pork, cubed	2 bell peppers, chopped
Salt, red pepper and garlic powder to taste	1 (10-ounce) can tomatoes with green chilies
1 pint vegetable oil	1 (8-ounce) can tomato sauce
4 pounds smoked pork sausage, sliced	1 cup ketchup
4 pounds boneless chicken, chopped	1 (10-ounce) can mushroom soup
6 pounds onions, chopped	4½ quarts water
6 ribs celery, chopped	12 cups rice

Season pork with salt, pepper and garlic powder. Heat oil in a large pot and add pork. Cook 30 minutes. Remove pork and set aside. Add sausage and chicken to pot. Cook 20 minutes. Remove sausage and chicken. Set aside. Add onion, celery and bell pepper, sauté 20 minutes. Stir in tomatoes with green chilies, tomato sauce, ketchup, soup, pork, sausage and chicken. Cook 20 minutes. Add water and bring to a boil. If needed add additional salt, pepper and garlic powder. Add rice. Cook 20 minutes. Reduce heat to low. Cook covered stirring every 5 minutes until rice is cooked.

Serves 50 to 60

Hint: *For every 1 cup of rice use 1½ cups water.*

Jesse Dugas &
"The Cajun Chefs"
Paincourtville, Louisiana

JJ's Meaux Jeaux Pork Medallions

Pork Medallions

6 boneless pork chops (about 1½ pounds total)
¾ cup JJ's Herb Dressing and Marinade
2 tablespoons olive oil
1 cup sliced onion
2 tablespoons dry sherry
1 tablespoon minced garlic
½ cup chopped gold bell pepper
1 teaspoon dried parsley
1 teaspoon lemon pepper
2 teaspoons cornstarch, dissolved in ¼ cup water
¾ cup sliced green onions

Sauce

Juice of 1 lemon
Juice of 1 lime
⅓ cup orange juice
½ cup chicken broth
4 tablespoons salsa
4 tablespoons sweet orange marmalade
2 tablespoons JJ's Herb Dressing and Marinade
1 tablespoon Worcestershire sauce
1 tablespoon dark brown sugar
Orange slice

Rinse pork and place in shallow glass pan. Coat with JJ's Herb Dressing and Marinade. Chill 30 minutes while preparing remaining ingredients. To make sauce combine sauce ingredients in a small glass bowl set aside. To make pork medallions, place a nonstick skillet over medium high heat until hot. Add 2 tablespoons olive oil and 2 tablespoons JJ's Herb Dressing and Marinade, swirling to coat bottom of pan. Add pork chops and brown for 2 minutes on each side remove from pan. Add onion and reduce heat to medium. Sauté until onion is brown on edges. Add sherry and swirl to deglaze pan. Sauté 1 to 2 minutes. Add garlic, bell pepper, parsley and lemon pepper to pan and stir well. Sauté 3 minutes over medium

continued next page

JJ's Meaux Jeaux Pork Medallions *continued*

heat. Return pork chops to pan reduce heat to low. Pour sauce over the chops, cover and simmer 20 minutes, turning chops once. Uncover skillet and stir in cornstarch solution and green onions. Simmer uncovered 5 to 6 minutes, turning chops once. Place pork medallions on platter and top with sauce. Garnish with orange slices.

Serves 6

Chef Johnny "Jambalaya" Percle
Johnny's Bayou Bistreaux
Thibodaux, Louisiana

SEAFOOD GUMBO

¼ **cup flour**	1 **gallon water**
¼ **cup vegetable oil**	5 **bay leaves**
3 **pounds onions, chopped**	2 **tablespoons Tony's**
8 **ounces chopped celery**	**seasoning**
9 **ounces chopped green**	2 **pounds crabmeat**
onions	5 **pounds shrimp**
4 **pounds cooked okra**	

Make light roux with flour and oil. Add onion, celery and green onions. Cook until vegetables are soft. Add okra and cook 5 to 10 minutes. Add water, bay leaves and Tony's seasoning. Cook 1 hour. Add crabmeat and cook 20 minutes. Add shrimp and cook 30 minutes.

Makes about 2 gallons

Too's Seafood and Steak House
Sue Gaudet
Highway 70
Pierre Part, Louisiana

PEPPER LACED PORK ROAST

6 cloves garlic, minced

2 cups sliced green onions

⅛ teaspoon dried thyme

⅛ teaspoon dried basil

1 teaspoon salt

⅛ teaspoon black pepper

1 (5-6 pound) boneless Boston butt

¼ cup sliced Cayenne peppers

¼ cup sliced jalapeño peppers

Salt and black pepper to taste

Louisiana hot sauce to taste

¼ cup vegetable oil

2 cups diced onion

¼ cup diced celery

¼ cup diced bell peppers

¼ cup chopped parsley

1 cup beef stock

Preheat oven to 375 degrees. In a small mixing bowl, combine garlic, green onions, thyme, basil, salt and pepper. Pierce holes through roast and fill each cavity with mixture. Next, stuff peppers into holes, leaving approximately 2 inches of peppers exposed. Season roast with salt, pepper and hot sauce. In a 12-quart cast iron Dutch oven, heat oil over medium high heat. Sear roast in hot oil on all sides. Place onion, celery, bell pepper, parsley and beef stock in Dutch oven. Cover and bake 3½ hours or until tender Add water if necessary during cooking. Reserve broth for serving.

Serves 6

Chef John Folse
Gonzales, Louisiana

SEAFOOD AU GRATIN

½ stick butter
½ large onion, diced
2 pounds shrimp 90/110 count peeled
1 pound Louisiana crawfish tails, peeled
1 pound claw crabmeat
1 pint half-and-half
1 bunch green onions, chopped
4 dashes hot sauce
2 tablespoons parsley
1½ tablespoons onion powder

1½ tablespoons garlic powder
½-1 teaspoon Cayenne pepper
1 teaspoon white pepper
Salt and black pepper to taste
½ pound butter
1¾ cups flour
1 cup shredded Cheddar cheese

Melt ½ stick butter and sauté onion. Add shrimp and sauté till almost done (4 to 5 minutes). Add crawfish and crabmeat and sauté 2 minutes. Add half-and-half. Add green onions, hot sauce, parsley, onion powder, garlic powder, Cayenne pepper, white pepper, salt and black pepper. In a separate pot melt ½ pound butter and stir in flour. Stir constantly for 2 minutes and turn off fire. Bring seafood and half-and-half mixture to a simmer and slowly add small amounts of the roux while stirring. Add roux until desired consistency is reached. Spoon into oven proof serving dishes and sprinkle Cheddar cheese over au gratin. Melt cheese in broiler. Serve with toasted French bread slices.

Chef Kevin Templet
Flanagan's Restaurant
402 West 3rd Street
Thibodaux, Louisiana

BLACKENED SHRIMP WITH PINEAPPLE RUM BUTTER SAUCE

Blackening Spice Mix

¼ cup paprika

¼ cup chili powder

⅛ cup cumin

⅛ cup garlic powder

⅛ cup onion salt

⅛ cup Cayenne pepper

1½ teaspoons ground basil

½ teaspoon nutmeg

1½ teaspoons ground oregano

1½ tablespoons filé

Pineapple Rum Butter Sauce

6 ounces Chablis

16 ounces pineapple juice

½ teaspoon whole thyme

1½ tablespoons minced shallots (green onions)

1 teaspoon black peppercorn

4 bay leaves

⅔ cup heavy cream

1 pound unsalted butter

2 tablespoons rum extract

Blackened Shrimp

20 peeled, butterflied and deveined jumbo shrimp

½ cup oil

Blackening mix

Pineapple Rum Butter Sauce

4 pineapple rings

To make blackening spice mix, mix all ingredients together in a small mixing bowl. Set aside. To make pineapple rum butter sauce, combine Chablis, pineapple juice, thyme, shallots, peppercorn and bay leaves in a 2-quart saucepan. Simmer and reduce to a syrup consistency. Add cream. Simmer and

continued next page

Blackened Shrimp with Pineapple Rum Butter Sauce *continued*

reduce by ½. Cut cold butter into 1-inch cubes. Stir into the creamy base, 2 pieces at a time over medium heat until all butter is melted. Add rum extract. Strain before serving. This sauce can be maintained in a water bath of 120 degrees stirring occasionally. To prepare the blackened shrimp, heat a large black iron skillet until it is very hot! Dredge the shrimp in the blackening seasoning and dip in the oil. Place the shrimp split side down, into the hot skillet. After approximately 30 seconds roll the shrimp onto their sides. After another 30 seconds roll them to their other side. Do not burn! Shrimp size will determine cooking time. The shrimp are cooked when they are no longer clear in the middle. Put the rings of pineapple in the skillet and cook on each side approximately 1 minute. Put approximately 2-ounces of the pineapple rum butter sauce on each plate. Put a pineapple ring in the center of the sauce and surround with the blackened shrimp.

Serves 4

Louisiana Lagniappe Restaurant
Baton Rouge, Louisiana

Many times butterflies can be seen gathering around mud puddles. These are called "puddle clubs" and they gather here to drink the water that is a source of salt and other minerals.

GULF SHRIMP TORTELLINI

4 tablespoons butter
8 shrimp, 26-30 count, cleaned
Salt and pepper to taste
2 ounces mushrooms, sliced
1 tablespoon minced garlic
2 ounces Roma diced tomatoes

2 ounces dry white wine
2 tablespoons lemon juice
1 ounce diced green onions
10 ounces heavy cream
12 ounces Tortellini, cheese filled
½ cup grated Parmesan cheese

In a sauté pan, melt butter. Add shrimp. Sprinkle with salt and pepper. Sauté 2 minutes, then add mushrooms. Sauté 30 seconds then add garlic and tomatoes. Sauté 30 seconds more, not letting garlic burn. Add white wine and lemon juice. Cook 1 more minute. Add green onions and heavy cream. When cream comes to a boil, add the pasta and simmer until cream starts to coat the pasta. Add the Parmesan cheese. Finish reducing the cream and serve.

Makes 1 serving

Executive Chef Kevin Templet
Fremin's Restaurant
402 West 3rd Street
Thibodaux, Louisiana

"The green grass and the happy skies court the fluttering butterflies."

Astrid Alaude

MIKE'S SUPREME

2 cups chopped yellow
   onion
3 tablespoons chicken
   base
¼ teaspoon hot sauce
2 tablespoons yellow
   mustard
5 teaspoons ketchup
4 teaspoons black pepper
2 tablespoons plus 2
   teaspoons garlic salt

½ teaspoon lemon juice
2½ tablespoons
   Worcestershire sauce
2-3 cups cream sherry
2 sticks butter, melted
1 pound (16-20 count)
   shrimp, peeled and
   butterflied

In a large bowl, combine 1 cup onion, chicken base, hot
sauce, mustard, ketchup, black pepper, garlic salt, lemon
juice, Worcestershire sauce and sherry. Stir. Pour butter into a
shallow baking dish. Add seasoned mixture, remaining onion
and shrimp. Broil on high 4 minutes then stir. Broil another 4
minutes or until shrimp are done. Serve with garlic bread.

Mike Anderson's Seafood Restaurant
Highway 30
Gonzales, Louisiana

*"Where have those butterflies all gone that science may
have staked the future on?"*

Robert Frost

SHRIMP LAFOURCHE

2   tablespoons clarified
    butter
20 (40-50 count) shrimp
¼   cup Triple Sec
1   teaspoon Créole
    seasoning
1   teaspoon chopped green
    onions
1   teaspoon chopped
    tomato

½   cup heavy cream
10 ounces angel hair pasta,
    cooked
½   teaspoon chopped
    parsley
2   tablespoons each, diced
    red, yellow and green
    bell peppers
    Coarse black pepper to
    taste

In a saucepan, melt butter, add shrimp and cook 3 minutes.
Pour Triple sec over mixture and flame off alcohol. Add Créole
seasoning, green onions and tomato. Cook 2 minutes. Add
cream, bringing to a boil, add pasta and cook until pasta pulls
from side of pan. Add parsley and peppers. Heat and serve in
large pasta bowl. Garnish with black pepper.

Makes 2 servings

Chef Eric Weil
Café Lafourche
Donaldsonville, Louisiana

SHRIMP SCAMPI

1   pound shrimp, medium
1   stick butter
3   cloves garlic, minced

Green onions to taste
Salt and pepper to taste

Sauté shrimp in butter. Add garlic, green onions, salt and
pepper and cook down. Do not overcook. Pour over angel
hair pasta or serve with French bread.

Politz Restaurant
John and Betty Politz
Highway 1
Thibodaux, Louisiana

BREAD PUDDING WITH RUM SAUCE

Sauce

1   stick butter
1   cup sugar

2   (16-ounce) containers
     whipped topping
6   ounces rum

Pudding

1   cup water, warmed
¼   pound margarine, melted
1   loaf sliced white bread,
     broken in pieces
1   cup evaporated milk

½   teaspoon vanilla
3   eggs, beaten
1   cup sugar

To make sauce, melt butter. Add sugar and mix together in a bowl until sugar is dissolved. Add whipped topping and whip mixture with a wire whisk. Drizzle the rum into the mixture a little at a time. Cover and keep mixture in the freezer until ready to serve. To make the pudding, preheat oven to 350 degrees. Mix in a large bowl the water and margarine. Put broken bread into mixture and stir. Add milk and stir. Add vanilla, eggs and sugar. Stir well. Pour into a 12x16-inch pan and bake 1 hour. Serve warm, topped with rum sauce.

Serves 20

Chef Johnny "Jambalaya" Percle
Johnny's Bayou Bistreau
Thibodaux, Louisiana

WHITE CHOCOLATE BREAD PUDDING

Pudding

1 French bread, stale and cut into ½-inch slices	⅔ cup sugar
3½ cups whipping cream	2 cups white chocolate
⅔ cup milk	2 eggs, whole
	8 egg yolks

Sauce

1 cup whipping cream	1 cup white chocolate

To make pudding; lightly spray the bottom of a 14x18-inch baking pan with a vegetable spray. Put one layer of bread slices in bottom of pan. Heat whipping cream and milk in a pot just until it is ready to boil. Stir in sugar and white chocolate. Turn off heat and continue stirring until white chocolate is melted. Whisk eggs and egg yolks together in a large bowl until smooth. Slowly pour melted mixture into egg mixture, stirring constantly, so as not to let eggs curdle. Continue stirring until well blended. Pour ½ of the mixture over the first layer of bread. Let bread soak up mixture. Add another layer of bread and pour remaining mixture on top. Use your hands to feel bread to make sure it is has soaked up all the mixture and that the center is not dry. Cover with aluminum foil and bake approximately 45 minutes to 1 hour at 375 degrees. The bread pudding is done when the center of the pudding rises. Remove foil and bake about 5 minutes longer. Let bread pudding cool and "set" for about 15 minutes. When ready to serve, cut in squares or scoop out with ice cream scoop. To make sauce, heat whipping cream almost to the boiling point. Turn off fire and whisk in white chocolate until creamy and smooth. Spoon over bread pudding.

Grapevine Café and Gallery
211 Railroad Avenue
Donaldsonville, Louisiana

CHOCOLATE CHESS PIE

2 eggs
1 (14-ounce) can
    condensed milk
1 cup sugar
¼ cup cocoa

½ stick butter, melted
  Dash salt
1 teaspoon vanilla
1 (9-inch) pie shell

Preheat oven to 325 degrees. Mix together eggs, milk, sugar and cocoa. Stir in butter and salt. Stir in vanilla and pour mixture into pie shell. Bake 1 hour.

Beth Rivers
Café by the River
White Castle, Louisiana

LEMON PIE

Crust

1 (16-ounce) box Ritz
    crackers
¼ cup sugar

1 stick butter, melted
  Dash nutmeg

Filling

8 large egg yolks
4 (14-ounce) cans
    condensed milk

1 dozen lemons or limes,
    juice only

Preheat oven to 300 degrees. Crush crackers into very fine crumbs, add sugar, butter and nutmeg. Stir until well blended. Press into a 9x13-inch baking dish to make crust. To make filling, mix egg yolks, milk and lemon or lime juice and pour over crust. Bake 10 minutes, cool and place in refrigerator overnight to chill. Serve with fresh whipped cream and a sprig of mint.

Chef Eric Weil
Café Lafourche
Donaldsonville, Louisiana

LEMON ICE BOX PIE

Crust

1½ sticks butter

2 ounces brown sugar

⅔ teaspoon cinnamon

3 cups graham cracker crumbs

Pie filling

8 egg yolks

3 cans condensed milk

1½ cups lemon juice

Preheat oven to 350 degrees. To make the crust, in a medium saucepan, melt butter and brown sugar whipping until smooth. Mix cinnamon in graham cracker crumbs. Mix brown sugar and butter mixture into graham cracker crumbs. Press into pie pans forming crust. To make the filling, mix egg yolks and milk. Whip 5 minutes. Add lemon juice and whip again. Pour into crust, Bake 15 minutes. Chill well and cut into slices. Top with whipped cream.

Makes 2 pies

Huey's Blues, Beers & Burgers

Downtown
77 South Second Street
Memphis, Tennessee

Midtown
1927 Madison Avenue
Memphis, Tennessee

Lagniappe

Brenda Romero

Lagniappe

Lagniappe - an old Créole word meaning "something extra."

There are many things about Louisiana not known by most people. Louisiana is the number one producer of crawfish in America and also produces 24% of the nation's salt.

The Louisiana Commercial Sugar Cane Industry was founded over 200 years ago in the heart of New Orleans which is now Audubon Park. Two of the remaining operating sugarhouses in Louisiana are in Assumption Parish. Steens's Syrup Mill, located in Abbeville, is the world's largest syrup plant producing sugar cane syrup, and Tabasco, a Louisiana product, holds the second oldest food trademark in the U.S. Patent Office. Louisiana also is home to America's oldest rice mill, located in New Iberia.

In addition to all the good food in Louisiana we also have the birthplace of Jazz, New Orleans. Jazz gave birth to the "Blues" and "Rock and Roll" music. Louisiana's 63.5 million acres of wetlands are the greatest wetland area in America. **Vive la Louisiane!**

KID'S KING CAKES

1 box food coloring,
  assorted colors
1 (16-ounce) container
  vanilla cake icing

1 box honey buns
1 container sugar sprinkles,
  assorted colors

Mix food coloring with icing in 3 separate plastic cups until you get desired colors of green, yellow (gold), and purple. Spread all 3 colors of icing on each honey bun. Sprinkle top with sugar sprinkles. It's carnival time, so eat up!

Hint: *Cream cheese icing can replace the vanilla. Directions on back of food coloring box shows mixing of different colors.*

MUFFIN CONES

24 ice cream cones, flat
   bottoms
1 (18-ounce) box yellow
  cake mix

1 (18-ounce) box butter
  cream frosting
  Food coloring
  Sugar sprinkles

Preheat oven to 350 degrees. Place cones in muffin cups or on a cookie sheet and set aside. Prepare cake mix according to directions on box. Spoon mixture into each cone filling about ⅔ full. Bake about 20 minutes or until a toothpick in the center comes out clean. Cool. Prepare frosting according to directions on box. Color with food coloring. Frost muffins and decorate with sprinkles.

CAKE MIX COOKIES

1 (18-ounce) box yellow or   2 eggs
   white cake mix   ½ cup vegetable oil

Preheat oven to 350 degrees. Grease a cookie sheet and set aside. Mix cake mix, eggs and oil until well blended. Drop by teaspoonfuls onto prepared cookie sheet and bake 8 to 10 minutes.

Hint: *Use 1 cup white or chocolate chips, pecans or raisins for variety.*

CANDY CONES

6 ice cream cones, flat   1 (8-ounce) container
   bottoms   whipped topping
1 cup chopped peanut   Sprinkles
   butter cup candies

Place cones in muffin cups and set aside. Stir candy into the whipped topping and carefully spoon into the cones. Shake sprinkles over each. Serve immediately. Refrigerate or freeze until ready to serve.

Hint: *Use candy of your choice, chocolate bars and various colored sprinkles.*

*"Like a butterfly emerges and unfolds its graceful wings,
a child grows and develops with the love a mother brings."*

Author unkown

CHERRY NUT ROLL

1 (14-ounce) box graham crackers	1 pound pecans, chopped
½ stick butter	1 (15-ounce) box raisins
1 (10-ounce) bag marshmallows	1 (6-ounce) jar cherries

Crush graham crackers. Reserve ¾ cup to coat rolls. Set aside. Melt butter and add marshmallows, stirring until melted. Add pecans, raisins, cherries with juice and graham crackers. Mix until well blended. Shape into rolls. Roll in reserve crumbs to coat. Wrap in waxed paper. Refrigerate. Slice to serve.

DIRT BALLS

1 (1-pound) package Oreo cookies	1 (12-ounce) package chocolate almond bark
1 (8-ounce) package cream cheese	1 (12-ounce) package vanilla almond bark

Crush cookies in food processor. In a large bowl, beat cream cheese with a mixer. Add cookies and mix well. Roll into small balls and place on a cookie sheet. Place in freezer for 15 minutes. Melt almond barks in separate bowls in a microwave about 1 minute. With a spoon dip each ball half in the chocolate and half in the vanilla until completely coated. Place on waxed paper until hardened. Refrigerate.

LADYBUG COOKIES

1 bottle red food coloring
1 (16-ounce) can white cake icing

1 (12-ounce) bag vanilla wafers
1 (6-ounce) bag chocolate chips

Mix food coloring with icing in a small container until icing is a dark red. Spread icing over the cookies. Decorate top with chocolate chips to resemble Ladybug dots. Eat your Ladybugs!

NO-BAKE COOKIES

½ cup light corn syrup
½ cup peanut butter

3 cups crisped rice cereal

Mix corn syrup and peanut butter together. Stir in cereal. Drop with a teaspoon onto waxed paper. Allow to sit until firm.

PECAN ROLLS

1 (14-ounce) can condensed milk

1 (12-ounce) box vanilla wafers, crushed
2 cups chopped pecans

Mix all ingredients. Shape into rolls and wrap in waxed paper. Refrigerate. Slice to serve.

SANTA'S WHISKERS

2	sticks butter, softened	¾	cup finely chopped candied cherries, red and green
1	cup sugar		
1	tablespoon milk	½	cup finely chopped pecans
1	teaspoon vanilla		
2½	cups flour	¾	cup flaked coconut

Preheat oven to 375 degrees. Cream together butter and sugar. Blend in milk and vanilla. Stir in flour, cherries and pecans. Form dough into 8-inch long rolls. Roll in coconut to coat all sides. Wrap in plastic wrap and chill. Cut in ¼-inch thick slices. Bake on a cookie sheet 15 minutes or until edges are golden brown.

. . . .

AFTER-SCHOOL SLUSH

1	cup strawberries or blueberries	1	cup milk
		1	cup yogurt

Put all ingredients in a blender and mix until smooth.

Hint: *Substitute skim milk and frozen strawberries or blueberries and strawberry or blueberry yogurt for variety.*

. . . .

NUTTY BANANA BREAKFAST SHAKE

1	banana, ripe	½	cup yogurt
2	tablespoons peanut butter	1	cup milk

Combine all ingredients in a blender and mix until smooth.

POP ROUGE ICE CREAM

1 (14-ounce) can
condensed milk

2 (12-ounce) cans
strawberry soda

Combine condensed milk and soda. Pour in ice cube trays or container for freezer. Place in the freezer and allow ice crystals to form. Remove from freezer and beat with mixer until ice crystals break and mixture becomes smooth. Return to freezer. Eat when frozen.

CINNAMON ORNAMENTS

¾ cup applesauce

1 (4-ounce) bottle cinnamon

Mix applesauce with cinnamon to form stiff dough. Roll to ¼-inch thickness. Cut with cookie cutters. Make a hole in top of ornament with a skewer or straw. Carefully lay ornaments on rack to dry. Let dry 1 to 2 days or until thoroughly dry, turning occasionally. Hang with decorative ribbon.

Makes 12 to 15

Hint: *May be decorated with decorator's paste.*

WRAP IT UP

1 (8-inch) flour tortilla
2 tablespoons peanut
butter

1 banana

Place tortilla between 2 sheets of paper towels. Microwave for 10 seconds or until soft. Spread with peanut butter and place banana on one end. Wrap and eat.

Popcorn Cake

½	cup popcorn kernels	1	stick butter
4	cups miniature marshmallows	1	cup M&M's

Pop the kernels according to directions on the package and set aside. In a medium pot, melt the marshmallows and butter over low heat, stirring constantly, until smooth. Combine the M&M's with the popcorn. Pour the marshmallow mixture over the popcorn mixture. Mix gently. Spoon into a 9x13-inch pan or a 2-quart oblong dish. Chill. Cut into squares.

Makes about 20

Caramel Popcorn

5	quarts popped popcorn	1	teaspoon salt
2	sticks butter	½	teaspoon baking soda
2	cups brown sugar	1	teaspoon vanilla
½	cup corn syrup		

Preheat oven to 250 degrees. Place popcorn in a large bowl and set aside. In a medium saucepan over medium heat, melt butter. Stir in brown sugar, corn syrup and salt. Bring to a boil stirring constantly. Boil without stirring 4 minutes. Remove from heat. Stir in soda and vanilla. Pour in a thin stream over popcorn, blending to coat. Place in a large baking dish and bake 1 hour stirring every 15 minutes. Remove from oven and let cool completely before breaking into pieces.

CHOCOLATE PEANUT BUTTER SANDWICHES

⅔ **cup sugar**

2 **tablespoons cocoa**

½ **cup evaporated milk**

½ **cup plus 1 tablespoon peanut butter**

4 **slices bread**

Mix sugar and cocoa, stir in milk. Add peanut butter and mix thoroughly. Spread on bread slices for sandwiches. Refrigerate leftover mixture.

HOT DIGGITY DOGS

8 **wieners**

8 **wooden craft sticks**

1 **(12-ounce) container refrigerated biscuits**

¼ **cup salad mustard**

8 **slices American cheese, halved**

Preheat oven to 350 degrees. Grease baking sheet and set aside. Insert a stick in each wiener and set aside. Roll biscuits out on a floured surface, in an oval shape, the length of the wiener. Spread each with mustard. Top each with 2 half slices of cheese and place a wiener in center of each. Fold each, enclosing the wiener. Pinch to seal. Place seam side down on prepared baking sheet and bake 20 to 25 minutes until golden brown.

Hint: *May be made without mustard. Serve mustard, mayonnaise and ketchup on the side.*

Cool Strawberry Cake

Cake

1 (18-ounce) box white cake mix	4 eggs
1 (3-ounce) package strawberry gelatin	1 cup strawberries, chopped
1 cup vegetable oil	1 cup pecans, chopped
½ cup milk	1 cup coconut flakes

Frosting

1½ cups strawberries, mashed	1 (3-ounce) package vanilla instant pudding
1 (8-ounce) container whipped topping	1 teaspoon vanilla
	Strawberries or pecans for garnish

Preheat oven to 350 degrees. Grease and flour three 8 or 9-inch cake pans. Combine cake mix and gelatin in a large bowl. Mix oil and milk. Add eggs, one at a time and mix well after each egg. Fold in strawberries, pecans and coconut. Pour into prepared pans. Bake 30 minutes. Remove from pans and cool. For frosting, mix together strawberries, whipped topping, pudding and vanilla. Spread between cake layers and on top and sides. Garnish with strawberries or pecans. Refrigerate

"If nothing ever changed, there would be no butterflies."

Author unknown

THINK PINK SUGAR COOKIES

Cookies

¾ **cup sugar**

½ **stick unsalted butter,
softened**

1 **egg**

½ **teaspoon vanilla**

3-4 **drops red food coloring**

1½ **cups flour**

1¼ **teaspoons baking powder**

¼ **teaspoon salt**

Icing

½ **cup confectioners' sugar,
sifted**

2 **teaspoons sugar**

1 **tablespoon egg white**

¼ **teaspoon cream of tartar**

2-3 **drops red food coloring**

Cream sugar and butter. Blend in egg, vanilla and food coloring. Beat at medium speed. Stir in flour, baking powder and salt. Wrap dough in plastic wrap and chill at least 3 hours. Preheat oven to 400 degrees. Divide dough in half and roll out on a floured surface to about ⅛-inch thick. Cut shapes with cookie cutters. Bake on a cookie sheet 8 to 10 minutes or until edges are lightly brown. Cool 2 minutes before removing to rack. To make icing, blend sugars, egg white, cream of tartar and food coloring. Beat until thick. Spread icing on cookies.

Makes 3 dozen

COMPANY'S COMING
STRAWBERRY DESSERT

1   (16-ounce) package
    frozen strawberries, in
    syrup
1   (10-ounce) angel food
    cake
1   (8-ounce) package
    cream cheese,
    softened

1   (10-ounce) can
    condensed milk
1   (12-ounce) container
    whipped topping

Set strawberries aside to thaw. Break cake into bite-size pieces
and place in a 9x13-inch dish. Blend cream cheese and milk
until smooth and pour over cake. Spoon the strawberries
evenly over the mixture. Spread on whipped topping.

Serves 10

DIVINE PINK DIVINITY

1   egg white
2   cups sugar
½   cup water
½   cup light corn syrup

1   teaspoon vanilla
1-2 drops red food coloring
½   cup chopped pecans
    (optional)

Beat the egg white in a large bowl until foamy. Set aside. In a
medium saucepan, boil sugar, water and corn syrup. Stir gently
until the mixture forms a soft-ball when dropped into tap water
(235 degrees). Pour over the egg white, beating continually.
Add vanilla. Add enough food coloring to turn mixture pink.
Add pecans and beat until almost hard. Drop by teaspoonfuls
onto waxed paper.

Makes about 35 to 40 candies

Ping Pong Ice Cream

3   bottles strawberry soda
1   (12-ounce) can
   evaporated milk

1   (14-ounce) can
   condensed milk
1   teaspoon vanilla

Combine all ingredients and proceed according to directions on your ice cream maker.

Strawberry Lemonade

1   cup sugar
1   (3-ounce) package
   strawberry gelatin
1   cup hot water

6   cups water
1   cup fresh lemon juice
1   cup sliced strawberries

In a 3-quart pitcher, dissolve sugar and gelatin in hot water. Add 6 cups water, lemon juice and strawberries. Add ice cubes before serving.

Pink Team Punch

1   (20-ounce) can frozen
   orange juice
1   (46-ounce) can
   pineapple juice

1   (2 liter) bottle lemon lime
   soda
1   (1 liter) bottle ginger ale
2-3 drops red food coloring

Mix together orange and pineapple juices until well blended. When ready to serve add soda, ginger ale and food coloring. Stir until blended.

Makes 40 (4-ounce) servings

NECTAR SODA

Syrup

3 cups sugar	4 tablespoons almond extract
6 cups water	2 teaspoons red food coloring
1 (10-ounce) can condensed milk	
4 tablespoons vanilla	

Soda

Nectar syrup	1 liter club soda
1 quart vanilla ice cream	

On low heat dissolve sugar and water. Bring to a boil. Cool. Add condensed milk, vanilla, almond extract and coloring. Stir well. Refrigerate. To make a soda, pour 1-inch of the syrup into a 16-ounce glass. Add 1 scoop of ice cream. Fill with club soda and mix well.

Hint: *May be served with whipped topping and a cherry on top.*

PINK SATIN PUNCH

1 (2 liter) bottle lemon lime soda	1 quart apple juice
1 quart cranberry juice	1 cup sliced strawberries

Fill an ice cube tray with lemon lime soda and freeze. Chill the remaining lemon lime soda, cranberry and apple juices. When ready to serve, pour the soda and juices over the ice cubes and add strawberries.

Serves 30

PINK SUNSET SMOOTHIE

2½ **cups orange juice**
2¼ **cups vanilla ice cream or**
frozen yogurt

1½ **cups frozen strawberry**
sorbet
Fresh strawberries for
garnish

Combine all ingredients in a blender and puree until smooth.
Pour into glasses and garnish with fresh strawberries.

Serves 6

FROZEN PINK SALAD

4-5 **bananas**
1 **lemon, juiced**
1 **(8-ounce) package**
cream cheese
¾ **cup sugar**
1 **(8-ounce) container**
whipped topping

1 **(10-ounce) package**
frozen strawberries
1 **(10-ounce) can**
pineapple, drained
slightly

Slice bananas and toss in lemon juice. Mix cream cheese,
sugar and whipped topping. Add bananas, strawberries and
pineapple. Freeze in a 9x9-inch pan. Remove from freezer 1
hour before serving. Serve on lettuce leaves.

Hint: *Fruit Fresh may be used instead of lemon juice to prevent*
discoloration.

PINK STUFF

1	(8-ounce) container cottage cheese	¼	cup chopped maraschino cherries
1	(3-ounce) package strawberry gelatin	1	(16-ounce) container whipped topping
1	(16-ounce) can crushed pineapple		

Mix cottage cheese and gelatin together until well blended. Stir in pineapple and cherries and add whipped topping. Chill at least 12 hours before serving.

*"When a small child, I thought that success spelled happiness.
I was wrong, happiness is like a butterfly which appears and delights
us for one brief moment, but soon flits away."*

Anna Pavlova

For a water bath, place jars in a canning pot with a rack or a pot large enough to completely immerse the jars. Heat in boiling water for 15 to 20 minutes. This seals the jars.

BLUEBERRY JAM

4   cups crushed blueberries
1   (6-ounce) box pectin
4   cups sugar

2   tablespoons fresh lemon juice

Place berries in a large pot. Add pectin and stir. Cook over high heat bringing to a rolling boil. Add sugar and lemon juice. Stir until dissolved. Bring to a rolling boil that cannot be stirred down. Boil hard for 1 minutes and 15 seconds. Remove from heat and skim with a metal spoon. Pour into sterilized jars to within ¼ inch of the top. Wipe tops and seal with new lids. Process in a water bath at simmering for 10 minutes.

Makes about 7 half pints

MOCK STRAWBERRY JAM

4   (3-ounce) packages
    strawberry gelatin
½   cup water

6   cups sugar
7   cups peeled figs
    Pinch of salt

In a medium saucepan over low heat, dissolve the gelatin in water. Add sugar, figs and salt. Cook 1 hour. Spoon into hot sterile jars and seal.

PEPPER JELLY

⅓   cup chopped hot
    peppers
1⅓ cups chopped bell
    peppers
6   cups sugar

1½ cups apple cider vinegar
1   (6-ounce) box fruit pectin
    Red and green food
    coloring

In a saucepan mix hot pepper, bell pepper, sugar and vinegar. Bring to a full boil. Boil 2 minutes, Remove from heat and allow to cool 5 minutes. Add pectin. Divide into 2 batches. Color one batch red and one batch green. Mix well. Let stand 5 minutes. Stir and pour into eight (8) 4-ounce jars.

Hint: *Makes a great Christmas gift.*

FIG PRESERVES

1   **gallon figs**   1   **quart sugar**

Wash figs and remove stems. Place figs in a large pot and cover with sugar. Bring to a rolling boil. Reduce heat and cook 1 hour. Remove from heat. Cover and cool in order for figs to become plump. Heat again to boiling. Remove from heat and spoon into sterile jars. Wipe rims and cover with sterile lids. Process in a water bath for 20 minutes.

Figs are one of the most perishable fresh fruits. Pick when fully ripe, handle carefully and use quickly because they spoil so readily.

PEAR PRESERVES

8   **cups sliced, peeled and**   3   **cups sugar**
     cored pears   1   **lemon, seeded and sliced**
1   **tablespoon water**   **thin**

Place pears, water and sugar in a large pot. Bring to a boil. Reduce heat, cover and cook on low about 2 hours or until pears are soft. Add lemon slices and cook 1 hour. Spoon into sterile 8-ounce canning jars. Process in a water bath 15 to 30 minutes.

À la Créole – Dishes prepared with tomatoes, green peppers and onions as key ingredients.

À la king – Dishes prepared in a rich cream sauce.

À la mode – Desserts prepared or topped with ice cream

Andouille – A hard, smoked, highly-seasoned pork sausage of Créole origin.

Au gratin – French term meaning a dish prepared with oven-browned topping of bread crumbs and cheese.

Au jus – Served in juice, or natural meat drippings.

Au lait – Made with milk.

Beignets – Créole version of doughnuts. Deep-fried dough sprinkled with confectioners' sugar.

Bisque – A thick gravy containing fish, game or vegetables.

Bon appétit – Good appetite

Bouillon – A clear soup stock made from beef, game or fowl, cooked with seasonings, then strained.

Boulette – Seasoned meatball

Café au lait – Hot black coffee and hot milk in equal proportions.

Canapé – An appetizer

Candied – Cooked in sugar until transparent.

Chevrettes – Shrimp

Chicory – A white root that is dried, roasted and then ground. Combined with coffee for a very distinctive taste.

Cochon de lait – Translated means roast suckling pig. It is roasted over a hickory fire until the outside is blistered and the inside is juicy tender.

Corasse – Fried dough

Court-bouillon – A thick fish stew served over rice.

Crêpes – Thin French pancakes.

Cuisine Créole – A style of preparing food characterized by the use of rice, okra, tomatoes, peppers and high seasonings. Créole cooking

Créole – Used to describe regional products and the people of Acadiana.

Echalote – A bulbous herb whose flavor resembles an onion. Also called green onions, scallions and in Louisiana shallots. The term applies to the green tops as well as the bulb.

Écrévisse – A small fresh water crustacean related to the lobster. Called a crawfish

Étouffée – Method of cooking (fish, shrimp, okra) along with seasonings in its own juices until tender. Cooked over a low flame and tightly covered.

Filé – Dried, ground leaves of the sassafras tree. Sprinkled over gumbo as a seasoning or thickening agent.

Fricassée – Chicken or rabbit cut into small pieces and added to a strong thick sauce.

Gambo (gumbo) – A thick soup, usually containing a variety of seasonings with chicken and seafood. Thickened with okra, roux or filé.

Gâteau de sirop – Syrup Cake

Glacé – To chill, make cold.

Graton – The crisp pork rind that remains after the skin has been rendered lard. Called a crackling.

Grillades – Beef or veal cut into small squares and cooked in rich dark gravy and served over grits or rice.

Gruyère – A cheese made of cow's milk.

Hors d'oeuvres – French appetizers.

Jambalaya – A mixture of any combinations of seafood, meat, poultry, sausage, vegetables and seasonings simmered with raw rice until the liquid is absorbed.

Lagniappe – An old Créole word used for "something extra."

Mirliton – Vegetable that looks like a pale, green squash. Also called vegetable pear or alligator pear.

Mélasse – A by-product of cane sugar. Known as molasses.

Okra A long tapered vegetable pod used in gumbos.

Pain perdu – Lost bread or French toast.

Patate douce – A tropical, trailing plant of the morning glory family. A fleshy, brownish tuber like root used as a vegetable. Yams in Louisiana are a new world plant much like the original sweet potato that was brought from Africa.

Poisson – Fish.

Praline – A candy made with sugar and pecans.

Riz au lait – Rice pudding.

Roux – A mixture of flour and oil (or butter) cooked until it is about the color of peanut butter. The darker the color the stronger the taste. Used for thickening gravies and gumbos.

Sauce Piquante – A thick, sharp-flavored sauce made with roux and tomatoes highly seasoned with herbs and peppers and simmered for hours.

Saucisse – Sausage

Sauté – Cook in a small amount of fat for a short time, stirring frequently.

Tarte à la bouillie – Sweet pie dough filled with a cooked custard filling and baked.

Tortue – Turtle

Vive la Louisiane – Long live Louisiana

Salade aux pomme de terre – Potato salad

PINK TEAM

Aucoin, Marguerite
Aucoin, Sharon
Baker, Kay
Banta, Joy
Barbera, Dawn
Barbera, Lori
Barbier, Bonnie
Barriente, Connie
Bergeron, Cheri
Bird, Terri
Blanchard, Catherine
Blanchard, Faye
Blanchard, Norma
Blanchard, Rhea
Blanchard, Sharon A.
Bouchereau, Brandi N.
Bourg, Shauna
Breaux, Iris C.
Breaux, Jeanette
Breaux, Ruby
Brister, Scottie
Brown, Lou
Carmouche, Marie
Carrier, Pat
Castro, Margo
Castro, Renee
Clement, Barbara
Comeaux, Connie S.
Daigle, Caryn
Daigle, Glenda R.
Daigle, Heidi
Daigle, Janet
Daigle, Jennifer
Daigle, Patsy
Daigle, Paula
David, Laurie
Delhommer, Dawn
Dizney, Karen
Dugas, Dot

Dugas, Gina
Dunn, Amy C.
Esneault, Juanita
Esneault, Shirlene
Falcon, Kristin
Falterman, Toni
Gaudet, Christy
George, Liz
Gonzales, Brigid
Gremillion, Melissa
Gros, Tammy
Guillot, Jane
Harrison, Cheryl
Hebert, Susan
Hock, Tootie
LaFleur, Shirley
Lagrange, Nadine
Landry, Brenda D.
Landry, Darlene
Landry, Dawn
Landry, Donna
Landry, Harriet
Landry, Ida
Landry, Kathy
Landry, Robin
Landry, Rosie
Landry, Tina
Larrison, Sherlyn B.
Latino, Lorie
LeBlanc, Darlene L.
LeBlanc, Phyllys
LeBlanc, Rhonda
Marquette, Cindy
Marquette, Geraldine
Martin, Loretta
Mattingly, Heidi R.
Mayeaux, Patricia
Morales, Chastity
Naquin, Barbara

Newchurch, Martha
Orillion, Cecile
Ourso, Caroline
Rivere, Debbie
Robichaux, Becky
Rowland, Stacie D.
Savoie, Grace
Simoneaux, Jannelle
Smith, Gretchen
St. Germain, Boogie
St. Germain, Karen
St. Germain, Mel
Suarez, Butsy
Talbot, Carolyn
Talbot, Sue
Theriot, Barbara
Thibodeaux, Marcy
Viator, Allison
Vicknair, Tammy
Watson, Erin
Woods, Beryl

FRIENDS

Ackerman, Linda
Adams, Barbara
Adams, Lillie
Alanzo, Peggy
Alleman, A
Alleman, Edna
Antoon, Evelyn
Arvel, Patrice R.
Attuso, Louise
Attuso, Lucien, Jr.
Aucoin, Mae
Badeaux, Scott
Baldwin, Wendy
Banta, Gene
Barbera, Alan
Barbera, Shelia
Barbin, Allison
Barbin, Jeff
Barriente, Deborah
Bass, Judy
Becnel, Frances
Bergeron, Betsy
Bergeron, Bud
Bergeron, Diane
Bergeron, Eva
Bergeron, Jan P.
Bergeron, Sophie
Bessonet, Sera
Billig, Craig
Blanchard, Christy
Blanchard, Donald
Blanchard, Floret
Blanchard, Glenda
Blanchard, Jenny
Blanchard, Marian
Blanchard, Minette
Blanchard, Myrt
Blancq, Terry
Bolotte, Irvin
Bolotte, Sandra
Bouchereau, Ted
Boudreaux, Brenda
Boudreaux, Cynthia

Boudreaux, Geisel
Boudreaux, Leroy
Boudreaux, Linda L.
Brame, Kellie
Breaux, Anne L.
Breaux, Booster
Breaux, Elizabeth
Breaux, Gayle
Breaux, Patsy
Brower, Maxine
Burleigh, Vickie
C F Industries D Shift
Campesi, Shirley
Cancienne, Betsy
Cancienne, Sally
Cardinal, Margaret
Cardwell, Rhoda
Carrier, Andrea
Carter, Odile
Cassard, Mary B.
Catrow, Patricia
Cavalier, Bonnie
Cavalier, Norris
Chachere, Donald, Jr.
Chiasson, Crystal D.
Clause, Margie
Cole, Heather
Cox, Georgiana
Daigle, Cecile S.
Daigle, Dodi
Daigle, Gloria
Daigle, J. Wilfred Jr.
Davis, Frank
Day, Mary Ellen
Dell, Val
Disterfano, Lucille L.
Dowing, Lana
Dugas, Carmen
Dugas, Donna
Dugas, Floyd Sr.
Dugas, Kay
Dugas, Marguerite
Dunn, Amy

Dunnehoo, Evelyn
Duplantis, Kendall
Duplantis, Loretta
Dupré, Cathy
Esneault, Betty
Esneault, Cassie W.
Evans, Diane
Falcon, Gloria C.
Falcon, Laurie
Falcon, Michelle
Falcon, Percy
Falgoust, Rita
Falterman, Anthony
Faneca, Julie
Ferguson, Sherry
Foret, Michelle
Fr.Labbé, Jason
Frey, Debbie
Gardner, Rose
Folse, Shirley
Gaudet, Tatty
Gautreaux, Laura Lee
Gautreaux, Susan
George, Tillie
Gravois, Helen
Griffin, Betty
Grisaffe, Brenda
Guillot, Dobbins
Guillot, Frank
Guillot, Marlene R.
Hales, Cindy
Harang, Becky
Hardwell, Hartford
Hargis, Sylvia
Hartman, Karen
Hebert, Myrle
Hebert, Sharon
Hendricks, Ruth
Henry, Pam
Higginbotham, Carole
Hilburn, Meme
Himel, Tonya
Hodson, David

FRIENDS

Hodson, Mary
Hodson, Melodie
Hollis, Henry
Hood, Alma
Horrocks, Ruth
Hulbert, Rebecca K.
Hurdle, Lorraine
Hymel, Lois R.
Hymel, Mary Jo
Hymel, Tonya
Ieyoub, Caprice
Iver, Robyn
Jarvis, Cathie
Johnson, Pat
Kern, Edith
Kern, Ida Mae
Kessler, Madeline
Lafleur, John
Landry, Betty
Landry, Brenda B.
Landry, Bridget C.
Landry, Charles, Jr.
Landry, Charles, Sr.
Landry, Charlotte D.
Landry, Felix, Jr.
Landry, Felix, Sr.
Landry, Gary
Landry, Gerry
Landry, Gloria D.
Landry, Janet S.
Landry, Judy R.
Landry, Mason
Landry, Shaina
Landry. Gerry
Landry. Ivy
Latino, Billly
LeBlanc, Betty Jane
LeBlanc, Don Michael
LeBlanc, Elnora
LeBlanc, Leroy J.
LeBlanc, Paulette
Lee, Leo
Leonard, Janel

Levert, Juanda
Mabile, Mary Jane
Maggio, Susan
Marmande, S. Ann
Martinez, Cheryl
Mattingly, Chris
Mayeaux, Beverly
Mc Gee, Ken
Mc Gee, Susan
Mc Nemar, Randy
Miller, Barbara
Miller, Sherry
Mitchel, Jeanette
Monson, Cynthia
Moore, Gayle
Morales, Carolyn
Naquin, Jeanie L.
Noel, Nancy
Noto, Mary
Odom, Simone
Orillion, Sonny
Oubre, Connie
Pate, Connie
Perque, Essie
Poche, Wayne
Prejean, Christy
Prejean, Hazel T.
Primeaux, Donnie
Primeaux, Payton
Primeaux, Stacy
Revere, Moss
Richard, Helen
Rivere, Yvette
Robichaux, Shannon
Rodrigue, Kye
Rome, Agnes
Rome, Debbie
Rousseau, Alma
Rumfola, Jenny
Russo, Annie
Sagona, Virginia
Samuels, Dr. Julie
Savoie, Don, Jr.

Savoie, Kathleen
Savoie, Mabel
Savoie, Nellie
Savoie, Rufus
Shaheen, Lorrraine
Simoneaux,
  Herman "Bill"
Simoneaux, Theresa
Simoneuax, Gertrude
Simpson, Joan
Simpson, Paula
Sirois, Linda
Skidmore, Comiella
Skidmore, Consuella
Smith, Linda
Sotile, Becky
St. Germain, Angelle
St. Germain, Gerald
Stamm, Arlene
Stauter, Marion
Stelly, Jaclyn
Stevens, Dave
Taylor, Andree C.
Templet, Angela
Templet, Liz
Templet, Lucille
Templet, Sundy M.
Theriot, Judy
Thibodeaux, Betty
Thibodeaux, Emma
Tramonte, Elaine D.
Varnadoe, Linda
Viallon, Berta
Waguespack, Heloise
Waguespack, Jill B.
Waits, Jean R.
Walker, Katherine
Warner, Marla
Williams, Christine
Winston, Roy "Moonie"
Winston, Yvette B.
Woods, Misty

4-H

Adolph, Spencer
Alleman, Jessie
Bergeron, Karen
Blanchard, Dylan
Blanchard, Kaitlyn
Breaux, Lindsay
Comeaux, Grant
Comeaux, Jamey
Crochet, Ben
Crochet, Haley
Daigle, Bailey
Daigle, Lucy
Daigle, Saulden

Falcon, Jared
Falterman, Imogene
Finger, Atticus
Gauthier, Jennifer
Gauthreaux, Kacie
Gonzales, Connor
Gravois, Allison
Gros, Kristi
Hebert, Hailey
Landry, Hannah
Landry, Tyler
LeBlanc, Taylor
Mabile, Zack

Marceaux, Carissa
Milazzo, Brooke
Pennison, Colleen
Rivere, Cody
Rivere, KayLynn
Sagona, Ashley
Talbot, Logan
Templet, Maria
Veron, Whitney

IN MEMORY

Achee, Fedora D.
Barber, Beth
Barrilleaux, Adam "Doc"
Bergeron, Eva H.
Blanchard, Helen M.
Blanchard, Jackie
Breaux, Aline
Burleigh, Edward
Cancienne, Betty
Clement, Billy
Daigle, Norris
Emory, Judy

Evans, Dorothy
Gonzales, Georgette
Grisaffe, Heloise
Guillot, Patty
Hula, Emma
Hymel, Deedy
Johnson, Shirley R.
Kessler, Betty
Lagrange, Wilma
Landry, Ida L.
Landry, Lena D.

Landry, Velsie
Leggio, Annie
Minton, Shelia
Newchurch, Jeremy
Robichaux, Henry
Sagona, Shirley
Savoie, Donald Sr.
Simmons, Lucy
Templet, Anne
Theriot, Eno
Williams, Gracie

We would like to take this opportunity to thank everyone who sent in a recipe or helped in anyway with the publication of "Butterflies For Life". Many recipes were received without names; therefore, if anyone has been left off the contributors list we are truly sorry and we do apologize.

The Pink Team of Assumption

butterfliesforlife.org

Butterflies For Life
The Pink Team Of Assumption
P.O. Drawer "D"
Paincourtville, Louisiana 70391

Please send me information on ordering additional copies of
"BUTTERFLIES FOR LIFE".

NAME_____

ADDRESS_____

CITY _____ STATE_____ZIP _____

PHONE (_____) _____

- -

butterfliesforlife.org

Butterflies For Life
The Pink Team Of Assumption
P.O. Drawer "D"
Paincourtville, Louisiana 70391

Please send me information on ordering additional copies of
"BUTTERFLIES FOR LIFE".

NAME_____

ADDRESS_____

CITY _____ STATE_____ZIP _____

PHONE (_____) _____